WEYERHAEUSER ENVIRONMENTAL BOOKS

WILLIAM CRONON, EDITOR

Weyerhaeuser Environmental Books explore human relationships with natural environments in all their variety and complexity. They seek to cast new light on the ways that natural systems affect human communities, the ways that people affect the environments of which they are a part, and the ways that different cultural conceptions of nature profoundly shape our sense of the world around us.

A complete list of the books in the series appears at the end of this book.

SEEKING REFUGE

BIRDS AND LANDSCAPES
OF THE PACIFIC FLYWAY

ROBERT M. WILSON

FOREWORD BY WILLIAM CRONON

UNIVERSITY OF WASHINGTON PRESS

SEATTLE AND LONDON

Seeking Refuge: Birds and Landscapes of the Pacific Flyway *is published with the assistance of a grant from the Weyerhaeuser Environmental Books Endowment, established by the Weyerhaeuser Company Foundation, members of the Weyerhaeuser family, and Janet and Jack Creighton.*

University of Washington Press
PO Box 50096, Seattle, WA 98145, USA
www.washington.edu/uwpress

Library of Congress Cataloging-in-Publication Data
Wilson, Robert M., 1971–
Seeking refuge : birds and landscapes of the Pacific flyway /
Robert M. Wilson.
p. cm. — (Weyerhaeuser environmental books)
Includes bibliographical references and index.
ISBN 978-0-295-99211-2 (pbk. : alk. paper)
1. Bird refuges—West (U.S.)
2. Migratory birds—Effect of habitat modification on.
3. Wetland conservation—West (U.S.)
4. Wetland management—West (U.S.)
I. Title.
QL676.56.W3W55 2010   598.156'80979—dc22   2010004332

CONTENTS

FOREWORD: A WILDERNESS ON WINGS

WILLIAM CRONON

ONE OF THE DEEPEST CONVICTIONS that geographers bring to every subject they study has to do with *scale*, a concept they understand with far greater rigor and subtlety than those who have never had to grapple with the befuddling complexities of mapmaking. The rest of us more often than not rely on spatial common sense as we navigate our daily life. We typically imagine that the places we visit exist pretty unambiguously at a singular location that can easily be visited if only we are able to find our way to the fixed position on a map where that place resides. Unless we're trying to estimate distances, we don't think very much about those little rulers that declare how many inches on the map correspond with how many miles in the real world. And unless we're lost or find ourselves wondering whether a map on which we've relied might somehow have led us astray, we don't much worry about the accuracy with which maps represent places we take for granted as "real."

Yet even a moment's reflection will suggest that the relationship between place and scale is far from straightforward, so much so that places can appear sharp or fuzzy or disappear altogether depending on the ways maps represent them. To demonstrate this phenomenon for yourself, try the following experiment. Visit a website like Google Maps or Mapquest to search for California's Sacramento National Wildlife Refuge, a place about which the historical geographer Robert Wilson has much to say in this thought-provoking book. You will initially see on your screen a drab polygon containing a few curving blue lines representing watercourses, a few gray lines representing roads, and not much else. It isn't quite a blank spot on the map, but almost. If you press the button to request a satellite view, however, the image suddenly morphs into an astonishingly complex maze of curving greens and browns and blues. Even more strikingly, you can now see the surrounding grid of rectilinear roads and fields that explain why the place is called a refuge. It is an island in a vast landscape of agricultural fields. At first glance, the refuge has an organic look and feel, though on closer examination its lines and shapes display considerable evidence of human engineering. The scale of the map, and the choices you make about what it represents, radically alter what you do and do not see within the boundaries of this place.

But the geographer's essential insight is not that we see more details when the scale of a map is large than when it is small. It is rather that we see *different* details—and therefore different *places*. When your view of this wildlife refuge is zoomed in close enough to see its interior watercourses, you cannot see the state of California, even though the one exists within the other. This is because places are inherently nested inside each other, and their nested identities wax and wane depending on the scale of the map that represents them. If you zoom back far enough to see all of Colusa County, in which the Sacramento National Wildlife Refuge is located, the refuge becomes little more than a brown blotch on your computer screen. If you pull back farther still to see the entire Sacramento River watershed, of which this place is such an important component, you can barely make out the refuge at all. Zoom back farther so you can progressively make out the places called "California" or the "Pacific Coast" or the "American West" or the "United States" or "North America" or the "Western Hemisphere," and the Sacramento National Wildlife Refuge disappears altogether.

Different places, in other words, exist on different scales, and the consequences of this truth are far from trivial. Although there is a long tradition in the history of conservation of seeking to protect nature by creating parks and wilderness areas in relatively isolated, self-contained units, in fact natural systems themselves are almost never coterminous with the boundaries we draw around them. Yellowstone National Park, for instance, is among the largest, most intact, and best-loved wild places legally protected in the Lower 48 United States, yet it measures less than 3,500 square miles—roughly sixty miles on a side. Especially the animals who live there—bison, elk, grizzlies, wolves, trumpeter swans, and others—have no conception of the park's boundaries, regularly crossing them to create a host of ecological, managerial, and political problems for human beings who care about these creatures. How to "protect nature" when nature perennially ignores the places we've set aside for it is the profound question that makes Robert Wilson's *Seeking Refuge: Birds and Landscapes of the Pacific Flyway* such a suggestive and important book.

No organisms demonstrate the geographical paradoxes of scale and place better than migratory birds. In one of the most remarkable evolutionary strategies in the history of life on earth, these species take advantage of their wings to move among far-flung ecosystems depending on the seasons of the year. During the warm summer months, they raise their young in the high latitudes of the planet, taking advantage of the intense productivity of northern and southern ecosystems at the time when all living things in subpolar regions race to complete their annual cycles before the return of winter. Migratory birds take advantage of abundant seasonal food supplies in territories with relatively low populations of native predators when vulnerable nestlings are least able to defend themselves. Once fledglings are older, they live with their parents in regions nearer the equator, where food is abundant even in winter—and when there is at least a fighting chance that young birds will be able to defend themselves against predators that are far more numerous here than near the poles. In between, during the spring and fall, these amazing creatures take to the air and travel many thousands of miles back and forth between their seasonal homes.

Most Americans, no matter where we live, think of ducks and geese as sharing the ecosystems in which we make our own homes. They certainly do this—but not all the time. Only at particular moments and for relatively brief periods do they sojourn in any particular locale. Their own home environments exist on a geographical scale that is hemispheric in scope. That is why, when the United States government began trying in the late nineteenth and early twentieth centuries to create wildlife refuges to protect the migratory and breeding territories of these species, it faced different challenges than had been involved in setting aside parks like Yellowstone or Yosemite. It was not just that such refuges involved wetlands that had not formerly received much attention from conservationists. It was that they needed to be strung together, like jewels on a necklace, separated by distances determined by how far a flock of birds might fly in a day.

A place like the Sacramento National Wildlife Refuge, where Robert Wilson begins this book, thus gains its ecological significance only in relation to the much larger geography on which avian life cycles express themselves. At the heart of Wilson's story is the invention during the 1920s of the concept of "flyways" by the federal biologist Frederick Lincoln, who worked with ornithologists in both the United States and Canada. A flyway was a new kind of place in the history of human consciousness, abstracting and labeling the aggregate movements of millions of birds traveling across space to connect their summer and winter homes, with all the stopover rest areas in between. The U.S. Bureau of Biological Survey, Lincoln's employer, and its successor, the U.S. Fish and Wildlife Service, popularized this idea of a flyway to help voters and taxpayers understand why the survival of migratory birds required a vast network of refuges along the corridors used by these species on their annual journeys. (Four such flyways were eventually identified for North America: the Atlantic, Mississippi, Central, and Pacific.) Authorized by the Migratory Bird Conservation Act of 1929, the agency began acquiring land with the express goal of creating refuges along the flyways to provide safe passage for birds. Wilson's book is the first comprehensive environmental history that traces in fine detail the linked stories of these refuges and flyways on the very different geographical scales that each implies.

The system of refuges that emerged over the course of the twentieth century is remarkable not just for its far-flung scope but also for its relationship to the larger landscapes in which it is embedded—and for the unabashed artificiality of the way it protects wild creatures. The rectilinear agricultural fields surrounding the Sacramento Refuge, for instance, are all too typical of the system as a whole. They reflect the nationwide grid of private property, dating back to the 1785 Land Ordinance and before, which transformed wild nature and Indian territory into the real estate that now underpins the U.S. economy. (The relationship of this abstract national grid to the rectilinear local parcels Americans now own is another striking example of the different geographical scales with which we conceive of the world around us.) A very large share of the wetlands on which migratory birds depend had already been drained and converted to farmland by the time the federal government began to create refuges. The Sacramento Refuge is a perfect case in point. When the Fish and Wildlife Service and the Civilian Conservation Corps began work on the site in 1937, it consisted mainly of dry alkaline lands whose waters were already being used for irrigation by nearby farms. A whole new drainage system had to be engineered to supply the refuge with the life-giving liquid that would transform an arid plain into the wetland it had never been before. Furthermore, efforts by engineers to deliver water to the refuge would have been meaningless without efforts by lawyers and managers to establish the legal right to that water and its equitable division with nearby irrigators.

Artificial wetlands, excavated canals, water contracts: these are only the beginning of the complexities and contradictions that Robert Wilson traces so deftly in the pages of this book. Wildlife managers had likewise to contend with the problem of assuring that their postage-stamp-sized refuges could support the immense numbers of passing birds that briefly relied on such places, and so found themselves raising and purchasing large quantities of grain to supply domesticated food to these wild animals. By the mid twentieth century, wildlife refuges could legitimately be regarded as "duck farms." Furthermore, birds had to be discouraged from snacking on nearby crops, so elaborate techniques had to be developed for frightening them away from adjacent farmlands so they would dine at the refuges instead. Just as farms had to be protected from the effects of birds, birds had to be protected from the effects of farms, a problem that became all the more challenging as the growing use of pesticides after World War II threatened avian populations worldwide. And, of course, the management of this ever more complicated system had to be paid for, whether through the sale of duck stamps and hunting licenses or through direct appropriation of tax dollars. Bird biology became ever more entangled with human politics.

Robert Wilson tells these and many other stories far more effectively than I can, so let me close with one last observation. The contrasting geographical scales of flyways and refuges are a potent reminder that the boundaries between the human and the natural exist far more in our minds than in the real world. Few things on earth more powerfully symbolize the wonder of nonhuman nature than the extraordinary movements of millions of birds from poles to equator and back again as they repeat their annual cycles. If there is wildness on this planet, surely we see it in the sky each time these magnificent creatures pass above our heads. Yet to think of them and their world as somehow separate from ours is not only to misconceive the nature of geographical boundaries and nested scales; it is in fact to put these animals deeply at risk. If they are unable to make safe passage through the landscapes we have made our own, if they cannot find food or refuge as they travel, then they and their wild beauty will vanish forever. We too live in their flyways and must share our homes with theirs if the places and creatures we care about are to be saved for all of us.

ACKNOWLEDGMENTS

I STARTED THIS PROJECT while a graduate student in the Geography Department at the University of British Columbia. I was fortunate to have a talented and supportive graduate committee. Cole Harris read more drafts of these chapters than I care to count, and his door was always open if I needed to discuss ideas with him. Some of my fondest graduate school memories are of the field reconnaissances he led into the British Columbia interior. Matthew Evenden was very helpful. While a visiting student at the University of Washington, I met Richard White and he was generous enough to join my committee. I owe the most to Graeme Wynn. He was an excellent supervisor, incisive critic, and rigorous editor. I thank him and Cole for introducing me to historical geography.

While I attended UBC and lived in Vancouver, I was sustained by fellow graduate students and others outside the university. I thank Pascal Haegeli, Stephanie Meyn, Andrew Murphy, Richard Powell, Jean-Francois Proulx, Étienne Rivard, Magdalena Rucker, and Jenny Salmond. I appreciate the many discussions I had with John Thistle about historical geography and environmental history at the Cedar

Cottage and elsewhere. Arn Keeling is a great scholar and an even better friend. It was a pleasure to go through graduate school with him. His partner, Shannon Fraser, was supportive, too, and carefully copy edited one of the chapters. While researching much of this project, I lived in a basement apartment beneath a wonderful family. I thank Anita and Robert Fashler and their rambunctious, delightful daughters: Elizabeth, Danielle, Samantha, and Robyn. They became like a second family to me, and my time in Vancouver would have been poorer had I never met them. My roommate Mark Veselinovic was there when I needed him. People beyond Vancouver also helped. Bob and Henrietta Mountz purchased another computer for me when my laptop was stolen. I literally could not have written this book without their help.

The U.S. Fish and Wildlife Service generously offered assistance with this research. Refuge staff granted me access to their "archives," which often consisted of old file cabinets in basements. At one refuge, I had to don work gloves to protect myself from black widow spiders while searching for documents in an equipment storage shed. Such unexpected occupational hazards were well worth the trouble. In particular, I thank the staff at the Klamath Basin and Sacramento National Wildlife Refuge Complexes, who cleared space for me to work and allowed me to photocopy documents.

This book took shape at a number of different locales. The first was the Department of History and Philosophy at Montana State University-Bozeman, where I spent a year as The Postdoc. Conversations with colleagues and their suggestions on how to improve my work benefitted me enormously. I thank Kirk Branch, Rob Campbell, Jennifer Chrisman, Edward Flashman, Dale Martin, Mary Murphy, Cindy Ott, Sara Pritchard, Robert Rydell, Bill Wyckoff, and Yanna Yannakakis. During my tenure there (and in the years since then), Brett Walker was an outstanding colleague and a source of wisdom. My closest friend and confidant there, Michael Reidy, introduced me to the history of science as well as his unorthodox teaching style. Billy Smith offered good advice on presentations related to this project, despite his apparent disdain for environmental history and those of us who practice it. Whether he cares to admit it or not, he is on his way to becoming a great environmental historian. I will always fondly remember my conversations with him, Peaty, and other colleagues at the 320 Ranch.

After my postdoctoral fellowship, I had the good fortune to land at Syracuse University, which has a fabulous geography program and is one of the leading centers for historical geography research in the United States. I could not ask for a more supportive group of colleagues. My thanks go to Jake Bendix, Peng Gao, Susan Millar, Mark Monmonier, Anne Mosher, Jane Read, David Robinson, and John Western. Tod Rutherford has been a friend and excellent chair of the department. Don Mitchell, who was also chair, has also offered sound advice and served as a model of a good scholar. During my time at SU, I have been fortunate to get to know Don Meinig. Over our monthly lunches, I have valued our conversations and his advice as a mentor. Jamie Winders has been a trusted friend since graduate school, and I am lucky now to have her as a colleague. Tom Perreault is another colleague and friend. I have benefited from our conversations in his office, over barbeques, and on the ski trail. Sarah Pralle is a political scientist, though I will always consider her an honorary geographer. She is a talented environmental scholar and a trusted friend. Many thanks to our staff cartographer, Joe Stoll, who made all the maps for this book. The SU Geography Department is also blessed with excellent graduate students. As professors, we too rarely acknowledge all we learn from them. In particular, I thank Beatriz Bustos, Barbara Green, Matt Himley, Reccia Orzeck, Effie Scott, Marla Torrado, and Evan Weissman. I also thank my two doctoral students, Brent Olson and Jeremy Bryson. A supervisor could not ask for two better students to advise.

My circle of support in Syracuse extends beyond the department. I am grateful to them for more than I can express. I would rather thank them all individually, but I will only list them here: Sarah Brouillette, Elizabeth Cohen, Mike Goode, and Jolynn Parker.

I completed the final edits for this book while working as a visiting scholar at Stanford University's Bill Lane Center for the American West. I thank co-directors Richard White and David Kennedy for accepting me into the program. I appreciate the conversations I had with them and the helpful comments about my work from visiting scholars Peter Alagona, Matt Booker, Jon Christensen, Judy Pasternak, and Gregory Simon.

One of the greatest benefits of being an academic is getting to know other scholars. I appreciate those who have taken the time to talk with me about this project: Laura Cameron, David Demeritt, Mark Madison, Neil Maher, Liza Piper, Paul Robbins, Helen Rozwadowski, and Aaron Sachs. Nancy Langston read the entire manuscript carefully and offered incisive comments. Anyone familiar with her work will see her influence here. I owe an enormous debt to Mark Fiege, who has not only read many versions of this work, but also serves as a sterling example of a scholar. So, too, has Matt Klingle, whose advice has helped me in ways too numerous to count. I also appreciate Jay Taylor's help throughout the years. I am privileged to count them all as friends.

This book could not have found a better home than with the University of Washington Press. Julidta Tarver was the editor when I first approached the press with this topic. Marianne Keddington-Lang, who took the reins after Julidta retried, has been an exemplary editor. I thank them both. Most of all, I thank Bill Cronon. His excitement about the project buoyed me as I finished the book. It is an honor to join the group of authors he has assembled for this series.

Finally, I thank my family. My grandmother, Jane Rountree, and my father, Allan Wilson, passed away before I finished the book. I wish only that they could have lived to read it. My mother, Jan Wilson, and siblings, Christy and Ben, have always been there for me. While completing this manuscript, I was fortunate enough to search for and find my birth mother, Taylor Johnson. I thank both of my mothers for their enthusiasm and support. I hope this book was worth the wait.

Finally, I dedicate this book to my wife, Dawn. I could not ask for a more lovely, enthusiastic, or supportive spouse. Her joy and humor sustain me. I thank her for migrating across the continent to be with me.

SEEKING REFUGE

INTRODUCTION

ONE OF AMERICA'S GREAT WILDLIFE SPECTACLES is found not in Yellowstone National Park or the backwoods of Alaska, but at the Sacramento National Wildlife Refuge beside Interstate 5 in California's Central Valley. Situated amid the vast rice farms that carpet this part of the state, the refuge seems uninviting at first glance, particularly in the summer when its ponds shimmer in the heat and the surrounding dry grass is baked brown by the harsh sun. In the fall, its character changes entirely as tens of thousands of migratory birds crowd into the refuge. Standing near the edge of it, as I did one October day at dusk, you can watch countless snow geese, pintails, and other waterfowl pour out of the marshes and spread across the valley to feed on nearby farms. With so many birds aloft, the sky seems stratified like a layer cake. For someone like me, more accustomed to the occasional crow or pigeon in my city neighborhood rather than stupendous flocks of geese, viewing this incredible display of wildlife was a revelation.

The Sacramento Refuge and other ones like it in the Central Valley are essential habitat for birds along the Pacific Flyway, the westernmost of four primary migratory bird corridors in North America.[1]

MAP 1 *The Pacific Flyway*

Not all of the birds found within the Sacramento Refuge migrate, but for someone visiting during the fall, the flocks of migratory ducks and geese are by far the most conspicuous. Whether loafing in refuge ponds or flying overhead, the Central Valley is a haven for these birds. The valley is where over 60 percent of migratory waterfowl along the Pacific Flyway spend the winter months. In the spring, these birds return to places across western North America to breed: Alaska's Yukon-Kuskokwim Delta, lakes in Canada's boreal forests, and the freshwater marshes of the prairie states and provinces. Central Valley refuges are key parts within a constellation of wetland habitats scattered unevenly across the breadth of the continent.

The immense flocks of ducks and geese on the Sacramento Refuge are impressive, but their numbers are only a fraction of what were found in the valley just sixty years ago.

Ornithologists estimate that fifty to sixty *million* waterfowl may have wintered in the area during the late 1940s.[2] They fed and rested amid the tapestry of marshes, sloughs, and vernal pools. The valley served then, as it does today, as a vital resting and wintering area for migratory birds.

Where tens of millions of ducks and geese once found shelter in wetlands, acres of farms now cover the valley. The Central Valley is the most productive agricultural region in the United States. According to geographer Richard Walker, "California is probably the most intensely farmed landscape in the world . . . and the most prosperous agricultural region of the advanced industrial nations."[3] At the heart of the state's agricultural cornucopia is the Central Valley. Creating this landscape required an environmental transformation matched in few places in North America. The Sacramento River, which once regularly flooded the northern part of the valley and created an ephemeral inland sea, has been diked and dammed. The river's major tributaries are also controlled, and irrigators have diverted much of the water that once sustained the valley's wetlands. Instead of flowing down the river, it pours through a maze of irrigation canals to service these vast farms or California's thriving cities.

It would be easy to see the marshes and fields within the Sacramento Refuge as simply environmental relics of a bygone era. But these ponds and marshes have a history. Like the nearby farms, this is a constructed landscape, sustained by irrigation water. Before the U.S. government created the refuge in 1937, the area was mostly a dry plain that attracted geese that fed on grasses, but served as poor habitat for most other birds. To a large degree, human actions account for the ability of the refuge to support such congregations of geese, ducks, and other wetland dependent birds.

From the air, refuges such as the Sacramento are tiny units within the grid of irrigated, industrial agriculture. During the twentieth century, waterfowl found much of the area outside refuges inhospitable. This was partially because irrigators and reclamation agencies had destroyed so many of the wetlands the birds once used. Yet some of the crops that grew in areas where marshes once existed proved beneficial for waterfowl. Soon after they were created, waterfowl descended on the fields of rice and consumed acres of grain. Sportsmen also hunted the birds outside the refuges, though eventually the U.S. Fish and Wildlife Service (FWS) opened it to hunting. In effect, the refuges served as places of relative sanctuary amid this unwelcoming landscape. Whether they are in Washington State or central California, most refuges share the same predicament. They lie amid intensely used agricultural landscapes in which the birds are, at best, merely tolerated, and at worst, a nuisance.

This book examines the development and management of Central Valley refuges and others like them along the Pacific Flyway during the twentieth century. It builds on a substantial literature addressing the history of protected areas and water development in the West.[4] Unlike national parks or national forests, migratory bird refuges are very small—most are only a few thousand acres. More than these other sorts of protected areas, actions outside wildlife refuges had significant impacts on the wildlife found within refuge borders. They lie within productive human landscapes where people live and work. Furthermore, irrigators and cities had diverted the water needed to support the marshes and ponds waterfowl used for other uses. This story is about how the wildlife managers carved out refuges amid these agricultural landscapes and sought to secure the water necessary for them to function.

Yet on a deeper level, this is a story about the intersection of mobile nature with the grid.[5] By the late nineteenth century, Americans had carved much of the western landscape into a patchwork of private, state, and federal lands. In the wake of the Euro-American conquest of western North America, settlers constructed rigid boundaries between parcels of private and public lands, between states and provinces, and between countries. This system fostered rapid settlement and aided economic development, but such boundaries made little ecological sense. Nature was not so tranquil. Fires respected no borders as they burned across the landscape and weeds moved from one farm to the next, often despite the best efforts of farmers to curtail their movement. Wildlife traveled across the landscape, too, often confounding the efforts of state game wardens and hunters to fix them in place.[6] Life within this sort of gridded landscape was, in the words of historian Mark Fiege, a "struggle to reconcile abstract boundaries with material conditions, to contain things that were inherently uncontainable."[7]

No group of animals crossed more boundaries than migratory birds. They traversed every border the modern nation state constructed. A snow goose hatched on Wrangel Island in Russia migrates across much of western North America until it finally arrives in the Central Valley of California, where it rests and feeds during the winter. Indeed, it was not until the twentieth century that people even understood the routes these birds traveled between their breeding and wintering areas. To complete these annual journeys, the birds depended on wetlands and other environments along their migration routes. Pristine habitat in one part of the migration route meant little if habitat elsewhere was degraded or destroyed. Like links in a chain, such travels worked only if all aspects of the migration route remained intact. For migratory waterfowl, the wetlands of western North America functioned as one habitat used at specific times during different seasons.

By the time federal and state governments began establishing refuges and providing the funds to maintain them, most western wetlands were already gone and their sources of water dammed, diked, or diverted. To maintain viable refuges, wildlife agencies had to connect them to the irrigated countryside. In so doing, they became another unit within the grid of irrigated agriculture, a landscape where users precisely allocated water to support crops on farms and marshes on refuges. Irrigators and reclamation agencies destroyed much of the wetland habitat in the wintering range of the Pacific Flyway, but wildlife managers would use their tools to create refuges for migratory birds. Over time, the fates of irrigated agriculture and refuges became intertwined. Flying birds and flowing water linked these ostensibly separate types of landscapes in complicated and surprising ways.

Farmers, irrigation agencies, and wildlife officials often had different visions for the lands they managed. Yet all believed in what William Cronon calls a zoned landscape, where individual places were rigidly defined.[8] Wildlife belonged on refuges and commercial crops on farms. After much conflict, the federal government created wildlife refuges in the irrigated landscapes of the West, but under the condition that birds remain in the places allotted to them. Unfortunately, nobody informed the birds of this, and they continued to land in farmers' fields and devour crops. Farmers harassed birds with shotguns and flares to clear their fields of waterfowl. When that did not work, they insisted that wildlife officials do this for them. Agency officials took to the air, dropping hand grenades among flocks of geese and then herding the startled birds into the refuges. In effect, the federal government segregated wild animals into the wild places designated in the countryside for the birds' benefit.

Federal agencies such as the FWS created refuges and policed their borders at the local level, but they were concerned with other scales, too. Managing waterfowl required the FWS to work on a continental scale, since the birds had such lengthy migration routes. The American and Canadian governments recognized this when they signed the Migratory Bird Treaty of 1916, one of the first and most successful conservation treaties during the Progressive Era.[9] In later years, the two governments developed a system to track and survey migratory waterfowl to better understand the birds' movements and populations. This book examines these efforts, especially the development of the flyway concept and its impact on migratory waterfowl management. Managing migratory birds had a transnational dimension that resources managed by other agencies lacked. Wildlife officials went to great pains to make bird migration *legible* through maps and charts.[10] Furthermore, they sought to use this information to make decisions at the scale of small refuges in places such as Oregon and California.

Refuges could not escape the context in which they were embedded. On a map, the refuges appeared like tidy boxes with clear boundaries dividing public spaces for wildlife and private ones for farmland. In reality, these were messy boundaries regularly transgressed by not only birds, but water, pesticides, weeds, insects, and other aspects of the nonhuman world. Of course this is true of all protected areas; even the largest national parks are typically surrounded by more heavily used lands. But compared to these parks, wildlife refuges were small—some only a few thousand acres. The refuges were too small, and frankly, the FWS too weak, to prevent serious encroachments from the surrounding areas. The rural West was a crowded landscape with many powerful interests. For the past century, the FWS has tried against long odds to create a place for wildlife amid a landscape that was created for other purposes and that was largely inhospitable to migratory birds.

Yet this is not a simple story of a lost wildlife Eden. In the midst of these changes, sport hunters and other bird enthusiasts sought to protect and restore wetland habitat for migratory birds. This book examines federal efforts to construct a viable system of refuges to sustain migratory birds amid this onslaught from agriculture and urbanization. This program involved the work of many groups, including sport hunters, bird watchers, as well as state, federal, and nongovernmental agencies. Each of the many groups involved has their own history. To provide some order to this story, I focus primarily on one agency, the U.S. Fish and Wildlife Service (formerly known as the Bureau of Biological Survey), and its attempts to develop a network of refuges throughout the United States to support migratory birds, particularly in the highly threatened wintering range. I do this for a number of reasons. First, the FWS was one of the first agencies, governmental or private, that attempted to create large refuges to protect birds. Second, unlike state and nongovernmental agencies, the FWS attempted to chart migration and survey bird populations over much of the birds' vast migratory territory. The efforts of the states and the provinces in Canada were very important, but only the FWS was involved at all scales, from the refuge to continental. Also, I devote relatively little space to nongovernmental groups such as Ducks Unlimited. Organizations like this have played a major role in the conservation of wetlands and game birds. This organization deserves its own book. Addressing all the state and non-state organizations involved in conserving Pacific Flyway birds would have led to an unwieldy study. I hope other interested scholars will see this book as a necessary starting point for more detailed work on these sorts of organizations.[11]

One of the main arguments of this book is that the habitat within the refuges was produced more than protected. By the time serious refuge creation and management began in the 1930s, reclamation and urbanization had destroyed many of the wetlands in the western United States, especially in California, which lost over 90 percent of its wetlands.[12] Moreover, the rivers and streams that once carried water from the Cascades or Sierra Nevadas were now dammed or diked and the water redirected to irrigate agriculture. To develop viable refuges, the FWS had to carve out new spaces within this irrigated, industrialized agricultural landscape. The agency came to depend on the same sorts of knowledge and technology of irrigated agriculture to maintain the refuges. Over time, FWS employees became astute water managers, directing water throughout the refuge to support marshes, crops, and ponds. They grew acres of wheat, barley, rice, and other crops to feed hungry waterfowl. By the 1950s, the FWS regularly sprayed its refuges with the insecticide DDT and herbicide 2,4-D to combat pests and weeds that might threaten refuge crops. Such dependence on pesticides would have deleterious consequences as the chemicals made their way through the refuge food chain.

What emerged from the efforts of the FWS was a hybrid landscape in which human artifice and nonhuman nature merged. I argue that refuge managers adopted models from irrigated industrial agriculture when constructing and managing these refuges. A farm is a type of hybrid landscape in which people modify the landscape and coax an often recalcitrant nature to produce more commodities for market. Refuge managers did not grow crops to sell, but they did hope to simplify the landscape to foster a better habitat for a very select number of species, namely, ducks and geese.[13] The goal of this hybrid landscape was to produce more waterfowl for hunters, an understandable aim given the threats faced by these birds. Yet through the decades the FWS learned that this narrow view of the refuge purpose would have serious ramifications for other species that used these places.[14]

If waterfowl were the intended products of the refuges, than hunters were the designated consumers. The needs of hunters informed refuge managers from the earliest days of the refuge system. The first refuges were designated as sanctuaries where hunting was prohibited. This was done primarily to protect birds from the ravages of hunters who hunted for market, but also to save some from the growing number who hunted for recreation. Even so, the FWS felt these sanctuaries ultimately benefited hunters, since they served as protected reservoirs from which birds could flow out over the countryside. After the Second World War, the growing number of recreational hunters pressured the FWS to open previously closed sanctuaries to hunting as well as create new refuges that would also serve as public shooting grounds. In effect, the FWS was expected to provide public spaces for sportsmen to hunt ducks and geese, a public resource under the management of the FWS and state wildlife agencies. This book is not primarily about hunting, but at numerous points I emphasize the way refuge managers made management decisions in what it thought was the best needs of hunters. As the environmental movement grew into a serious political force during the 1970s and beyond, the FWS was forced to seriously consider the needs of other species besides boosting the number of waterfowl for sport hunters.[15]

What follows is a complicated story. Environmentalists—and often environmental historians—have shown a fondness for declentional narratives that move from splendor to desolation. Certainly the history of migratory birds and wetlands in the Far West—California, Oregon, Washington, and British Columbia—would partially support this interpretation. Duck and geese populations once numbered in the tens of millions during the winter months in California, and lush wetlands once cloaked many of the arid basins in the region. But despite this loss, refuge managers, sportsmen, and other conservationists have developed a tenuous but viable system of wetlands and protected areas for these animals.

This book charts the development of refuge landscapes throughout the Far West for migratory birds. Landscape formation and interpretation is a perennial topic of interest for geographers. My approach to studying the landscape differs in many ways from most historical or cultural geographers. Until the early 1980s, most examined material features on the landscape—homes, crops, roads—to understand more about the groups that made them. For these geographers, nature was seen as a raw material with which people created a distinctive cultural landscape.[16] By the late 1980s and early 1990s, a new generation of cultural geographers was criticizing these earlier landscape studies for their rather static view of culture and inattention to how different social groups contested over the development of the landscape or its meaning.[17]

No matter what approach these geographers adopted, they shared an inattention to animals, wild or domestic. Not only was nature rendered as passive in their accounts, the animals that inhabit landscapes were absent. For most geographers, studying landscape is a way to understand the cultural groups that created them. In this book, I place the birds and the habitats they use at the center of analysis rather than a particular group of people. The development of landscapes has had enormous impacts on other creatures, arguably nowhere more so in places such as the Klamath Basin and Central Valley. In both places, a rich mosaic of productive wetlands was replaced with a grid of irrigated agriculture. This had serious ramifications for the animals that used these places, especially migratory birds. This study attempts to rectify this blindness in landscape studies by examining how landscape transformations affected other species, and just as importantly, how government agencies and concerned citizens created a landscape of refuges to ensure the survival of migratory birds.

This story begins in the mid-nineteenth century, before people drained western marshes and created wildlife refuges. Chapter 1 examines the geography of the Pacific Flyway and how bird migration linked wetlands in western North America. Bird enthusiasts have often framed wetland loss in terms of a static nature drastically altered by American and Canadian society. But wetlands within the intermountain West and California were highly dynamic environments prior to Euro-American and Euro-Canadian settlement. Shallow lakes covered the valleys of the Great Basin at the end of the Pleistocene, and in the mid-Quaternary, freshwater marshes replaced them. Meanwhile, deglaciation of the northern part of the continent opened immense areas of land for the birds to utilize during their breeding seasons, and migratory routes changed accordingly. Native peoples harvested these birds and used an assortment of other organisms from these wetlands. Unlike Euro-American land use, Native use of birds and wetlands did not require the rigid division between water and land promoted under western private property regimes. For migratory birds, the shifting biogeoclimatic patterns of postglacial North America allowed them to travel to sources of abundance separated by hundreds of miles. But this left the birds vulnerable to environmental changes along the flyway.

The next chapter focuses on the impact of new settlers on bird habitat and early bird protection efforts. As Euro-American and Euro-Canadian settlement proceeded and Native people were pushed to the margins, newcomers began draining wetlands to create farmland. They also harvested enormous numbers of birds for market and sport. Unlike recent studies of wildlife conservation during this era, this book focuses on the West Coast states and not the nation as a whole.[18] At the beginning of the twentieth century, California and Oregon lay on the periphery of the bird protection movement. Groups such as the National Association of Audubon Societies (NAAS) were strongest in the Northeast United States, where they used their influence to convince President Theodore Roosevelt to establish wildlife refuges in the region, as well as in Florida and other Gulf Coast states. In the West, where there were fewer NAAS members, there was less enthusiasm for refuge development. Oregon diverged from this pattern. It had a vigorous and influential NAAS chapter led by two intrepid wildlife photographers, William Finley and Herman Bohlman. Their writings and photographs of birds in eastern Oregon galvanized interest among bird enthusiasts and ornithologists to protect Lower Klamath and Malheur Lakes as sanctuaries patrolled by the U.S. Bureau of Biological Survey wardens. Even with federal protection, irrigators and the U.S. Bureau of Reclamation destroyed some or all of these refuges.

Chapter 3 examines the development of the flyway concept and the creation of a network of refuges for waterfowl. During the 1920s and 1930s, Bureau of Biological Survey biologist Frederick Lincoln, in cooperation with Canadian and American ornithologists, bird watchers, and sport hunters, developed the idea of flyways. The concept revolutionized migratory bird management and gave the Biological Survey a powerful tool for selecting refuge sites. Lincoln developed the flyway concept at a time when duck and goose populations were in steep decline and when the bureau was enlarging the refuge system. The Biological Survey (renamed the U.S. Fish and Wildlife Service in 1940) used funds and labor provided by New Deal programs to restore damaged wetlands. The agency constructed dikes, built canals, and planted aquatic vegetation to rehabilitate damaged marshes in Oregon and California. Remaining wetlands and ponds were divided into diked units to facilitate the management of water. Such development enabled the agency to deal with the recurring problem of avian botulism and cholera that afflicted western waterfowl. With these developments, however, nearby farmers expected the agency to contain the birds within the refuges to prevent waterfowl from damaging crops.

As duck and goose populations increased during the 1940s, the refuges proved unable to provide sufficient food for the birds. By the end of the Second World War, a rising number of waterfowl hunters in Los Angeles and San Francisco, combined with the continuing loss of wetland habitat throughout the flyway, placed enormous pressures on these small refuges. Farmers continued to insist that wildlife managers remove waterfowl from rice and barley fields, yet sport hunters used their growing influence to maintain refuges and establish others in the Central Valley of California. The emerging geography of wildlife refuges in the valley was the result of intense political battles among different groups who had claims on the spaces used by birds.

Chapter 4 moves from local to regional scales as it follows attempts by the FWS to alter the rhythm of bird migration during the fall. It also considers the ramifications of the agency's farming program to grow crops for waterfowl. The agency's narrow focus on grain production for ducks and geese had disastrous consequences for other species of birds. DDT and other pesticides applied to refuge crops found their way into wetlands where pelicans, grebes, and other fish-eating birds died from the pesticides found in the fish.

The final chapter discusses how endangered species legislation and water policy in Oregon and California during the past decade affected wildlife refuges. The passing of the Endangered Species Act (ESA) in 1973 had far reaching consequences for the Fish and Wildlife Service and the refuges it managed in Oregon and California. The FWS was the agency primarily responsible for enforcing the act. It gave the agency increasing power over how private lands were managed throughout the nation, and it had important implications for refuge management. The ESA forced the agency to consider the welfare of threatened species other than waterfowl on its refuges. The agency was slow to adapt to these changes since it had long grown accustomed to managing refuges primarily for ducks and geese. But the ESA was a double-edged sword. On the one hand, it gave the agency more power. On the other hand, efforts to protect endangered species like salmon often had far-reaching consequences for refuges. Water that would have once been diverted to refuges now remained in rivers and streams to protect endangered salmon. Refuges still depended on water from nearby irrigation districts to support the refuges. When endangered species received water instead of irrigators, the refuges suffered. Water transferred from agricultural to urban users had a similar effect. Irrigation districts and farmers proved increasingly willing to sell water to municipalities. This diversion of water often meant that less water was available for wildlife such as migratory waterfowl. Entering the new millennium, the FWS found its refuges in a precarious position. This chapter examines these issues by focusing on recent conflicts over water and endangered species in the Klamath Basin, the Central Valley of California, and the Imperial Valley.

Although this is a history of past efforts to conserve migratory birds, it has considerable salience today, even for those not primarily concerned with birds. At its most basic, this is a story about protecting wild nature in working landscapes. For the past century, we have tried to segregate wildlife from parts of the countryside devoted to productive uses. Wildlife managers may no longer bomb waterfowl and herd them into refuges, but there is still a sense among farmers and the public that waterfowl belong in designated spaces. The western landscape is a shared space, and the refuges are part of the irrigated landscape, even if the two appear clearly separated on maps. If migratory birds are to have a future during an era when our demands on the land and water are increasing—and they face one of their greatest threats from global warming—we must recognize these relationships and foster common spaces where both people and wildlife can thrive.

1

THE WETLAND ARCHIPELAGO

THE WORD "FLYWAY" conjures up visions of an aerial highway that birds follow up and down the continent, taking rest stops along the way. But the word is misleading. There is no interstate in the sky for the birds to follow. Ornithologists realize that beneath the simplicity of the flyway concept lays a very complicated network of crisscrossing migration paths. Despite these limitations, wildlife managers still use flyways as a management tool. In the words of one nature writer, the Pacific Flyway is a "way of thinking about ducks."[1] Although biologists now have more sophisticated understandings of bird migration than they did when the concept was developed in the 1930s, it does capture one basic fact of North American bird migration: along the Pacific coast, waterfowl migrate between the ocean and the flanks of the main mountain ranges. Birds can and do cross these mountains while migrating, but many species of waterfowl follow the general north-south trending ranges.[2]

Except for the northern part of the continent, where wetlands were extensive and plentiful, most of the area encompassed by the Pacific Flyway was useless to waterfowl even before people began draining wetlands on a large scale in the late nineteenth century. Ducks, geese, and swans need wetlands to survive, and the degree of their dependence varies by species. Most waterfowl nest on or near wetlands. Although birds migrate across vast distances, their journeys bring them to environments similar to ones they left. A goose would breed in a wetland in Alaska, stop to feed in a wetland in British Columbia or Oregon, and spend the winter in a wetland in California.[3]

Until the nineteenth century, people did not radically alter or drain wetlands along the Pacific Flyway on a large scale. This does not mean that they were pristine sites free from human use. The enormous productivity of wetland environments made them attractive to Native peoples from Alaska to Mexico. Although they had a significant impact on wildlife numbers using these wetlands, their technologies limited their ability to alter the hydrology of western marshes and estuaries. Native peoples neither diverted major rivers nor filled wetlands. Until the nineteenth century, the distribution of wetlands, and their formation or disappearance, was largely the product of natural forces.[4]

Yet the fact that humans had only minimal impact on the hydrology of western wetlands does not mean that these wetlands were timeless. Change defines the natural history of these places. Focusing on the wetlands just prior to their destruction in the nineteenth century can create a misleading impression of their characteristics. Wetlands were dynamic environments before people began to drain, dike, and fill them, and the degree of dynamism differed from area to area. This dynamism operated over short courses of a few years and over longer periods of centuries and millennia. During the Pleistocene, for example, ice covered most of the current breeding range of migratory waterfowl. Waterfowl were therefore geographically limited to regions south of the ice sheets that covered most of present-day Canada and Alaska. As the ice sheets retreated between 10,000 and 12,000 years ago, many areas were opened to colonization by plant species and, eventually, by migratory birds. Waterfowl migration is partially an adaptation to this change.[5]

By migrating, waterfowl and other birds were able to take advantage of the seasonal abundance of resources available in the Arctic and subarctic during the summer, and then retreat to lower latitudes before the onset of winter. But long migratory journeys exposed them to dangers en route, as well as to the possibility that drought would dry up wetlands in either the wintering or breeding range. For many species of birds, migration was necessary and unavoidable, but it exacted a cost. The cost became all too apparent to conservationists hoping to save migratory waterfowl as western marshes and estuaries were lost to agricultural and urban development.[6]

THE PACIFIC FLYWAY WATERSCAPE

Pacific Flyway birds annually migrated to wetlands separated by thousands of miles. Prior to the nineteenth century, wetlands were more common in the northern reaches of the flyway than in the southern portion, where aridity and topography restricted their development. Although wetlands and lakes were abundant in the Arctic and subarctic, they were not all equally useful for waterfowl. River deltas supported the highest numbers of waterfowl. During their annual migrations, birds migrated from these northern wetlands to marshes and estuaries in the western United States and Mexico. Their journeys took them from Arctic deltas to wetlands in some of the driest deserts in North America.

The Yukon-Kuskokwim Delta on the west coast of Alaska formed the largest and most important wetland complex in this northern region. Between the lower stretches of these major rivers, a tapestry of bogs and marshes formed that covered over 26,000 square miles. During the summer breeding season in peak years, over 750,000 ducks and 500,000 geese could be found within this delta. All the cackling Canada geese found in North America nested in the delta, and most of the white-fronted geese that traveled along the Pacific Flyway bred there, too. For snow geese migrating from their breeding ground on Wrangel Island in Siberia, the Yukon-Kuskokwim Delta was an important stopover on their journey to California's Central Valley. The upper regions of the Yukon River (known as the Yukon Flats) were also critical habitat for waterfowl. Over 40,000 ponds and lakes flanked the river. Together, these wetlands provided nesting habitat for a significant portion of Pacific Flyway waterfowl.[7]

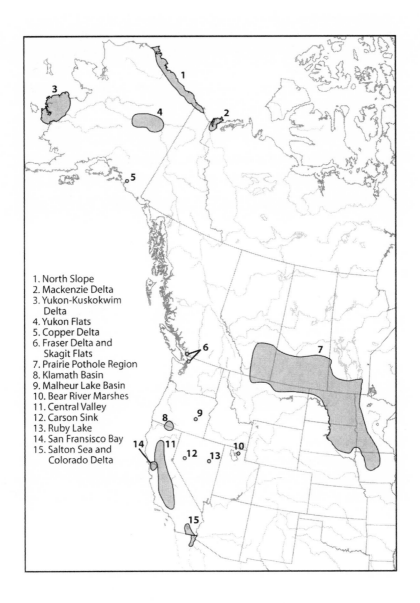

1. North Slope
2. Mackenzie Delta
3. Yukon-Kuskokwim
   Delta
4. Yukon Flats
5. Copper Delta
6. Fraser Delta and
   Skagit Flats
7. Prairie Pothole Region
8. Klamath Basin
9. Malheur Lake Basin
10. Bear River Marshes
11. Central Valley
12. Carson Sink
13. Ruby Lake
14. San Fransisco Bay
15. Salton Sea and
    Colorado Delta

MAP 2 *Nesting, staging, and wintering areas of the Pacific Flyway*

The drainage basins of other major rivers also provided habitat for ducks, geese, and swans. The Mackenzie River was the most important in northern Canada. Waterfowl researchers in the 1960s compared the Mackenzie River system to a giant staircase stretching from the Arctic into more southerly parts of Canada. Inland deltas were found along each step or landing along the Mackenzie River and its major tributaries. Toward the headwaters of this system, the Peace and Athabasca rivers formed a delta on the southeast shore of Lake Athabasca. The remnants of meander channels from both rivers created an ideal habitat for waterfowl. Ducks and geese fed on marsh plants like sago pondweed and alkali bulrushes that grew in abundance. The most serious threat to birds using the area was not drought, but flooding, which could wipe out waterfowl nests. This could have severe consequences if a flood occurred in the peak nesting season (June and July). The population of waterfowl using the delta during the summer could range from 84,000 to 250,000 birds. Other rivers in this system also formed deltas when they entered large lakes. The Slave River, for instance, formed a delta when it reached Great Slave Lake, which served as an aquatic nursery for waterfowl. The largest delta formed where the Mackenzie River emptied into the Beaufort Sea.[8]

Widespread though they were, the wetlands and river deltas of the north were not nearly as productive per acre as wetlands farther south, particularly on the Canadian and American prairies. Wetlands were common in the northern boreal forests, but the soils were poor and supported fewer of the marsh plants ducks and geese needed. Since drought occurred less often in the north than it did on the prairies, the northern wetlands were nonetheless more dependable from year to year. The sheer size of the northern wetland area also meant that it could support large waterfowl populations. Also, the dispersal of waterfowl over the vast territory meant that poor conditions in one part of the region would not have devastating consequences to waterfowl in other parts. Even more importantly, the northern region served as a place to which ducks and geese could retreat when droughts dried up wetlands on the prairies. Therefore, in addition to being an important breeding area for waterfowl every year, northern wetlands and deltas functioned as a safety valve for birds along the flyway. Ducks and geese could depend on the relatively pristine and drought-free areas in the north when conditions deteriorated on the prairies. As we shall see, the situation was considerably different in the wintering range.[9]

These northern areas were an opportunity and a problem. Although Alaska and northern Canada made up one of the largest wetland complexes in the world, waterfowl could only use them during the warmer months each year. Once winter arrived, waterfowl needed to migrate to areas where food was plentiful and open water was available for feeding and resting. Waterfowl migrated to the northern reaches annually, but they had to retreat quickly at the end of summer. Without dependable, high-quality wintering habitat, these northern areas were useless to waterfowl.

None of the wetlands in northern Canada or Alaska could compare to the incredible productivity of the Prairie Pothole area, a region of thousands of small ponds and marshes straddling the Canada-U.S. border. Although the area only contained a tenth of the duck-breeding area in North America, the Prairie Potholes supported between 50 and 80 percent of the continent's breeding ducks during the summer. Since most of these ducks migrated along other flyways, the region contributed fewer ducks and geese to the Pacific Flyway than the northern regions. If the Pacific Flyway were a river, the waterfowl from the Prairie Pothole would be tributary to the main stem of birds coming from Alaska and northwestern Canada.

The reason for this area's productivity lay in the extensiveness and types of wetlands found there. The region is dotted with small ponds and marshes (most only a few acres in size) that formed at the end of the Pleistocene when the Laurentide Ice Sheet retreated, leaving blocks of ice in what is now southern Alberta, Saskatchewan, and Manitoba. These "potholes," known as kettles, later became ponds and marshes. In some places the density of potholes reached almost 40 per square kilometer. The exact number of potholes that existed prior to agricultural settlement of the Prairies is difficult to estimate because they were so numerous; some studies suggest that over ten million existed in Canada and one million in the United States.[10]

Changes in precipitation in the region from year to year made the potholes dynamic environments. In the fall, most potholes were dry or contained very little water. During the spring, they refilled with melting snow or rainwater, which evaporated over the course of the spring and summer. By late summer or early fall, many potholes would be dry once again. The way waterfowl used these freshwater marshes differed by species, but the diversity of pothole types and the length of time they contained water was part of what made them so attractive to these types of birds. Mallard and pintail ducks used a number of different types of potholes throughout the breeding and wintering season. Seasonal potholes often had plentiful insects in the late spring, which was when ducks had higher protein needs for breeding. At other times, ducks sought out potholes with dense vegetation to shelter their young. Over the course of the breeding season, ducks used between seven and twenty-two different potholes. Although each pothole was important, the assemblage of wetlands is what made this area so vital for waterfowl.[11]

Waterfowl could not rely on the availability of pothole wetlands every breeding season. During drought years, potholes often failed to fill with water or the water evaporated early in the season. Without pothole wetlands, waterfowl were forced to fly elsewhere to find breeding habitat. This usually meant flying farther north to wetlands in the boreal region or river deltas. Although wetlands in northern areas were less prone to drought, they were not as productive as prairie wetlands. Even with these "back-up" northern wetlands, drought years led to sharp declines in waterfowl populations. Yet this dynamism was partly responsible for the productivity of prairie wetlands: the repeated drying and flooding of potholes allowed emergent marsh vegetation to flourish.[12]

Prairie Pothole wetlands were extremely vital for North American waterfowl as a whole. Yet they contributed fewer birds to the Pacific Flyway than they did to the continent's other principal migration routes. The pothole region was the primary breeding ground for the ducks that migrated along the Central and Mississippi flyways. There were exceptions to this general trend. For instance, most northern pintails and mallards found along the Pacific Flyway bred in the Prairie Potholes and wintered in the Central Valley of California. The relatively small contribution of Prairie Pothole birds to the Pacific Flyway had a number of implications. It meant that the draining and filling of Prairie Potholes in the twentieth century would have less impact on Pacific Flyway waterfowl populations than on the waterfowl of other flyways; most of the wetlands in the breeding range of migratory waterfowl along this flyway were not seriously affected. Even in the late twentieth century, northern wetlands in Alaska and Canada remained little altered by humans. Also, drought cycles, which periodically dried pothole marshes, were common in the Prairie Pothole region, but occurred less frequently in the breeding range of most Pacific Flyway waterfowl.[13]

Unlike the primary breeding areas for Pacific Flyway waterfowl, which were extensive and continuous, the wetlands in the wintering range were more like an archipelago. Much of the West Coast was too mountainous for extensive wetlands to form. Along the coast, fjords between Alaska and southern British Columbia were not conducive environments for the creation of wetlands. Waterfowl flying to wintering grounds beyond Alaska's Copper River Delta would not encounter another estuary of comparable size until they reached southwestern British Columbia. There, the Fraser River formed a large delta where the river entered the Georgia Strait. Birds congregated there, and at Sumas Lake sixty miles east of the delta. Marshes were also abundant on the Chilcotin Plateau in British Columbia's interior, but like the wetlands farther north, they were used by waterfowl only in the warmer months. In coastal areas, where the temperatures were mild, migrants could live in large numbers throughout the winter. Because of this, most British Columbia wetlands were primarily breeding and staging areas for birds that wintered to the south.[14]

The lowlands surrounding the Strait of Georgia and Puget Sound were also valuable habitat for migratory waterfowl. Bogs and marshes formed in the depressions left by retreating glaciers were common throughout the area. As in the far north, the river deltas were the most important areas for migrating ducks and geese. Largest among these was the Fraser River Delta, but the deltas of the Skagit, Duwamish, and Nisqually also attracted waterfowl. These lowlands were transitional areas for migratory waterfowl. Some species or populations of waterfowl ventured no farther and wintered in these sites. Others used them as staging sites before continuing on to other wintering areas. It was this mosaic of habitats that attracted the birds.[15]

Many large wetlands were found in the wide depressions of

the Great Basin, a physiographic province encompassing most of Nevada as well as southeastern Oregon, western Utah, and southern Arizona. Without any natural outlet, the rivers flowing from the north-south trending mountains in the region drained into basins, where, over time, much of the water evaporated. In an environment with such high evaporation rates and no drainage, the remaining lake water became hypersaline. The Great Salt Lake in northern Utah was the largest of these lakes. Smaller lakes like Lake Abert in Oregon, Pyramid and Winnemucca lakes in Nevada, and Mono and Owens lakes in California were also important. These lakes were particularly valuable for non-waterfowl species like American avocets, snowy plovers, phalaropes, and eared grebes, which could tolerate the saline water and feed on the relatively small number of species living in the lakes. Most Great Basin lakes were too saline to support abundant wetlands, but extensive marshes could form where modest drainage occurred or when rivers emptied into the lakes. This was the case in the Malheur and Klamath Basins of central Oregon. In both areas, there was sufficient drainage to prevent lakes from developing salt levels that would inhibit wetland development.[16]

More than any other areas along the Pacific Flyway, the lakes and marshes of the Great Basin were subject to change that likely affected the distribution of waterfowl. During the Pleistocene, immense lakes such as Lake Modoc, Lake Lohontan, and Lake Bonneville connected most of the now-dry valleys.[17] Over the past 12,000 years, the distribution and size of Great Basin lakes changed in response to the climate. Most of these lakes disappeared as the climate warmed, but between 10,000 and 8,000 years ago, many of the valleys within the Great Basin contained substantial marshes. Paleoecologists and geologists have found evidence of cattails and other marsh vegetation from that time in the Las Vegas Valley of southern Nevada. Scientists also believe that the marshes at Ruby Lake in central Nevada were deeper and more extensive than they are today. The bones of ducks and other wetland-dependent bird species found in the basin sediments from this period show that waterfowl used the area extensively. Presumably, other valleys in the Great Basin also had lakes and marshes during this era. These marshes disappeared as the southern Great Basin became drier and warmer about 7,000 years ago. Until approximately 4,500 years ago, Great Basin conditions were hotter and drier than they are today. Cooler conditions after that time enabled some marshes to form, but neither these wetlands nor the lakes were as extensive as they were during the early Holocene.[18]

Because of these long-term alterations in Great Basin climate and hydrology, waterfowl had to adapt to changing environments well before the arrival of Euro-Americans. No doubt waterfowl numbers rose and fell in relation to the conditions of the lakes and marshes in the Great Basin. Other wetlands and lakes were available in other parts of the wintering range, and migratory routes likely changed as wetlands were created, destroyed, or altered.

Migratory waterfowl used the lakes and wetlands of the Great Basin primarily as staging areas during migration. The largest and most important of these areas was the Klamath Basin on the Oregon-California state line.[19] More than 80 percent of Pacific Flyway waterfowl funneled into the basin during their migration to use the basin's wetlands. Although a small number of birds remained in the high, cold basin during the winter, most used it as a staging area, feeding and resting for a few days or weeks before continuing on to wintering grounds in California's Central Valley or western Mexico. The exact number of birds using the basin before the twentieth century is impossible to determine, but as late as 1958, five to six million ducks, geese, and swans were found in the area's lakes and marshes during the peak of the fall migration.[20]

The Klamath Basin had a unique waterscape that contributed to its importance as a staging area for migratory birds. Waterfowl stopped in the basin during fall and spring migrations to rest and feed before continuing on to the wintering or breeding areas. Since all of the lakes in the basin had at least partial drainage, none of them became hypersaline. Still, not all of the lakes were attractive to waterfowl. Most of Upper Klamath Lake was too deep to support wetlands, but like the lakes in the Great Basin, freshwater marshes formed on the lake's margins, such as where the Williamson River emptied into the lake. Clear Lake, surrounded by sagebrush on a high plateau of the Klamath Basin, was fringed by freshwater marshes. The best waterfowl habitat, however, was found on Lower Klamath Lake and on Tule Lake. Although called lakes, both areas were a mixture of marshes and open water. The diversity of marshes and water depths attracted the largest congregations of ducks and geese in the Klamath Basin.

Water for Lower Klamath Lake came from the Klamath River via Klamath Straits, a channel that connected the river to the lake. During spring freshets, water flowed from the Klamath River into Lower Klamath Lake. When the river subsided, water flowed from the lake back into the Klamath River. This seasonal flow of water into and out of the lake prevented the lake from becoming hypersaline like lakes in the Great Basin. Although Lower Klamath and Tule lakes were only a few miles apart, they were in different watersheds (a ridge separated the two lakes). Tule Lake received its water from Lost River, which originated at Clear Lake and took a circuitous path flowing northwest before altering course southward into Tule Lake. Even though Tule Lake lacked a surface outlet, it never became hypersaline. Geologists suspected that water seeped through the vesicular basalt underlying the southern portion of the lake.[21]

The wetlands in the Klamath Basin and Great Basin were important stops for migrating waterfowl, but few birds wintered in these areas. The frigid winters common throughout the inland West forced the waterfowl to travel to more hospitable climates. The ultimate destination for many of these birds was the Central Valley of California, the wintering grounds for 60 percent of Pacific Flyway waterfowl. Hemmed in by the Coast Range to the west and the Sierra Nevada Mountains to the east, the Central Valley stretched for four hundred miles through the heart of California. In fact, the Central Valley was divided into a northern portion, the Sacramento Valley, and a southern portion, the San Joaquin Valley, each drained by a river named after its respective valley. The confluence of these two rivers formed an enormous delta. Riparian forests once cloaked the banks of the rivers and the meandering channels in the delta. Freshwater marshes formed on the floodplains of the river and saltwater marshes rimmed the edges of the bay. Together, these extensive wetlands served as habitat for the largest wintering population of waterfowl in the United States.[22]

This is surprising given the aridity of the region. The annual rainfall in the valley ranges between eight and twenty inches. But the Sacramento and San Joaquin rivers were fed by melting snow pack and rainfall in the Sierra Nevada Mountains. In the northern part of the valley, the Sacramento River often flooded, creating a vast, temporary inland lake. Although much of this water receded through the summer months, it nourished the freshwater marshes on the floodplain, particularly along the lower stretches of the river near the delta. Flooding was less common along the San Joaquin River (which had a much smaller annual discharge), and marshes were restricted to riparian areas and the lower reaches of the river. The most abundant habitat for migratory waterfowl in the San Joaquin Valley was in the Tulare, Buena Vista, and Kern lakes, in the southern part of the valley. Until the mid-nineteenth century, Tulare Lake was the largest freshwater lake in the western United States. Tules and other marsh plants were so thick on the edges of the lake that it was difficult to see open water from shore. When spring river flows were particularly heavy, sloughs connected the three lakes, creating an important hydrologic network in this arid region. During wet years, wetlands covered up to two-and-a-half million acres of the valley floor.[23]

Because detailed surveys of the waterfowl populations did not begin until the 1950s, determining the number of ducks and geese that wintered in the Central Valley prior to the twentieth century is difficult. The environmental historian Ann Vileisis used the relationship between average waterfowl population in the 1980s and available Central Valley wetland habitat at the time to estimate the number of ducks and geese wintering in the valley before Euro-American settlement. Using this technique, she calculated that approximately thirty-five million Pacific Flyway ducks, geese, and swans wintered in this part of California.[24] Some waterfowl biologists make even higher estimates: Guy A. Baldassarre and Eric G. Bolen estimate that the waterfowl population may have been fifty million as late as the 1940s.[25] Today, only three to four million ducks and a million geese winter in the Central Valley.[26] Although we will never have more than a rough gauge of the number of waterfowl that wintered in the valley before the twentieth century, it is clear the population was far higher than it is today.[27]

Some Pacific Flyway birds continued their southward migration beyond the Central Valley to wetlands in northern Mexico. One of the largest was the Colorado River Delta, located just south of the California-Mexico border. Covering over 3,300 square miles, the delta was a vital oasis for migrating birds along this part of the flyway. The Sonoran Desert, one of the hottest and driest parts of North America, surrounds the delta. Within this desert region, the delta's thousands of acres of marshes, sloughs, and lagoons provided habitat for many species of ducks and geese. The rarity of such habitat in the U.S.-Mexico borderlands is what made the area so crucial for migratory birds. The highly variable flow of the Colorado River also contributed to the delta's productivity.[28]

As in the Central Valley, there were no detailed surveys of waterfowl populations in the Colorado River Delta during the early twentieth century. The area remained poorly known by American ornithologists. Aldo Leopold ventured into the delta region by canoe in 1922 on a hunting expedition, which he described over two decades later in *A Sand County Almanac*. For two weeks, he and his brother hunted geese and paddled through the lush lagoons of the delta. When he climbed a cottonwood to survey the area, he saw the delta spreading in all directions toward the horizon. To Leopold, this land of abundant bird life was a "milk-and-honey wilderness," a memory that stayed with him for the rest of his life. Flocks of snow geese and sandhill cranes flew overhead. He and his brother were "sharing our wilderness with the wildest of living fowl. We and they have found a common home in the remote fastnesses of space and time; we were both back in the Pleistocene."[29]

Within the span of a few weeks or months, Pacific Flyway waterfowl traveled between radically different surroundings. Some started their journey in Arctic or subarctic river deltas amid a patchwork of wetlands extending for hundreds of square miles. As they flew farther south, the birds entered arid western North America, where the wetlands were restricted to the valleys between mountain ranges of the deltas of major rivers like those of the Sacramento–San Joaquin and the Colorado. Compared to the extensive northern wetlands, these areas were like an archipelago surrounded by deserts. In places such as the Klamath and Malheur basins, the marshes were large enough to support millions of birds for a few weeks during the fall and spring migrations. Even though they lay within deserts, the frigid temperatures made it impossible for most waterfowl to remain throughout the winter. Compared to other parts of the country, the total acreage of wetlands in the western states was meager. Because of this, ducks and geese congregated in the few wetland areas in greater numbers than any other part of the United States. The multitudes of waterfowl were a reflection of the scarcity of habitat, not its abundance. If these wetlands disappeared, there would be nowhere for the birds to retreat.

LINKING WETLANDS

Wetlands in western North American supported hundreds of different types of animals, but none of them were more prominent than ducks and geese. It was common to see tens of thousands of them in the tule marshes of the Central Valley or in the channels of the delta of the Sacramento and San Joaquin rivers. Migratory waterfowl were so numerous that they became as closely identified with western marshes and estuaries as bison were with the Great Plains and salmon with the rivers of the Pacific Northwest.[30]

The degree to which waterfowl depend on wetlands varies by species, since some are better able to survive on food outside of wetlands. Swans and geese, for instance, are herbivores that feed on grasses as well as wetland plants. These types of waterfowl would later prove adept at eating cultivated plants such as barley, wheat, and rice. Other waterfowl species, including dabbling ducks, feed on wetland plants and invertebrates. The diet of ducks and geese also varies throughout the year. During the winter, most waterfowl tend to eat plants for the abundant carbohydrates they need to carry them through the season. In the breeding season, however, many species of waterfowl need more protein, which they obtain by eating insects. The availability of insects partly affects the nesting sites chosen by mallards, northern pintails, and other ducks.[31]

Although the migration of birds is commonly associated with the onset of fall or spring, birds do not migrate primarily to escape winter. If food is plentiful, waterfowl can handle very cold temperatures. They are forced to leave the Arctic and subarctic because food is extremely scarce or covered by snow. Finding food generally means traveling southward. Despite the different migration strategies of other avian species, the general north-south pattern most people associate with bird migration holds true for waterfowl in the northern hemisphere.[32]

Defining migration is not as easy as it seems. Although most people use the term loosely in reference to the movement of someone or something from one place to another, biologists employ more precise definitions. Migration is a coping mechanism for dealing with the uneven distribution of resources across time and space. Birds can exploit the often seasonally available resources in northern latitudes even though such places cannot support them throughout the entire year. Since other animals such as terrestrial mammals or amphibians are unable to travel great distances, they must adapt to the lack of resources during the winter months by hibernating or using other survival strategies to make it through to spring.[33] Birds can overcome the distances and geographical constraints that other animals cannot.[34]

The biologist Hugh Dingle offers a more nuanced view of migration. He sees it as a very specific kind of movement used by many types of organisms. Rather than providing a simple definition for the term, he examines some of the more important characteristics of migration. First, migration is a persistent movement that lasts longer than the normal, everyday journeys an animal might make. Waterfowl fly within a limited range to find food on a daily basis, but while migrating, the birds can fly nonstop for many hours (in some cases, days) until they reach their destination. Second, the movement is linear and lacks the frequent changes of direction common in everyday flights for food and shelter. Migrating species will not eat during their journey until they deplete their fat reserves. For birds, this means often ignoring food sources and resting sites such as wetlands until they complete their journey or are physically incapable of continuing.[35]

At first glance, migration might appear to be the perfect solution to dealing with widely separated, seasonally available resources. Birds can feed on the vegetation available in the northern latitudes during the warmer months and then fly to places with more hospitable climates for the rest of the year. After reaching lower latitudes, they can take advantage of the food sources available during the winter season before returning north. But these advantages are not without difficulty. Many of the birds that leave northern breeding ranges never reach their destination. Storms blow the birds off course or force them to land prematurely. A poor year for food in the breeding range can leave waterfowl with insufficient fat reserves to make the migratory journey.[36]

Because waterfowl depend on widely dispersed wetlands along their migratory routes, they are particularly vulnerable if conditions lead to depleted resources in any of these habitats over the course of the year. Pristine breeding grounds are of little use if there are no wetlands in the birds' wintering range. The destruction of habitat in one part of the flyway can have distant geographical ramifications. Although these birds need wetlands in different places throughout the year, the way they use them differs depending on the season. In the winter or nonbreeding season, waterfowl need wetlands for resting and food. Since geese and swans are able to eat non-wetland vegetation, they can also feed in upland areas away from wetlands. During the breeding season, the habitat needs of waterfowl are more restricted. They depend on wetland vegetation to build their nests. More importantly, they need protein from wetland insects in order to produce viable clutches of eggs.[37]

Different species of waterfowl and populations within species show affinities for particular areas, often traveling from the same wintering to breeding grounds each year. Although birds might travel from each place annually, these routes are not fixed. Waterfowl can and do adapt to new environmental conditions. Although waterfowl have an innate ability to orient themselves during migration, finding appropriate wintering and breeding grounds is often a learned behavior. Waterfowl are particularly adept at learning migration routes from other ducks, geese, and swans. "The timing of migration seems to be innate, as is a very general compass bearing," writes Scott Weidensaul. "A duck raised in isolation knows *how* to migrate, but not specifically *where*. Among these birds, and unlike almost all others, the details are bound up in tradition, passed on by older generations."[38] In effect, each new generation of ducks and geese becomes familiar with migration routes from older waterfowl. When food is available year round, some waterfowl species stop migrating altogether. This strategy can persist only when local resources are abundant. If habitat conditions change years later, the population of waterfowl no longer knows the migration routes traveled by its ancestors. On the other hand, since the exact routes of migration are not genetically determined, waterfowl can adapt to the loss or creation of new habitats along the flyway. In the twentieth century, drastic habitat transformations along the Pacific Flyway forced just such changes in migration and behavior.[39]

Although there were broad similarities in the routes and wetlands used by Pacific Flyway waterfowl, the individual paths and specific habitats they used varied by species. Take the snow geese, for instance. Pacific Flyway snow geese bred in a relatively small number of places, most notably Wrangel Island just north of Russia and the Mackenzie River Delta and Banks Island in northern Canada. The migration path of the snow geese originating on Wrangel Island took them across the Gulf of Alaska and then the mouth of the Columbia River. After resting and feeding there, they continued their journey to the Central Valley of California, the largest wintering ground for Pacific Flyway snow geese.[40]

Other waterfowl species were even more restrictive in their breeding range. For instance, Pacific Flyway white-fronted geese breed exclusively in the remote marshes formed in the delta of the Yukon and Kuskokwim rivers. Unlike other geese, white-fronted geese fly to staging areas without stopping and arrive there earlier than many other waterfowl. Some would arrive in the Klamath Basin by the first week of September before the bulk of them continued to winter in the Central Valley.[41]

Pintails, a dabbling duck, have a breeding area in a completely different part of North America. Most originate in the small marshes of the Prairie Pothole region. This vast reservoir for ducks contributes birds to all the major flyways. As with snow and white-fronted geese, the winter home of most pintails was the Central Valley, though roughly a quarter of Pacific Flyway pintails would continue on to Mexico. In the 1960s, the wintering population of pintails was a staggering two million, easily making them the most common duck in these areas.[42]

Regardless of the species, the wetlands of the Far West served as essential links in the annual migratory journeys of waterfowl. By migrating, waterfowl were able to gain access to the abundant resources available in northern latitudes (particularly within Arctic and subarctic river deltas) during the summer months. Unlike non-avian or marine species, migratory waterfowl were able to leave these areas quickly before colder temperatures made them inhospitable. Within the wintering range of the Pacific Flyway, migratory waterfowl found food in western marshes and estuaries as well as open water for resting.

Migration came with substantial costs, too. Storms could blow migrants off course or force birds to expend so much energy that they were unable to reach their wintering quarters. Droughts could dry up wetlands in parts of the flyway. Migratory paths were flexible enough to enable the birds to adapt to these changes. They could cope with the loss of some wetlands along the flyway. But the system was not infinitely flexible. Migrants still needed wetlands in both the breeding *and* wintering areas: abundant wetlands in good condition in one part of the flyway meant little if wetlands were unavailable in another part. Like a chain, the flyway was only as strong as its weakest link.[43]

Over the course of the twentieth century, reclamation and water diversions destroyed most of the wetlands in the wintering range of the Pacific Flyway. The waterfowl that survived this loss of habitat congregated in smaller pockets of wetlands, particularly in the Central Valley of California. Although wetlands had disappeared in the past, particularly during wet-dry cycles of a few years or more, these losses were not usually permanent, except over the long term. The destruction of wetlands occurred within the context of dynamic environments to which waterfowl had adapted. Yet their ability to cope with these changes had limits. They could survive if wetlands remained in both the wintering and breeding ranges, but not if the wetlands disappeared entirely in either area.

2

ELUSIVE SANCTUARIES

DURING THE EARLY TWENTIETH CENTURY, the tapestry of wetlands along the southern portion of the Pacific Flyway largely disappeared. Although government agencies did not tally the disappearance of marshes at the time, more recent studies provide some sense of what was lost. By the 1930s, states such as Washington had lost nearly 31 percent of wetlands and Oregon 38 percent. As bad as this was, it could not compare to the staggering losses in California. In the great Central Valley, the prime Pacific Flyway wintering area, more than 90 percent of wetlands were destroyed, a loss unmatched by any other state in the country. Farmers, irrigation districts, and reclamation agencies systematically destroyed western marshes and other riparian areas to clear the way for farmland and, to a lesser degree, growing cities. Boosters called this process "reclamation"—as if the land was a fallen sinner awaiting salvation. Americans and Canadians transformed western rivers, lakes, and wetlands to a scope unseen since the last Ice Age. Migratory birds continued their annual migrations, but in their wintering range they found fewer marshes for food and rest. At the same time, hunting pressures increased. Amidst diminished habitat and growing threats, waterfowl struggled to survive.[1]

Migratory waterfowl faced many threats in the early twentieth century, but these threats were not evenly distributed along the flyway. The vast marshes of Alaska and northern Canada, the nurseries for many Pacific Flyway ducks and geese, were virtually unscathed during this period. The region was also sparsely populated and largely inaccessible to all but subsistence Native hunters. Wetland drainage and overhunting was overwhelmingly concentrated in the wintering range of flyway birds. Yet since migratory waterfowl depended on wetlands at both ends of their journeys, the loss of habitat took a toll on birds overall even though in the north such pressures were slight.[2]

This destruction went largely unopposed. Despite their many divisions, most American and Canadian settlers agreed on one thing: wetlands were valueless unless drained. But in a few places, some challenged the reclamation drive, not because they valued marshes in and of themselves, but because of the wildlife they sustained. Sport hunters and bird protectionists convinced the federal government to establish bird sanctuaries along the Oregon-California border and in central Oregon. Hunting was prohibited in these protected marshes. Along with stiffer hunting regulations, bird conservationists hoped these protected areas would stop migratory bird numbers from plummeting. Together, the Klamath Basin and Malheur Basin sanctuaries comprised the largest bird refuges in the nation.

This protection, such as it was, proved ephemeral. The marshes and sloughs within the refuge borders disappeared as irrigators diverted the water that once flowed into the wetlands to new farms. In the Klamath Basin, it was another federal agency, the U.S. Reclamation Service, which accomplished this transformation. Although presidential decree had created these refuges, the agency destroyed them with little opposition. Conservationists waged a prolonged, losing campaign through the 1910s and 1920s to halt this destruction, and later, to resurrect the marshes. They faced a government and public committed to wetland drainage.

More than anywhere else, the Klamath Basin exposed the U.S. government's Janus-faced approach to wetlands—an approach that endures in some measure to this day. On the one hand, the federal government through the U.S. Reclamation Service sought to transform the arid West into an irrigated garden. Using dams, dikes, and canals, it would convert "wastelands" such as marshes into productive farms. On the other, the federal government also hoped to sustain migratory birds by creating bird sanctuaries. In the case of the Klamath Basin, the government tried both simultaneously—and in the very same place. The result was a century of discord that exposed the contradictions and absurdities of the early refuge program. Such conflicts became common in later decades as additional refuges were established elsewhere along the Pacific Flyway.

RECLAIMING THE LAND, DRAINING THE SKIES

The desire to convert wetlands into productive farmland was a major impetus for the destruction of migratory bird habitat; the perceived unhealthiness of marshes, bogs, and other wetlands the birds used was another. In the late nineteenth and early twentieth centuries, Americans and Canadians shared a deep-seated belief that wetlands were noxious places. Swamps and marshes in California, historian Linda Nash writes, were "not merely an unsightly landscape, an inconvenience to travel, and a hindrance to agriculture—though they were all these; they were also a frightening source of disease."[3] Draining or diverting water that supported wetlands would not only aid the economic development of many areas of the Far West, it would also help foster a sanitary landscape. Given the economic imperatives and health concerns behind wetland reclamation, it is not surprising that farmers and government agencies destroyed so many wetlands.[4]

Canada held relatively little wintering habitat for Pacific Flyway waterfowl. An exception to this was the southwest portion of the country's mainland. Although much of British Columbia received abundant rainfall, extensive wetlands were uncommon west of the Coast Range and Cascade Mountains. Topography restricted B.C. wetlands to the narrow river valleys and estuaries of the rivers that poured into the ocean. Some of the most important wetlands were found along the lower reaches of the Fraser River, the largest river in the province. The broad plain formed by the river near its mouth (known as the Lower Mainland) held many freshwater and saltwater marshes, as well as Sumas Lake. In the late nineteenth century, the fertile soil in the Lower Mainland attracted non-Native settlers who cleared the forest and created farms. By the first decades of the twentieth century, settlers also sought to drain the valley's shallow lakes and wetlands.[5]

Sumas Lake was the site of the most ambitious draining program. For the Stó:lō people, whose territory included the lake, the area had long been a valued place to harvest resources. The Stó:lō captured large lake sturgeon, and when the waterfowl came in the autumn, they caught ducks and geese on the lake using nets strung between poles. In the late nineteenth century, Euro-Canadian settlers arrived and homesteaded land purchased under the Pre-Emption Act of 1860. In a highly contested process, the Stó:lō were relegated to small reserves on the margins of the lake to make way for these settlers. To facilitate the development of the wetlands into agricultural areas, the Dominion of Canada gave the Province of British Columbia control over the 45,000 acres of the lake and marsh area with a view toward development.[6]

Although sportsmen from Vancouver and other towns in the region hunted waterfowl on and near Sumas Lake, they could not stop plans to drain it in the early 1920s. This drainage was justified by proponents who wanted to open the area for agricultural settlement and for mosquito control. Even Gordon Hewitt, one of Canada's leaders in conservation, was a strong proponent of drainage. Hewitt, an entomologist employed by the federal government, argued that draining Sumas Lake seemed like the best way to reduce what most settlers considered a terrible nuisance. With the support of the Dominion of Canada, local groups constructed dikes and pumps to "reclaim" the lake. By 1924, the lake was gone. Locals said that for years afterward, waterfowl returned to the area and circled overhead searching for the lake that no longer existed.[7]

The massive government-directed engineering project at Sumas Lake was indicative of a different approach to the environment that emerged in the early decades of the twentieth century. Prior to that time, the Canadian and B.C. governments adopted a laissez-faire approach to agricultural settlement in British Columbia. Although they saw the development of an agricultural countryside as a laudable goal, in practice federal and provincial governments offered little direct assistance to would-be settlers. By the end of the First World War, government leaders had come to see an expanded role for government, particularly in environmental matters. These new liberals, as they came to be known in Canada, advocated for a more activist state to benefit society. Like earlier supporters of Canadian agriculture, these new liberals also sought to foster a landscape of individual farmers cultivating crops for market. To achieve this, however, new liberals believed the state needed to take an active role in reshaping the land to create a modern agricultural countryside. In the case of Sumas Lake, this meant constructing the dikes, pumps, and other apparatuses that drained the waters.[8]

Draining Sumas Lake was a deliberate, state-directed act. Reducing and altering the riparian areas along the margins of the Fraser River was unintended. Farmers and municipalities began constructing dikes along the Fraser River as early as the 1860s. Yet only after a devastating flood in 1894 did the province intercede to direct the reconstruction of dikes and provide funds for their maintenance. "The magnitude of the task places it beyond the ability of private enterprise and makes it clearly the duty of the State to undertake," said British Columbia Premier Theodore Davie.[9] Although it provided oversight, the province did not build the dikes. Private districts constructed them, and the province provided financial support when districts were unable to finance dike construction themselves. The dikes eventually protected over 160,000 acres of farmland, over a third of the agricultural land in the province. Although riparian marshes could develop between the dikes and the Fraser River, the rocky riprap placed along the sides of the dikes to protect them from erosion was a poor substrate for the development of wetlands. Taken together, these actions effectively starved floodplain wetlands of water, making it easier for farmers to transform former marshes into farmland.[10]

In the United States, federal legislation encouraged wetland drainage. In the mid-nineteenth century, the U.S. Congress passed several acts that gave the states greater legislative authority to acquire and drain wetlands. The Swamp Land Act of 1849 transferred ownership of swamplands from the federal government to the states along the lower Mississippi River; other acts in the next decade extended this arrangement to other states, including California and Oregon. The federal government expected the states to use money from selling these lands to fund wetland drainage. After the states drained wetlands, they could sell the reclaimed land to fund additional wetland drainage. In practice, most states lacked the funds or expertise to undertake the formidable task of reclaiming large wetland areas. Speculators and large landowners often purchased much of the swampland, though even these groups often lacked the means to drain the land. Although swamp land acts led to very little immediate drainage, they did show that state and federal governments sought to eliminate wetlands whenever feasible.[11]

The danger of flooding made it difficult for those who acquired land in the Sacramento Valley to reclaim it. The Sacramento River, which flows through the valley, carries snowmelt from the Sierra Nevada and Cascade Mountains each year. In the mid-nineteenth century, the river regularly flooded areas along the southern portion of the Sacramento Valley, inundating the newly established state capital.[12] These floods also nourished wetlands within the flood plain used by wintering migratory waterfowl. Although plans to dike the river were proposed as early as the 1850s, a concerted, state-directed effort at river management would not come until the twentieth century. Before that time, early efforts at managing the river consisted of individual farmers or towns building dikes to protect their property, similar to what occurred in the Lower Mainland of British Columbia. This often came at the expense of other people along the river who had smaller dikes or built them haphazardly, since torrents of water flowing down the Sacramento River often destroyed them. Even though farmers and speculators had used the Swamp Land Act to purchase most of the wetlands in the Sacramento Valley, it was difficult to use these lands fully until the river was controlled. Thus, the wetlands gained a temporary reprieve from growers who wanted to convert them into agricultural land.[13]

Although the laissez-faire approach to managing the Sacramento River predominated in the late 1800s, the California state legislature was more amenable to centralized planning after the turn of the century. Legislators could see the success that some of the valley's larger landowners had in diking and protecting their lands from floods. In

1911, the state created a reclamation board to oversee dikes and other flood control structures in the Sacramento Valley. Later, with the assistance of the U.S. Army Corps of Engineers, the state constructed the large dikes and bypasses necessary to control flooding on the Sacramento River. The Sacramento Flood Control Project took decades to finish, but the completion of each dike or levee eliminated more wetlands and made large floods less common. The completion in the 1940s of the Shasta Dam near the headwaters of the Sacramento River reduced the threat of flooding even further. The frequent flooding of the Sacramento River had sustained many of the freshwater marshes; now enormous levees and bypasses confined the flow. This enabled landowners to drain and farm land that once remained uncultivated due to the risk of flooding and severed the connection between the river and surrounding flood plain. By 1918, landowners had reclaimed over 400,000 acres of land in the Sacramento Valley. With the flooding threat reduced, railway lines proliferated to service the more intensive farming that developed in the valley.[14]

Although the Sacramento and Fraser rivers were in different countries, the diking of both rivers was part of flood control programs carried out by the state.[15] In the case of the Sacramento River, the U.S. federal government played a more instrumental role than did the Canadian federal government along the Fraser in British Columbia.[16] Diking the lower reaches of these major rivers occurred for the same reasons and had similar consequences for nearby wetlands. Wetlands were integral parts of fluvial systems, and the construction of dikes and levees ended this connection. With the serious threat of flooding over, farmers willingly reclaimed marshes protected by dikes. In the wake of dike construction, people built more permanent structures— railroads, homes, and towns—that either eliminated more wetlands or made it impossible to restore them.

In the San Joaquin Valley and Tulare Basin to the south, reclamation for agriculture rather than flood control destroyed most of the wetlands.[17] As they had to the north, farmers and speculators used the swamp land acts to purchase most of the wetlands in the valley. The Miller & Lux company owned the largest tracts of land; the company controlled a staggering 420,888 acres, mostly in the San Joaquin Valley. Unlike most other landowners with large tracts, Miller & Lux did not intend to sell off the land to others. Rather, the company constructed dikes to reclaim marshes and developed an elaborate network of canals to irrigate its land.[18] The development of water control structures also affected Tulare Lake, the largest freshwater lake in the western United States. The lake covered more than 700 square miles and supported a productive fishery and thousands of ducks and geese during the winter. Diversions of water for irrigation from the Kings, Kaweah, and Tule rivers caused the lake to contract. Eventually, the remaining lake became so saline that by the end of the nineteenth century few species could survive in it. One visitor to the basin at that time said that the lake "is devoid of a single element of beauty and its uses are few. . . . It is a great, unsightly mud-hole."[19] Most of the lake evaporated, and what remained became a sump for agricultural wastewater. With the disappearance of Tulare Lake went one of the most important wintering areas for migratory waterfowl along the Pacific Flyway.[20]

East of the Sierra Nevada Mountains, extensive marshes were less common, but two lakes—Mono and Owens—were of particular value for migratory waterfowl. Marshes rimmed the margins of both lakes and the rivers that emptied into them. Although the Owens Valley Paiute had practiced small-scale irrigation, large-scale water development occurred in this area only after the arrival of non-Native settlers. As their counterparts had done upstream of Tulare Lake, farmers in the Owens Valley reduced the size and depth of Owens Lake by diverting river water for irrigation. By 1890, the shoreline of Owens Lake had receded nearly a mile, and the lake level had dropped by fifteen feet. Irrigation took a toll on Owens Lake, but municipal water diversions ultimately led to its destruction. In one of the most famous episodes in the history of western water, the city of Los Angeles bought most of the water rights to the Owens River. In 1914, the city diverted much of the river's flow into an aqueduct from Owens Valley to the Los Angeles Basin. In little over a decade, what remained of Owens Lake evaporated into the high desert air.[21]

Elsewhere in California, the elimination of marshes was a more incremental process. Before the influx of settlers after the Gold Rush of 1849, San Francisco Bay and the Sacramento-San Joaquin River Delta were a maze of tidal marshes, ponds, and tidal flats. San Francisco Bay was the location of the most extensive salt-water marshes and the most important estuary in California. Beginning in the mid-nineteenth century, farmers diked land to create pastures for livestock, and companies built ponds on the former marshes for salt production. Other parts of the bay were filled to make space for urban and industrial development. Collectively, these actions eliminated nearly 80 percent of the tidal marshes in the Bay Area. Some of the largest wetlands in the Bay Area, such as Suisun Marsh in the east bay, were almost completely destroyed. Of the 68,000 acres of existing marsh early in the nineteenth century, only 6,800 remained in the 1930s. The remaining wetlands comprised a discontinuous patchwork. Although some new wetlands formed on sediments deposited by the Sacramento River, they were not nearly enough to compensate for the thousands of acres of wetlands lost due to diking, draining, and filling.[22]

Although irrigation projects eliminated most of the wetlands and many of the freshwater lakes in California, they occasionally created habitat for migratory birds. The most important and unusual case was the creation of the Salton Sea in 1905. The sea formed in the Salton Sink, one of the lowest places in North America (a distinction it held with Death Valley to the north). Located near the California-Mexico border, the sink had been filled repeatedly in the distant past by the nearby Colorado River as it meandered to the Gulf of California. At the time American settlers came to the basin, the Salton Sink was a dry, blistering-hot playa. Beginning in 1901, the Colorado Development Company diverted water from the Colorado River into the basin, which George Chaffey, one of the founders of the company, had renamed the Imperial Valley. It was a stunning success. Within a few years, 7,000 people had moved to the valley and were using water supplied by the company to develop farms. In 1905, however, high flows on the Colorado River broke the diversion dam and sent the entire flow into the basin, where it continued to pour for nearly two years. The Colorado Development Company enlisted the help of the Southern Pacific Railway to plug the gap. By the time they stopped the flow, the dry basin had become an enormous lake fifty miles long and up to fifteen miles wide, making it easily the largest lake in California. The Salton Sink became the Salton Sea.[23]

An accident created the Salton Sea. Irrigation sustained it. In the decades following the flood, the Imperial Irrigation District (formed after the demise of the Colorado Development Company) brought most of the land bordering the northern and southern parts of the lake into agricultural production. The warm climate and the steady supply of water from the Colorado River made it possible to grow crops year round. Since the basin lacked a natural outlet, the irrigation drain water from the surrounding fields flowed into the Salton Sea, turning it into the largest sump in the western United States. Water diversions along the Colorado River eventually led to the drying up of the river's delta in Mexico. With the destruction of the Colorado River Delta, Pacific Flyway birds lost yet another key wintering area along their migratory route. Before this occurred, birds were already using the Salton Sea. The water development blunder that created the sea, and the irrigation water that supported it, came with a price. The evaporation of the lake left behind tons of salt. Over the decades, the salinity increased, making the sea unfit for many species. In the meantime, the sea became a haven for migratory birds.

Although these changes to the waterscape occurred for a variety of local reasons rather than as a result of one centralized program, Pacific Flyway waterfowl experienced it as a collective loss. Such a broad-brush summary cannot do justice to the nuances of water development activities in the West Coast states and provinces during the early twentieth century. Each place and era could receive—indeed, in many cases, has already received—careful scholarly analysis. Since there were no detailed censuses conducted at the time, precise estimates of bird populations are impossible. Eliminating wetland habitat at key sites along the migration route likely had a catastrophic impact on migratory bird numbers. Natural events like drought, which had always affected wetlands along the flyway, could now be disastrous. Formerly, if drought had led to the loss of wetlands in one part of the wintering range, waterfowl could potentially move to other areas where wetlands were still extensive. Now, with the elimination of so many wetlands due to water diversions, diking, and draining, there were fewer and fewer "safety valves" in the migration system. Reduced marshes endured, and formations of geese and ducks continued to cross western skies, but a half-century of transformations left the birds increasingly vulnerable to human and nonhuman threats. This posed severe ramifications for the future of migratory waterfowl.

What united proponents of wetland drainage was a conviction that the lands beneath the marshes would serve a more productive use as farms. In both Canada and the United States, a new political order that saw an increasing role for the state in reengineering the landscape, and particularly, draining lakes, diking rivers, and reclaiming marshes, resulted in drastic alterations of waterscapes. Since governments and most settlers valued wetlands so little, a geography developed that emphasized sharp divisions between water and land. Water did not disappear entirely from these new agricultural landscapes. Yet now it flowed within channels protected by dikes or in canals constructed by growers and reclamation agencies. In most places, water flowed across the land to support terrestrial plants, not wetland species that dominated the marshes. Rice in the Sacramento Valley proved an exception to this, since rice paddies were, in effect, a managed wetland. But even rice fields proved an unwelcoming landscape for the ducks and geese that sought refuge there.

SANCTUARY

Few protested this drastic reorganization of the Far West's waterscape. A broad consensus existed that, where possible, governments and irrigators should convert marshes into farmland. Where massive water development schemes threatened established uses, resistance flared, as when Owens Valley residents protested the diversion of water to Los Angeles. Others, such as John Muir and supporters of the Sierra Club, fought the damming of the Hetch Hetchy Valley in the 1910s. Yet by and large, few people thought water should remain unused or underdeveloped, particularly for the benefit of wildlife.[24]

There were some exceptions to this rule. In the Klamath Basin on the Oregon-California border and the Malheur Basin in eastern Oregon, sport hunters and bird conservationists successfully lobbied for federal refuges. In the Klamath Basin, the federal government undertook two experiments simultaneously: reclaiming arid lands and

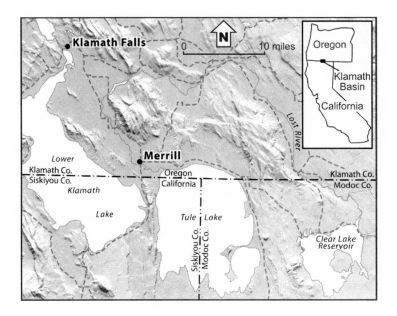

MAP 3 *Upper Klamath Basin, 1906*

creating large refuges for migratory birds. This "double agenda" of draining wetlands and protecting bird habitat proved incompatible.[25] Designating some of the lakes in the Klamath Basin as bird sanctuaries did not impede efforts by the Reclamation Service to destroy most of the basin's wetlands and attempt to create an irrigated landscape in their place. Bird protectionists collided head-on with the federal government's efforts to reclaim arid lands and transform them into an irrigated Eden for homesteaders.[26]

At first glance, the Klamath Basin might seem a poor choice for either migratory bird protection or federally sponsored reclamation. Straddling the California-Oregon border, the basin is more than four hundred miles from San Francisco and Portland—the two largest cities in the region—and east of the Cascade Mountains. Not only was it far removed from these centers of power, it had limited agricultural promise. Unlike the Central Valley to the south, where a productive and diversified agriculture had developed by the turn of the century, the economy of the Klamath Basin was limited mostly to ranching and a little farming. The railroad did not reach the basin until 1909. Before then, outsiders could reach it only by horse or wagon. Small irrigation companies had managed to deliver water to about 10,000 acres of land where ranchers grew hay and alfalfa for livestock. At an elevation of 4,000 feet and with a short growing season, the Klamath Basin seemed unlikely to support the lucrative and increasingly diversified agriculture found in the Central Valley or, later, in the Imperial Valley.[27]

Like parts of the Central Valley to the south, most of the wetlands in the basin had passed into the hands of the states of Oregon and California as part of the swamp land acts. The states were expected to undertake measures to drain the marshes and convert the lakebed into agriculture or to sell them to private companies that would do so. Like many states awarded wetlands under the act, Oregon and California failed to convert any of the marshes into farmland.

This failure is not surprising; formible engineering challenges faced anyone hoping to convert the Klamath Basin's marshes into an irrigated landscape. Unlike other water projects in the West, reclaiming the basin would require more than simply diverting water to dry land. Engineers needed to formulate ways to dewater the shallow lakes and marshes as well as build storage facilities to capture melting snow pack and construct canals and pumps to deliver water.[28] Given the region's distance from markets and its modest agricultural potential, the two states had made little effort to reclaim the basin.

The Reclamation Act of 1902 improved prospects for irrigating more of the Klamath Basin. In passing the act, Congress acknowledged that small, private ventures like the ones in the Klamath Basin could not undertake the projects needed to reclaim large expanses of western land. Only the federal government, with its engineering expertise and funds, could accomplish such programs. Thus, it fell to the federal government to continue the spread of the agricultural frontier that had stalled by the end of the nineteenth century. A newly created agency, the U.S. Reclamation Service, was charged with implementing the act. Using federal funds, the agency would build the irrigation structures necessary to supply homesteads with water on the public domain. The Reclamation Act stipulated that federal irrigation projects could supply water to farms of only 160 acres or less. Like farmers applying for land under the Homestead Act of 1862, the farmers homesteading on federal irrigation projects would have five years to build homes and cultivate the soil in order to gain title to the land. They would also pay the federal government a modest fee for the water in order to pay back the costs of the irrigation project.[29]

Between 1902 and 1905, the Reclamation Service surveyed the basin to determine whether it was a suitable site for an irrigation project. Surveyors concluded that the basin could be reclaimed but that doing so would require a multipronged approach that involved the forced evaporation of two shallow lakes and marshes, Lower Klamath Lake and Tule Lake; building dams to increase the storage capacity of Upper Klamath Lake and Clear Lake; and constructing primary canals and ditches to supply water to individual homesteads. Dewatering Lower Klamath Lake and Tule Lake was a challenge since neither lake had a natural surface outlet.[30] Water flowed into Tule Lake via Lost River, the source of which was Clear Lake to the east. Lower Klamath Lake received its water from the Klamath Straits, a short channel connecting the lake and the Klamath River. During the spring freshets, river water flowed into the lake. Once the river level subsided, water drained out of the lake and into the Klamath River. To reclaim the lakes for agriculture, the Reclamation Service would block the natural flow of water into these shallow lakes and marshes, and then let them slowly evaporate.[31]

Considering the hydrological challenges involved in "reclaiming" the Klamath Basin, it might have seemed wiser to choose other areas in Oregon and California for an irrigation project. The Reclamation Service chose the Klamath Basin less for its agricultural potential than for the fact that there were fewer private irrigation companies with which to contend. In the Central Valley, irrigation companies were supplying water to farms in the late nineteenth century. In order to build larger irrigation projects there, the Reclamation Service would have to purchase the water rights to the entire area, often at exorbitant prices. Moreover, many of the farms in the Central Valley were more than 160 acres, so technically it was illegal to service them with water. The Klamath Basin was attractive because irrigators had supplied water to only a small amount of land and because most of the area was owned by the states of Oregon and California. The states could transfer the land (primarily Lower Klamath Lake and Tule Lake) back to the federal government. Engineers were confident that they could dewater the marshes and build the water structures necessary to convert the area into an irrigated landscape. The Reclamation Service settled with the few irrigation companies in the basin and gained approval for the project in the spring of 1905.[32]

While the Reclamation Service finalized agreements that paved the way for an irrigation project in the Klamath Basin, two young wildlife photographers made their way to the basin from Portland. William L. Finley and Herman T. Bohlman visited Lower Klamath Lake and Tule Lake in the early summer of 1905 to photograph birds and other wildlife. Finley was president of the recently created Oregon chapter of the National Association of Audubon Societies (NAAS). The two photographers went at the urging of William Dutcher, a treasurer for the American Ornithologists' Union and an instrumental figure in the consolidation of state Audubon Societies into the NAAS. Reports had reached Dutcher and other eastern bird protectionists of market hunters slaughtering birds in the marshes of southern and eastern Oregon as part of the trade in bird plumes. By photographing birds in the area, Dutcher, Finley, and Bohlman hoped to show the abundant bird life in the region to eastern audiences and to build support for establishing federal bird reservations.[33]

Bird protection championed by organizations such as the NAAS had been common in the eastern United States for over two decades. George Bird Grinnell founded the first Audubon Society chapter in 1885 to stop the killing of birds for ornaments on women's hats and to stop the hunting of songbirds. Despite the initial enthusiasm by some for the project and the enlisting of more than 20,000 members, support for the organization quickly fizzled, and Grinnell abandoned the Audubon Society the following year. A decade later, Dutcher and others interested in bird issues started forming state Audubon Society chapters in the northeastern United States. The society tapped into the back-to-nature movement and gave a voice to those worried about the destruction of bird life. The NAAS started purchasing small plots of important breeding areas for birds along the East and Gulf coasts and employing wardens to patrol them. Until 1905, the young organization had not had much influence in the western United States. Finley and Bohlman's reconnaissance was one of the first extensions of the eastern-based bird protection effort into the Far West.[34] By the time they arrived in the basin, the NAAS had lobbied successfully for the passage of legislation to protect birds in general. The Lacey Act of 1900 made the interstate transport of birds killed in violation of state law illegal. In practice, the act made it more difficult for market hunters to transport plumes and other bird parts to market. Although a modest piece of legislation, it was one of the first national wildlife statutes and a demonstration that the federal government had a role in protecting wildlife.[35]

Finley and Bohlman spent nearly a month in the Klamath Basin taking photographs of pelicans, cormorants, gulls, terns, and other birds. In their photographs and in the articles Finley wrote for *National Geographic* and *The Atlantic Monthly*, they depicted the marshes as natural wonderlands teeming with life. Finley seemed overwhelmed by what he saw:

Here lay the land of my dreams. After nearly 20 years of waiting, I was looking over this place of mystery that lay far beyond the northern rim of my home hills. From the distance, where I stood the marsh was a level sea of green. As I discovered later, it was absolutely deceptive to its real character. The ocean tells nothing of its thousand hidden wonders; so the marsh. . . . The unmeasured stretch of tules is the same as when Lewis and Clark blazed a trail into the Oregon forest. . . . The lure of the marsh was its wildness.[36]

On the same trip, the two men traveled to the Malheur Basin in eastern Oregon and also marveled at the vast marshes there. Finley wrote of both places as though they were Eden before the fall, and Finley and Bohlman portrayed themselves as wide-eyed children on an adventure in the American West.[37]

Although wildlife dominated the photographs taken by Finley and Bohlman, the two men neither excluded themselves from their images nor from the narrative Finley wrote. To help viewers feel an attachment to the birds they photographed, Finley and Bohlman placed themselves in the images. In one photograph, Finley kneels with an immense camera taking a photograph of a flock of white pelicans only a few feet away. In another, Finley and Bohlman sit on the rocky shore of Tule Lake taking field notes and examining cormorant eggs. Finley's efforts to put himself in the action with animals became a hallmark of the photographs and motion pictures he would produce throughout his career. Finley and Bohlman depicted the basin's marshes as inviting places where one could have entertaining encounters with animals. In this way, Finley's photographs and films had more in common with the wildlife adventure stories later shown on Walt Disney television specials or *Wild Kingdom* than with the later artistic photographs of natural landscapes by Ansel Adams or Eliot Porter.[38]

For Finley, nature was a place for adventure filled with inquisitive, playful animals. During their time in the Klamath and Malheur basins in 1905 (and later when Finley returned on his own), they emphasized the adventurous aspects of their journey. The dozens of photographs from the trip show Finley and Bohlman making camp, moving equipment by wagon, and piloting their small row boat through the maze of tules on each lake. Although they do show some of the challenges they faced as well as the more unsavory aspects of the wetlands (such as the swarms of insects), for the most part the two men portray the remote Oregon marshes as spaces for playful recreation. Urban middle-class audiences in Portland as well as the eastern United States could easily imagine themselves touring with Finley and Bohlman in these natural wonderlands.[39]

The photographs and reports sent back to NAAS President Dutcher clearly had their intended effect. Following lobbying by bird protectionists and sportsmen across the nation, President Theodore Roosevelt established the Klamath Lake and Malheur Lake bird reservations in 1908.[40] Roosevelt had already demonstrated his commitment to bird protection by creating the first wildlife refuge for birds at Pelican Island, Florida, in 1903. He would set aside over fifty areas during his presidency. Although the Klamath and Malheur reservations joined a growing number of federal and private refuges owned by state Audubon societies, none of the other sanctuaries approached the scale of these Oregon refuges. Most of the refuges in the eastern United States were a few hundred acres at most; the Oregon ones encompassed thousands of acres of marshes and open water, and wetlands of a different sort than in the east. Like the eastern refuges, however, the Oregon areas were set aside to prevent the destruction of plume-bearing birds and to offer protection from the overhunting of migratory waterfowl by market hunters. Establishing the Klamath Lake Reservation was a relatively easy matter. Lower Klamath Lake had passed back into federal control when Oregon and California transferred ownership to the Reclamation Service in 1905 as part of the agency's plan to construct the Klamath Project. Roosevelt simply carved out a bird reservation within this newly acquired federal domain.[41]

Finley, the NAAS, and sport hunters considered the establishment of the two bird sanctuaries to be a major victory. Finley saw the protection of the refuges as the culmination of a struggle against ruthless plume and market hunters who had ransacked the most magnificent areas for birds in the entire United States. Soon after his journey to the eastern Oregon marshes with Bohlman, Finley became the NAAS's field agent for the Pacific Coast states. His annual reports to the society published in *Bird Lore*, the organization's magazine, showed his unbridled optimism and his zeal for bird protection. He helped assign wardens to guard the reservations from hunters and pushed for the strengthening of bird protection laws in Oregon, and to a lesser degree, in California. With the federal protection of such outstanding bird areas as Lower Klamath Lake and Malheur Lake, nothing, it seemed, could stop the crusade to protect migratory birds.[42]

With market hunting, plume-bearing birds such as egrets and herons had become yet another natural commodity harvested from western lands and marshes. Stiffer hunting regulations and the formation of sanctuaries were part of a counter effort to decommodify these birds. By prohibiting hunting in large western marshes, conservationists hoped to save such birds from extinction. But even as hunting plume-bearing birds was prohibited, other birds such as ducks and waterfowl continued to be legitimate prey for sport hunters.

Although the creation of a large bird refuge in the basin seemed like a major victory for bird conservationists, a close examination of the executive order establishing the Klamath Lake Reservation reveals that there was ample cause for concern. Lower Klamath Lake was the only lake in the region given protection; other lakes and marshes in the area used by migratory birds, such as Upper Klamath Lake, Clear Lake, and Tule Lake, were unprotected. Although the order prohibited the destruction of birds' nests and eggs and the killing of any birds within the reservation's borders, it did not ensure a water supply. The order explicitly stated that the management of the reservation was not to "interfere with the use of any part of the reserved area by the Reclamation Service."[43] In drawing the boundaries of the reservation, the creators of the order intended to include marsh areas that were expected to be unfit for agriculture. The Reclamation Service made it very clear as early as 1905 that it intended to divert most of the water that fed Lower Klamath Lake and Tule Lake for irrigation. As far as the agency was concerned, the Klamath Lake Bird Reservation was superimposed on the Klamath Project, and the needs of the project came before the needs of the refuge. The refuge only provided a temporary reprieve from the hunters. In time, the Reclamation Service would eliminate this avian wonderland altogether.

Roosevelt did not place the refuges under the care of a competent federal agency. Rather than create a new agency to oversee these refuges, Roosevelt and the U.S. Congress placed them in the hands of the Bureau of Biological Survey, a small agency in the Department of Agriculture. The agency had originally been established to assess the role of birds in controlling insect pests. It neither had a law enforcement role before it was placed in charge of the refuges nor were extra funds allocated to pay such personnel if it did. The result was that the Biological Survey lacked the capacity to staff the refuges and to resist the actions of other federal agencies that would damage the sanctuaries.[44]

Without federal money or personnel to manage the refuges, patrolling the Klamath Lake Reservation fell to a warden employed by the NAAS. As field agent for the West Coast states, Finley appointed the warden on behalf of the NAAS, a fitting task since he played so prominent a role in creating the sanctuary. He chose L. Alva Lewis, a former jeweler in Klamath Falls looking for a new line of work. Lewis's task was to patrol the reservation in *The Grebe*, a small motorboat bought with funds from the NAAS, searching for poachers and taking notes on the wildlife. To give him some authority, he was also commissioned as a state warden for Oregon and California, which allowed him to fine and arrest people breaking game laws in the two states. His authority as a federal warden on the reservation itself was unclear.

Who could he arrest? How was he to patrol such an enormous reservation? For the next few years, Lewis was the extent of federal wildlife protection efforts in the Klamath Basin. His reports provide a rare glimpse into the reservation after its founding and before its eventual destruction. The lack of support from the Bureau of Biological Survey and the many problems Lewis encountered are some measure of the federal government's timid role in managing the refuges.[45]

The very size of the reservation made it difficult to patrol. By his own admission, Lewis patrolled an area "as large as the state of Rhode Island."[46] He kept watch over the five or six channels among the tules on the northern end of the lake. It was unclear to him what he should do if he caught someone poaching. The NAAS and Biological Survey provided no set of regulations to enforce except for the state game laws of Oregon and California. No one had posted the reservation's boundaries, so hunters could always claim that they did not realize Lower Klamath Lake was now a bird sanctuary. Lewis worried that without stronger federal regulations, national efforts to protect birds would fail in the Klamath Basin and elsewhere. In fact, Lewis was surprised that people refrained from hunting on the reservation at all given the uncertainty about jurisdiction. "People will not always be ruled by bluff alone," Lewis wrote, "especially those who have hunted for market, and are now deprived of a valuable source of income and we should be prepared to meet them with weapons which are at once effective and relentless."[47]

Although market hunters sought birds on the lakes, nearby residents also hunted ducks and other waterfowl, often out of season. Lewis had better luck apprehending local violators than market hunters illegally using the Klamath Lake Reservation. In August 1909, he arrested four men for this offense after chasing them by boat across Tule Lake in the dark. Three of the four were prominent men in the area (one was the mayor of Merrill, a town bordering Tule Lake).[48] Lewis's willingness to apprehend such men shows how seriously he took his position. He also came across Native people in the area hunting on Lower Klamath Lake earlier that summer. "Two canoe loads of Indians were on the Lower Lake, out for the purpose of gathering eggs I suppose," Lewis wrote. He ordered them off the reservation, but they refused to comply. "They became quite ugly. . . . They were eight to one and so thought they had the balance of power. As soon as I saw they would not move out peaceably, I backed the launch off and suddenly ran forward and rammed one of the canoes giving it a glancing blow. The canoe turned over tipping the occupants out. I backed off preparatory to giving the other canoe a dose of the same medicine, but they surrendered."[49]

Given the number of wildlife in the marshes of Lower Klamath Lake and Tule Lake and Lewis's willingness to apprehend violators, it is surprising there were not more such incidents. The creation of the Klamath Lake Reservation had interfered with established uses of the marshes. Lewis's encounters with the two groups show that the lakes were recreational spaces for local sport hunters as well as a commons for Native people. Although Lewis was hired to stop market hunters, he rarely came across them. The lack of plume hunters and other market hunters on the reservation suggests that there must be other reasons for the decline in illegal hunting activity besides Lewis's vigilance. Granted, the reservation was large, but access to the lake was possible only by a few channels through the tules on the lake's margins, and the repeated shooting of guns by market hunters would have attracted attention. The decline in market hunters most likely reflects the diminishing demand for plumes in the early twentieth century. Bird protectionists had successfully targeted many of the consumers of bird plumes (namely women for fine hats), turning the wearing of bird feathers into a shameful act.[50]

Lewis's eagerness to arrest hunters on and off the reservation could easily have put his life in jeopardy. Although he escaped from these encounters unscathed, other wardens working for the NAAS were not so lucky. Occasionally poachers and plume hunters killed wardens when they tried to interfere. The most famous was the killing of Guy Bradley, a warden working near Fort Myers in the Florida Everglades. Ornithologists and other bird enthusiasts had long traveled to the remote parts of the state to see the colonies of waterbirds. Plume hunters also frequented the area, and their presence led early Audubon leaders to assign Bradley to locate and protect the last remaining colonies. These plume hunters considered Bradley a real threat, and in 1905, one of them shot him. A local grand jury refused to indict the accused killer, and no one was ever convicted for the murder. Among

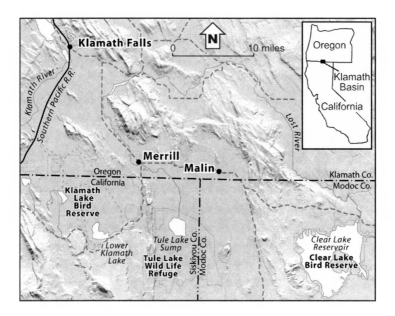

MAP 4 *Upper Klamath Basin, 1929*

eastern bird protectionists, Bradley became a martyr for the movement; his death testified to the dangers wardens faced. It also demonstrated that wardens often threatened long-established patterns
of resource use. Since wardens often worked alone in remote areas
confronting other men with guns, Bradley's death was not surprising.
Rather, it was surprising that plume hunters and poachers did not kill
more of them.[51]

When Lewis was not patrolling the reservation, he was either trying to shoot animals that he believed preyed on waterfowl in the area
or assisting other people in trying to do so. Lewis was particularly
worried about raptors killing the ducks in the marshes, and he regularly shot Cooper's hawks and other birds of prey. Like many conservationists of the time, he believed that raptors were vicious killers of
birds that needed to be eliminated. In one evening, he killed eight
hawks. "As these were off the Reserve, and knowing their character as
I do I considered I was doing good work killing them."[52] Trappers also
captured mink, raccoon, skunks, and weasels. Although the ability of

Lewis and a few trappers to affect the population of hawks or mammals was limited, their actions demonstrate a willingness to control many other species in order to protect waterfowl.[53]

A more substantial threat to the wildlife reservation came from the U.S. Reclamation Service, which still intended to dewater most of the reservation. Lewis informed Finley and the NAAS that this was a possibility as early as 1909, when the Southern Pacific Railroad constructed an embankment across the northwest corner of the reservation. The embankment had a small opening over Klamath Straits that allowed water to pass from the Klamath River into Lower Klamath Lake. For the time being the channel remained open. Lewis saw a calamity in the making if the Reclamation Service decided to close the channel, though initially, he worried more about how the blockage would interfere with his regular patrols rather than with the effect it might have on the lake.[54] The Reclamation Service left the channel open for another seven years as it focused on developing other parts of the Klamath Project. In 1917, however, it closed the straits and, in effect, starved the lake of water. Over the next four years, its waters slowly evaporated, leaving the vast tule marshes to wither and die.[55]

Finley and other conservationists were livid. An immense marsh that supported an extraordinary profusion of bird life was turned into a desert waste. Once the waters receded and exposed the tules, fires burned the drying vegetation.[56] Smoke and dust from the dry lakebed clogged the skies over the towns of Merrill and Klamath Falls, occasionally closing schools and businesses. Years later, when Biological Survey ornithologist Frederick Lincoln visited the area, the sight of the former reservation disgusted him. "It doesn't even support a good crop of weeds. . . . A jack-rabbit would starve on it."[57] Many of the waterfowl that crowded into the small, muddy remnant of the lake perished from avian diseases, most likely botulism.[58]

What incensed Finley and others even more was that the drainage was done for an agricultural scheme of dubious value. An evaluation by soil scientists in 1909 concluded that most of the soil underlying the lakebed was too alkaline to support most crops. Farmers successfully cultivated some of the land, especially north of the California-Oregon border, but much of the soil was as poor as the soil survey said it would be. Many homesteaders never secured title to their land because of repeated crop failures.[59]

To make matters worse, executive presidential orders reduced the size of the reservations. A number of executive orders signed by Presidents Woodrow Wilson and Warren Harding between 1917 and 1921 eliminated parts of the bird sanctuary to open them for homesteading.[60] Such legal reductions hardly seemed necessary when closing the Klamath Straits had effectively starved the reservation of water and the Klamath Bird Reservation had proved not to be an impediment in the Reclamation Service's plans for the Klamath Basin. Other nearby bird refuges could not compensate for the lost marshes. Clear Lake, one of the primary storage facilities for the Klamath Project, was designated as a refuge in 1911. However, the Reclamation Service adjusted the level of the lake based on the needs of irrigators downstream. Annual water fluctuations destroyed most of the marshes rimming the lake, limiting its usefulness for birds. Even prior to its appropriation as an irrigation reservoir, Clear Lake supported far fewer birds than Lower Klamath Lake or Tule Lake.[61]

It seemed as though the Malheur Lake Bird Reservation, the other federal refuge in Oregon, might meet a similar fate. Although the Reclamation Service chose not to pursue an irrigation project in the Malheur Basin, it later supported the dewatering of Malheur Lake for agricultural purposes. In 1916, a report created by the Oregon State engineer and a federal reclamation official recommended diverting the Blitzen and Silvies rivers, which flowed into Malheur Lake, for use by irrigators. Five years later the Blitzen River Irrigation District was organized to construct the needed canals and other irrigation apparatus to provide water for farms.[62] Finley tried to rally the support of the Oregon State legislature and bird lovers across the country to stop these schemes.[63] The State of Oregon laid claim to the lake, saying that the state had rights over any navigable body of water—a particularly dubious claim given the shallowness of Malheur Lake. Newspapers in Portland claimed that the refuge stood in the way of progress. "*The [Portland] Spectator* is heartily in favor of bird refuges, but is much more in favor of bringing into cultivation the small fraction of Central Oregon lands that can be cultivated, even if the entire Malheur reservation should thereby be destroyed. Let us not by our votes doom Eastern Oregon to remain a howling wilderness."[64] Countering such claims and protecting the few remaining areas for migratory birds from irrigators would require "eternal vigilance" from conservationists.[65] The fate of the reservation would remain in limbo until the 1930s, when the federal government finally bought out the groups that controlled the water and riparian areas along the rivers that fed the lake.

The Bureau of Biological Survey had largely forgotten these sanctuaries in Oregon and California. H. F. Stone, the man in charge of the bureau's refuges, took an inspection trip of the nation's sanctuaries in 1920. He wrote that the refuges were underfunded and managed by an incompetent staff. Lower Klamath was merely the most egregious example of the neglect common to all of the nation's federal refuges. On the Malheur Lake Bird Reservation, for example, locals did not take the bureau seriously. "There is already a feeling in Burns that the Bureau is handling this reservation in a weak manner and without any definite policy," Stone wrote. "As a result of this feeling, I am told that the opinion is openly expressed that there would be no danger in local people using the reservation as they see fit." Stone's report showed a refuge system in disrepair and a bureau with only a tenuous hold on these western sanctuaries.[66]

While fighting threats to the Malheur Basin marshes, William Finley never gave up trying to restore those of Lower Klamath Lake. It had become obvious, even to the Bureau of Reclamation, that the irrigation project it planned for the area had largely failed.[67] Few farmers had successfully homesteaded on the lakebed, though some had managed to raise crops on the land once covered by tules. Instead of cultivating the lakebed, the Bureau of Reclamation decided to convert it into a sump for wastewater from part of the Klamath Project.[68] Finley and others wanted the entire area restored and the channel connecting the Klamath River and the Lower Klamath lakebed reopened. The Bureau of Reclamation rejected this proposal, stating that it would need to construct a dike to protect the farms that settlers did establish from rising lake water. Also, diverting water from the Klamath River into the lake might diminish the flow downriver through a new hydroelectric dam.[69] The Biological Survey commissioned a report by drainage engineer L. T. Jessup to investigate the feasibility of the sump serving as the new basis for the Klamath Lake Bird Reservation. Jessup concluded that even though the sump would cover part of the former lakebed, without drainage it would quickly become too alkaline to support wildlife. Neither Jessup nor the Bureau of Reclamation considered building a drain between the lake and the Klamath River, which is how the Klamath Straits had functioned during times when the river level was low.[70]

There were more than technical impediments. Restoring the lake would require significant changes to how irrigators, power companies, and the Bureau of Reclamation divided the basin's water. By the 1920s, users had appropriated all the water in the basin, including water from the Klamath River, the potential source for reflooding Lower Klamath Lake. Even if the technical problems could have been overcome, there was no water available. The Bureau of Reclamation could divert water from the Klamath River for the purposes of irrigation. But due to the legislation that ceded control of Lower Klamath Lake from the states of Oregon and California back to the federal government, it could not be used for other purposes, such as reflooding the lake. In short, the Bureau of Reclamation could dewater the lake but claimed it lacked the authority to restore it.[71]

Instead of restoring Lower Klamath Lake, the agencies proposed to enlarge marshes and ponds located on the margins of the Great Salt Lake, over four hundred miles to the east in Utah. Private sport hunting groups had already constructed dikes and canals to increase the freshwater marshes along the Bear River, one of the main sources of water for the lake. With more work and federal funds, the Biological Survey hoped to convert this area into the largest wetland for migratory birds in the western United States. Yet it was unclear how waterfowl that once used the Klamath Basin would know to fly to the Bear River marshes rather than the Klamath Basin. In fact, later migration studies would reveal that Bear River was a major nesting site for waterfowl that would then fly to marshes in Oregon and California to winter. Since waterfowl used the Klamath Basin marshes primarily as a stopover point during autumn and spring migrations, merely increasing the marsh area in Utah did little good for the birds that traveled through the West Coast states. Those birds required marshes for resting and feeding as they migrated—functions once provided by the wetlands in the Klamath and Malheur basins.[72]

To placate conservationists, President Calvin Coolidge established two new Klamath Basin refuges, Tule Lake and Upper Klamath Lake, in 1928. By this time Tule Lake, which once had covered over a hundred thousand acres, had been reduced to little more than two thousand. A diversion dam constructed on the Lost River, the source of water for the lake, had led to the contraction of the lake as the water evaporated. Although homesteads had only begun to establish farms on the former lakebed, the Bureau of Reclamation had allowed farmers to lease land near the edges of the lake for farming or grazing. The Upper Klamath Refuge included only the marshes at the northern end of the lake. Because of its greater depth, the lake had never been as important for migratory waterfowl as Lower Klamath Lake and Tule Lake. Even though there were four wildlife refuges in the Klamath Basin by the 1920s, reclamation had either destroyed or drastically compromised their usefulness for migratory birds.[73]

It was clear to Finley and the leadership of the Bureau of Biological Survey that, without adequate habitat, migratory waterfowl throughout the western United States might perish. Edward Nelson, chief of the Biological Survey during the early 1920s, criticized the recklessness shown by many drainage schemes. Like Finley, he was reluctant to condemn all wetland drainage, but pointed out that what was gained in agriculture often came at a high price for migratory birds and other species of wildlife. The modest growth in migratory waterfowl populations since the passage of the Migratory Bird Treaty Act of 1918 had stopped, and Nelson feared that the number of migratory waterfowl would plummet if more was not done to protect and restore wetlands. The existing refuges were quickly reaching capacity. The thousands of birds concentrated on such refuges left them susceptible to starvation, lead poisoning (from spent ammunition), and disease. The government and private landowners across the country needed to realize that "water and water areas have a community value entirely apart from that of private ownership, and this relationship should be borne in mind when drainage operations are being considered." Without substantial federal intervention, Nelson, Finley, and other bird conservationists feared a catastrophe for the continent's migratory birds.[74]

Livestock grazing also took a toll on the Clear Lake and Tule Lake refuges. Citing the fact that these refuges were superimposed on the Klamath Project, and therefore that the Bureau of Reclamation's needs came first, the agency authorized livestock grazing on both of these refuges during the late 1920s and early 1930s. For many conservationists, allowing livestock to graze on the refuges was a disaster for migratory birds and yet another demonstration of the Bureau of Reclamation's disregard for wildlife. Livestock trampled nests and ruined the vegetation birds needed for protection. Both Finley and the federal warden in the area, H. M. Worcester, complained to the Bureau of Reclamation about the problem to no avail. In a detailed response to their protests, the chief commissioner for the agency, Elwood Mead, wrote that ranchers had the right to graze between the maximum level of the lake and the current level. He added that most of this grazing occurred during the winter months, not during the summer when the birds nested. Regardless of the true environmental impact, conservationists considered it absurd that grazing should continue, particularly without consulting the Biological Survey, which managed the refuges.[75]

Livestock grazing pushed aside hunting as the most pressing issue on the Tule Lake Refuge in the early 1930s. The Bureau of Reclamation issued grazing permits to cattle and sheep owners living nearby that allowed them to graze livestock on the refuge. The agency granted a handful of permitees grazing privileges to large tracts of refuge land; one sheep outfit received a lease for 3,850 acres, over one-third of the refuge. Hundreds of sheep grazing on the refuge had a disastrous effect on the grasses and tules used by waterfowl for nesting. During the fall migration, geese regularly fed in the grass-covered areas between the dikes separating the leased farm land and the open water of Tule Lake. With the grasses the birds ate either trampled or eaten by livestock, the geese flew to the leased farmland nearby and caused further depredations.[76]

The Bureau of Reclamation rarely consulted the Biological Survey before issuing grazing leases on the refuge, but the survey vigorously protested permitting grazing on Tule Lake after it learned of the bureau's plans. The Biological Survey struggled through the early 1930s to exclude grazing from the refuge. Without restrictions on grazing, field officers with the survey stationed in southern Oregon questioned whether the refuge would have any value as a migration stop or nesting area for migratory birds. William Finley, who continued to protest the activities of the Bureau of Reclamation in the 1930s, echoed these concerns. In 1934 he wrote, "If we can't protect the birds on a federal reservation established by Executive Order, these sanctuaries have no specific value."[77]

Finley argued that the potential environmental cost of grazing to migratory bird habitat was severe, but that its benefit to stockmen was minimal. To provide a paltry amount of forage and to collect small fees from livestock owners, the Bureau of Reclamation allowed the destruction of cover and vegetation in what remained two of the most important refuges in the United States. In one of many angry letters to Commissioner Mead, Finley argued that "I cannot see why one department of the government concerned with the uses of land and water is so utterly thoughtless of resources in charge of another department. . . . The Reclamation Service has gained a few thousand dollars in rentals, but I feel that this does not pay for the damage to bird life. A natural resource belonging to the public has been lost."[78] Finley also sent complaints to Secretary of the Interior Harold Ickes and met with the new head of the Biological Survey, Jay "Ding" Darling. Despite years of protest and the continued erosion of the few sanctuaries established for migratory birds, the Biological Survey had virtually no say in the management of these protected areas. They remained hollow sanctuaries.[79]

While Finley and the Biological Survey were fighting the Bureau of Reclamation over livestock grazing, they also sought to reflood Lower Klamath Lake. With the onset of the Great Depression, farmers in the Klamath Drainage District had difficulty making their payments to the Bureau of Reclamation. To aid the farmers on the Klamath Basin and other Bureau of Reclamation projects, the federal government placed a moratorium on all payments beginning in 1930. With the drainage district in poor financial shape, Finley saw this as an excellent opportunity for the federal government to buy out the district using funds acquired from federal hunting permits known as Duck Stamps. As it had many times before, the Bureau of Reclamation provided a list of reasons why the plan was impossible. The federal government would need to purchase land from approximately fifty landowners. Since water to reflood the lake would come from the Klamath River, the federal government would need to compensate the California Oregon Power Company for the loss of river water used to power downstream generators. Even if the water were available, the Bureau of Reclamation argued that it was prohibited from using the water for nonirrigation purposes. Once again, conservationists had offered a creative solution to restoring Lower Klamath Lake only to have the Bureau of Reclamation stonewall them.[80]

By the early 1930s, the Klamath and Malheur basin refuges, as ones elsewhere in the nation, were shattered remnants of a decrepit system. Such areas were as precious as refuges as Yosemite and Yellowstone were as national parks, but arguments on their behalf failed to sway irrigators or the Bureau of Reclamation. To the bureau, protests against the destruction of Lower Klamath and Tule lakes were like mosquitoes harassing a camper on a summer evening—a nuisance, yes, but ultimately not a real threat.

The Bureau of Reclamation had reengineered the basins' lakes and waterways to serve the needs of irrigated agriculture. This did not always entail obliterating the preexisting waterscape. Indeed, when it suited its purposes, the bureau modified lakes to serve as reservoirs and rivers to drain irrigation wastewater. Upper Klamath Lake and Clear Lake survived, but only because the agency needed them as reservoirs for project irrigation water. A comparison of maps of the Klamath Basin landscapes in 1905 and 1935 showed an area harnessed to serve the needs of irrigated agriculture. Any attempt to restore the basin's marshes for migratory birds would have to account for this fact. Ironically, the failure of the bureau to adequately plan for the disposal of wastewater would provide conservationists in the 1930s with an opportunity to resurrect the lost splendor of Lower Klamath and Tule lakes.

Migratory birds were the collateral damage of irrigated agriculture and river improvements in the Far West, which transformed the waterscape in the southern portion of the Pacific Flyway during the early twentieth century. The Central Valley—a region where more than 60 percent of migratory waterfowl spent the winter months—lost most of its wetlands. Diking along the Sacramento River and water diversions along the San Joaquin River resulted in the destruction of marshes on the flood plain. Important lakes used by migratory waterfowl, such as Tulare Lake and Owens Lake, vanished altogether. Just beyond the California and Mexico border, the Colorado River Delta still supported a network of marshes and lagoons until the 1930s, but after the completion of Boulder (Hoover) Dam in 1936, the Colorado River would cease to reach the delta at all. Without the fortuitous creation of the Salton Sea decades earlier, there would have been no major lakes or marshes left for migratory waterfowl in this portion of the flyway.

Decades of activism on behalf of the birds that used these wetlands barely slowed the reclamation movement. Although Finley's vision of a bird paradise had captured the imagination of many amateur bird watchers, sport hunters, and ornithologists, it paled in comparison to the reclamation drive. Most Americans still considered wetlands as impediments to progress and supported efforts by the Bureau of Reclamation to drain western marshes. This would change in the 1930s, just as the migratory waterfowl populations were at their lowest and many feared for their survival. During later years of that decade, the federal government launched a major program to restore damaged wetlands throughout the nation. Wetlands along the Pacific Flyway would become testing grounds for the use of hydrologic engineering and the techniques of irrigators to construct industrial refuges. Irrigated agriculture—responsible for so much of the wetland loss in the Far West—would provide the tools to restore vanished marshes.

3

PLACES IN THE GRID

BY THE EARLY 1930S, migratory bird populations were plummeting. Although both the U.S. and Canada had implemented more stringent hunting regulations and had had some success curtailing market hunting, wetland drainage continued at an alarming rate. Farmers, often with the aid of government agencies, drained wetlands or diverted the water that nourished them for the benefit of agriculture. This onslaught took a devastating toll on the wetlands in the wintering range of Pacific Flyway birds. Major breeding areas for migratory waterfowl, such as the Prairie Pothole region in the upper Midwest and southern Canada, though less important for Pacific Flyway birds, also lost many wetlands. In a matter of decades, most of the wetlands in the wintering range of the Pacific Flyway had been destroyed. Conservationists feared that some species of ducks and geese might become extinct.

Yet by the late 1930s in the United States, the fortunes of migratory waterfowl—and the Biological Survey—began to change. An infusion of federal funds and labor allowed the agency to establish dozens of new refuges and rehabilitate the beleaguered wetland landscape.

It also drew upon new ornithological knowledge based on years of migration studies to create a more systematic refuge program. The agency also sought to replace its earlier ineffectual oversight with an increasingly rationalized waterfowl management program. Under the direction of new leaders such as survey chief Jay "Ding" Darling and J. Clark Salyer II, the head of the Biological Survey's refuge program, the scale and scope of waterfowl management changed considerably. From the level of the continent to individual refuges, agency managers sought to build a refuge system that would sustain migratory birds throughout their entire migration route.

Restoring marshes entailed reengineering the landscape. The complex patchwork of pools and marsh vegetation was replaced by grids of dikes and ponds (units) in which managers could regulate water levels. The agency showed a remarkable willingness to experiment and engineer the landscape within refuges in new ways. Sometimes this meant resurrecting ponds and marshes that irrigated agriculture had destroyed. But often it meant creating wetlands where few had existed previously or taking relatively poor waterfowl habitat and attempting to improve it. What emerged was a "complex machine aimed at increasing waterfowl production."[1]

The dire situation of migratory waterfowl in the early 1930s made conservationists more amenable to solutions that could create bird habitat quickly.[2] Other factors affected their decisions. Foremost among these was disease. Avian botulism (known as western duck sickness at the time) took a horrendous toll on ducks and geese in the Far West. Ornithological studies in the early twentieth century suggested that better management of water could reduce the severity of botulism outbreaks and save thousands of birds. Such careful management of water was only possible in an engineered landscape of dikes, ponds, and canals. More importantly, refuges were imbedded within an irrigated landscape in which the Biological Survey had only limited control. Water that had once nourished the Pacific Flyway had long since been diverted by irrigators for farms. The Biological Survey's solution was to make refuges within this new hydrologic system and carve individual refuges into diked units to facilitate the easy manipulation of water. In doing so, the agency sought advice from irrigation engineers and employed irrigation technologies. After fighting irrigators and the Bureau of Reclamation for decades, the Biological Survey now put the knowledge and tools of these groups into the service of restoring marshes they had damaged or destroyed.

THE NEW DEAL, PLANNING, AND WILDLIFE

This change of fortune resulted from federal responses to dire environmental and economic conditions plaguing the nation. The federal government sought solutions to both of these conditions at the same time. During the 1930s, the Biological Survey went from an ineffective bureau managing a tattered collection of refuges to a more robust agency with dozens of new refuges under its care. Birds and wetlands, once seen only as impediments to development, were now used to contend with the problems that plagued agriculture during the Great Depression. Amid this national trauma, the Biological Survey constructed a network of refuges—not only along the Pacific Flyway, but throughout the nation.

The populations of ducks and geese had increased briefly after the signing of the Migratory Bird Treaty Act of 1918, but began to decline shortly thereafter. Fewer market hunters killed ducks and geese in the 1920s, and stiffer hunting regulations limited the toll sport hunters exacted on waterfowl. Yet farmers continued to drain wetlands to expand crop production, particularly in the Prairie Pothole region of the United States and Canada where half of the continent's waterfowl nested. Drought conditions that began during the 1930s dried many of the remaining marshes on the prairies and elsewhere, leaving few places for waterfowl to nest in the summer or to live in the winter. For waterfowl, the Dust Bowl that consumed the Great Plains during the early 1930s was an ecological catastrophe.[3]

The drought hit the nation's farmers especially hard, many of whom were already under financial stress due to low crop prices during much of the preceding decade. To generate revenue, more land was brought into production, but the subsequent glut of crops depressed commodity prices even further. Midwest farmers were in a precarious position. Hard times left them without a cushion to soften the blow of the droughts that had often struck the plains states, and the drought that gripped the prairies between 1930 and 1936 pushed many farmers into financial ruin.[4]

In an effort to address the agricultural crisis, reformers suggested that the federal government purchase surplus crops, impose limitations on the amount of land farmers could cultivate, and remove marginal farmland from production. Agricultural reformers also sought to raise crop prices. By retiring marginal land from production, the federal government hoped to conserve soil and ultimately take excess crops off the market so agricultural commodity prices would rise. In early 1934, the National Recovery Administration began to pursue the latter strategy. Some of this land taken out of production was developed for recreation, transferred to Indian tribes, or given to the Biological Survey to convert into wildlife refuges. On the Great Plains, refuges were part of a larger conservation strategy to control wind erosion. The federal government hoped to address the plight of migratory waterfowl and farmers simultaneously.[5]

As these actions suggest, the protection of migratory waterfowl had become a priority for President Franklin D. Roosevelt, who formed a committee to develop solutions to deal with plummeting numbers of waterfowl. He appointed Thomas Beck, a businessmen and conservationist, as head of the committee, which also included Jay "Ding" Darling, who was a political cartoonist before he became head of the Biological Survey, and Aldo Leopold, then a professor in wildlife management at the University of Wisconsin–Madison. All three men were passionate conservationists, though they each had different perspectives on how to solve the waterfowl problem.[6]

Beck was a founder of the More Game Birds in America Foundation. This organization sought to apply the techniques of business management to wildlife restoration. In this view, waterfowl and other game birds were a crop, and with proper management techniques, conservationists could boost their numbers by applying business principles. Many sport hunters and wildlife officials agreed with this position. Implementing it meant purchasing land in the breeding grounds of waterfowl, supervising the reservations with trained personnel, growing food for the birds, eliminating predators, and suppressing fire. The Biological Survey had tried to implement just such an approach over the preceding decade, but lacked the funds to adequately do the job. Reflecting his organization's lack of faith in the Biological Survey, Beck advocated the private ownership of breeding and wintering areas as well as the artificial propagation of waterfowl through captive breeding programs.[7]

Leopold saw the need to protect wildlife habitat, but challenged many of Beck's suggestions. Shortly before joining the committee, Leopold had finished *Game Management*, a textbook that would have an enormous influence on wildlife conservation for decades to come. In it, he argued that conservationists should raise wildlife like a crop for the benefit of all Americans. Although Beck and Leopold both saw game as reproducible, Leopold realized that there were complex relationships between wildlife and the environment, and that wildlife managers needed to consider many intangibles if they wanted to perpetuate the resource. A more fundamental difference turned on Leopold's belief in the public ownership of wildlife and in keeping hunting areas accessible to all Americans as long as they honored necessary regulations. For much of his career Leopold had fought the "European model" of hunting, where game belonged to a wealthy elite on privately owned land. To Leopold, Beck's plan seemed an attempt to privatize America's public hunting commons.[8]

Darling lacked Leopold's scientific background in game management and Beck's experience managing a conservation organization, but what he lacked in scientific expertise, he made up for with political aptitude. He had a keen sense of the political process and of how to achieve results in Washington, D.C. Darling was one of the most influential political cartoonists of his day, and he was in a unique position to publicize his conservation views and criticize the federal government for its failure to protect migratory waterfowl. He lived in Iowa, a state where farmers had suffered greatly from drought and falling crop prices during the early years of the Depression. He had also seen thousands of acres of wetlands in Iowa drained to make way for agricultural land. A program that could remove marginal land from production and convert it into marshes for waterfowl, he believed, might save North American waterfowl from extinction.[9]

Despite the disagreements between Beck and Leopold, the committee reached an agreement and completed its report in February

1934. Leopold and Darling convinced Beck not to include suggestions for the artificial propagation of waterfowl and the abolition of the Biological Survey. Instead the group concluded that unwise development of marginal agricultural land was primarily responsible for the decline of waterfowl populations and that bird numbers would not be increased simply by imposing more stringent regulations. The committee proposed a nationwide restoration effort to include the purchase of four million acres of poor quality grazing and farm land to convert into refuges. Other money from New Deal agencies such as the Public Works Administration and the Civil Works Administration would go toward restoration work on newly acquired refuges or the poorly maintained refuges already in existence. The report had widespread support among dozens of the country's leading conservation organizations, including the National Association of Audubon Societies, the Izaak Walton League, and, even though the report lacked some of Beck's key suggestions, the More Game Birds in America Foundation.[10]

When Biological Survey chief Paul Redington resigned shortly after the committee submitted its report, Roosevelt and Secretary of Agriculture Henry Wallace offered Darling the position.[11] In accepting the post, Darling extracted a guarantee from Wallace that hunting club members would not dictate Biological Survey policy and a promise from Roosevelt to allocate one million dollars immediately for wildlife conservation. Wallace and Roosevelt agreed to this, though as Darling would learn, Roosevelt often failed to keep his promises. Four months later, Congress had not allocated the promised funds, and the Biological Survey's ambitious refuge enlargement program lay dormant. Darling asked Senator Peter Norbeck of South Dakota, who had supported conservation measures in the past, to attach a resolution to the Migratory Bird Hunting Stamp Act of 1934 (more commonly known as the Duck Stamp Act, which used funds generated from an annual federal waterfowl hunting stamp to finance refuge acquisition) granting one million dollars in unallocated relief funds to the Biological Survey. Norbeck agreed and raised the figure to six million dollars. The Senate passed the bill, and Roosevelt signed it without noticing the funds Norbeck had added. The new chief was a craftier politician than were previous chiefs of the agency, and it was clear that

Darling was willing to adopt creative tactics to further his conservation goals.[12]

The Biological Survey garnered funds from a number of sources, and it used money from the sale of Duck Stamps and the Emergency Relief Program to buy land for refuges. It also used funds and labor from the Civilian Conservation Corps (CCC), one of Roosevelt's most popular New Deal programs, to develop refuges. For the Biological Survey, which had never received sustained attention or adequate funding from the federal government, CCC labor was a windfall. By 1935, the CCC operated twenty-six camps on refuges throughout the country. Now the Biological Survey could implement a wildlife restoration program of sufficient magnitude to match the scale of the waterfowl crisis. The refuge system was growing, too. Between 1935 and 1937, the number of national wildlife refuges doubled; by 1940, the number doubled again.[13]

The CCC began in 1933 as a make-work program run by the U.S. Army to employ young men in forestry and soil protection projects throughout the nation. The men enrolled in the program lived in camps with military-style barracks and were subjected to the discipline of camp managers. The word "conservation" in the program's name had a dual meaning: Roosevelt wanted the program to help conserve natural resources *and* conserve the bodies of young men going to waste due to the Depression. The CCC would heal the wounds on the land created by years of neglect while restoring both the bodies and souls of the nation's youth.[14]

Darling and other Biological Survey officials were savvy enough to connect the agency's wildlife restoration efforts with other conservation initiatives such as the CCC. New Deal conservationists wanted to restore damaged land and distribute resources more equitably. Increasingly, the federal government saw ducks and geese as valuable resources for urban sport hunters now worried about the potential demise of game birds. To save them, the Biological Survey capitalized on the move to retire denuded farmland. The low land prices brought on by the Great Depression enabled the Biological Survey to acquire parcels for refuges that it would have been unable to afford during better economic times. Wildlife restoration and the refuges needed to achieve it were important components of federal conservation programs. But other developments during the New Deal conflicted with constructing habitats more beneficial for wildlife. For instance, the Bureau of Reclamation, whose irrigation projects had often been the subject of ridicule in earlier decades, emerged as a powerful agency during the New Deal. With the completion of the Boulder Dam (later renamed Hoover Dam) along the Colorado River on the border between Nevada and Arizona in 1935, the agency demonstrated it was capable of building large, multipurpose water projects that would satisfy both urban and rural residents in the West. The dam straddled the Colorado River and provided electricity for Los Angeles and parts of Arizona as well as water for the Imperial Irrigation District near the Mexico border in California. Similar multipurpose projects became commonplace after World War II as the Bureau of Reclamation and the Corps of Engineers undertook massive development projects on other western rivers such as the Sacramento and Columbia.[15]

The Biological Survey's refuge program formed but a small component of this massive reorganization of the West's waterscape. The survey enlarged its domain during the New Deal, but the resources at its disposal were modest compared to other federal agencies. Despite President Roosevelt's enthusiasm for conservation and the eagerness of his cabinet members to implement his initiatives, the president's wildlife recovery plan was riddled with contradictions. He was a fervent champion of large-scale water projects like Hoover Dam and the Central Valley Project, even though these projects often destroyed waterfowl habitat that the Biological Survey sought to protect. The small refuges created during the New Deal as well as the ones restored during this time could hardly withstand the onslaught of water development and the resulting widespread loss of essential bird habitat. Given the enormous resources directed towards dam construction and other forms of water development, aiming meager funds at wildlife protection was like throwing cash into a hurricane.

A BIRD'S EYE VIEW OF THE CONTINENT

The federal government had established and managed refuges long before the New Deal. But efforts during the 1930s were part of a systematic program to develop a refuge system congruent with the latest ornithological knowledge about bird migration.[16] Two Biological Survey officials were crucial in this process: Frederick C. Lincoln, an ornithologist, and J. Clark Salyer II, the bureau's chief of the Division of Wildlife Refuges. Lincoln provided a compelling framework for understanding North American bird migration; Salyer used this framework to determine where the agency should establish new refuges and focus its efforts. Together, they demonstrated a shift in focus of bird conservation from a local to national and even continental scale.

Although the Biological Survey had conducted research on bird migration since its inception in 1885, most agency research in the early twentieth century focused on how to use birds for controlling insect pests. In the wake of the Migratory Bird Treaty Act of 1918, the Biological Survey began a more concerted effort to understand the migration patterns of North American birds. To enforce the act and devise hunting regulations for migratory waterfowl, the Biological Survey needed a more detailed knowledge of bird migration. Ornithologists, however, were only just beginning to study the life histories and ecology of birds. Although some ornithologists had studied bird migration since 1883, the year the American Ornithologists' Union was founded, most ornithologists were preoccupied with collecting and classifying bird specimens. The Biological Survey and nongovernmental associations tried various means of tracking the arrival and departure dates of migrating birds. Only after the ornithologists began banding birds on a large scale did their migration patterns begin to come into focus. Ornithologists attached aluminum bands with the address of the bander or of a recording agency engraved in the metal to the legs of birds. When people killed or found banded birds, they could return the bands to the address with information on where they were found. Using this method, ornithologists were able to determine the sites used by birds and to devise theories about the routes the birds took between them.[17]

The Biological Survey hired Frederick Lincoln to manage its migration study. Formerly a curator at the Colorado Museum in Denver, Lincoln came to his new post with a reputation as a creative and efficient researcher. At the Biological Survey, Lincoln encouraged ornithologists and bird enthusiasts to band birds while raising the standards to certify them for the task. During the 1920s, he cultivated a network of volunteer bird banders throughout the United States and Canada that included both professional and amateur ornithologists. Sport hunters and others sent bands collected from dead birds to Washington, D.C. Lincoln and his staff matched the numbered bands with cards containing information on where and when the birds were banded. By 1930, volunteers had banded over 740,000 birds and returned 10,000 bands from dead birds to the Biological Survey.[18]

In effect, Lincoln had turned the research offices of the Biological Survey into what Bruno Latour calls a centre of calculation.[19] Lincoln and his staff were at the heart of a data collecting network that included bird banders, hunters, and, of course, the birds themselves. Under Lincoln's guidance, the Biological Survey was able to centralize the production of bird banding data. Instead of bands being sent to a number of different agencies or countries, under his program all bands were mailed to the bureau's offices in Washington, D.C.

As Lincoln mapped the banding sites and retrieval points for individual birds, a pattern began to emerge. The birds did not migrate to different areas year after year as previously thought. Rather, birds repeatedly followed the same route each season even though other members of the same species might travel elsewhere. For instance, although Canada geese had a continental distribution, and many of them bred in the Arctic, various populations wintered in different areas. What had previously seemed a confusing movement of birds south each fall became a set of paths that biologists could trace on maps. Lincoln called these broad migration paths flyways, and he named four of them: the Pacific, Central, Mississippi, and Atlantic.

Using the flyway concept, federal and state officials could compartmentalize space even further to manage waterfowl and the places they used during migration. Shortly after Lincoln developed the concept, the Biological Survey divided waterfowl management into four administrative regions that roughly corresponded to the flyway boundaries drawn by Lincoln. Region One, the area encompassing the American section of the Pacific Flyway, included all the West Coast states as well as Idaho, Nevada, and Arizona. Each region had a flyway biologist who reported on regional conditions and processed data on waterfowl populations. Fish and game departments in each state were responsible for enforcing hunting regulations. This bureaucratization of waterfowl management served to blur the distinctions between the biological flyway Lincoln described and the administrative structure constructed to manage it.[20]

CONSTRUCTING HEALTHFUL ENVIRONMENTS

While water diversions and grazing further decimated the Klamath Refuges during the 1920s, the Biological Survey began a massive engineering project on the shores of Utah's Great Salt Lake—a project that would serve as a model for refuge restoration elsewhere in the 1930s and 1940s. The Great Basin of the western United States had long been an area with limited wetlands, but the ones found in this arid region were vital for waterfowl. Among these desert oases, few could rival the marshes on the northeastern shores of the Great Salt Lake, where the Bear River emerged from the Wasatch Mountains and emptied into the lake's briny waters.

Under certain conditions, these marshes were lethal for waterfowl. In the early twentieth century, what was then known as western duck sickness killed hundreds of thousands of waterfowl in the Bear River marshes. Research on the causes of the malady affecting ducks and geese would lead the Biological Survey to make its first forays into large-scale water development to foster a healthful environment for birds. The Bear River marshes became a laboratory for early research on the source of the disease and the environmental conditions that fostered its spread. Alexander Wetmore, an assistant biologist with the Bureau of Biological Survey, was one of the first scientists to investigate it. During the summer seasons between 1913 and 1916, Wetmore retrieved carcasses and examined birds stricken with duck sickness in the marshes around Utah's Great Salt Lake. Residents had told him of a massive die-off of waterfowl in 1910. The number of dead birds was "said to have been almost beyond belief. Dead birds rotting in the sun dotted the water in shallow bays, and long windrows of bodies were blown up on the shorelines and against the rushes."[21] Up to half-a-million birds died that year. Between 1910 and 1925, seven million birds may have perished due to the disease.[22]

The cause of the disease eluded early researchers such as Wetmore, but it was clear to him that the physical environment played some role in the illness. He considered a number of possible causes, including industrial pollutants and sulphuric acid in springs near the Great Salt Lake, but he eventually concluded that alkali salts ingested by the birds acted as a toxin. Since duck sickness was most common in marshes lying in the arid parts of the western United States, the alkali salts that accumulated in such environments seemed likely culprits. Later studies demonstrated that while aridity contributed to the spread of the illness, the bacterium *Clostridium botulism* (more commonly known as botulism) was the source of the disease. The disease spread quickly due to a series of events that often spiraled out of control. First, waterfowl ingested spores containing the toxin (which could lie dormant for years in marshes). After the bird succumbed to the disease, maggots consuming the carcass concentrated the toxin; they were eaten in turn by other ducks and geese. This eventually caused the death of yet more birds whose decomposing bodies served as fertile environments for the disease to spread. Thousands of birds could die in a matter of weeks before anyone could stop the outbreak.[23]

Waterfowl faced the threat of botulism before the twentieth century, but the onslaught of water diversion and the growth of irrigated agriculture at the expense of wetlands made it much worse. The destruction of wetlands forced surviving populations of ducks and geese to congregate in small areas of remaining habitat. Overcrowded on small refuges and forced to linger there throughout the wintering season, flocks of birds were highly susceptible to the malady. Droughts, which were all too common in the arid landscapes of Oregon and California, also forced birds into shrinking ponds and marshes. Since waterfowl are gregarious by disposition, epizootics of botulism could devastate birds on a given refuge very quickly. Migrating birds could also carry the toxin to other wetlands and refuges along the flyway.[24]

This situation posed a particularly vexing conundrum for anyone hoping to create viable refuges, either at Bear River or elsewhere in the West. Wildlife refuges provided rare sanctuary amid landscapes

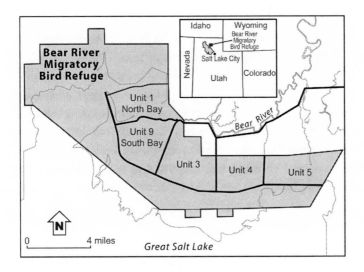

MAP 5 *Bear River Migratory Bird Refuge, 1950*

that once contained plentiful wetland habitat. Yet these same refuges crowded the waterfowl unnaturally and left them susceptible to epizootics of botulism. One of the primary means to control such outbreaks was to carefully adjust refuge water levels and distribution. Refuge staff learned that botulism thrived in very shallow ponds and marshes, which warmed quickly during the summer months. When an outbreak started in one part of a refuge, wildlife managers drained the pool where the afflicted birds congregated, hoping that healthy birds would move to other parts of the refuge that were free of the toxin. Of course, to drain or raise water on demand, wildlife managers needed a network of canals to carry water, pumps to move it, and dikes to contain it. Protecting birds from botulism meant that refuge staff had to regulate water with the same care and foresight as the farmers irrigating crops nearby.[25]

At the mouth of the Bear River, the Biological Survey sought to transform the marshes where duck sickness festered and fashion a more healthful environment for migratory birds. In 1928, the federal government established the Bear River Migratory Bird Refuge, and quickly thereafter, the Bureau of Biological Survey commenced an ambitious engineering project to improve the habitat for waterfowl. Converting a landscape of disease and death to one of health required a deeper manipulation of the area's hydrology than it had at any other refuge. To achieve this, the agency constructed a set of ponds and marshes divided by dikes. It diverted water from the Bear River into these ponds. Fresh, clean water would prevent the development of alkaline conditions that refuge managers assumed was the source of the disease. Failing this, refuge staff could always drain ponds where the disease emerged, collect dead birds, and dispose of their carcasses to stop the perpetuation of the outbreak. "Instead of a death trap," the Biological Survey proudly stated, "the area will become a supply depot for the surrounding region, producing vastly increased numbers of wild fowl."[26]

The dikes and ponds served other purposes, too. The Great Salt Lake was extremely shallow and had no outlet; lake levels could vary a great deal annually. In heavy snow years, snowmelt poured off the mountains and into the lake, leading to the migration of the shoreline as the lake level rose. Rather than nourishing the marshes, this intrusion of hypersaline water proved devastating to marsh plants and creatures adapted to freshwater conditions. To prevent this, the Biological Survey constructed a dike to separate freshwater on refuges from salty water in the lake.

The thousands of waterfowl using the marshes vividly confirmed the area's importance for waterfowl. Yet the results of migration research demonstrated the importance of Bear River even more. "The significance of these facts is that they prove the Bear River Marshes to the central distributing point, supplying wild fowl to the Rocky Mountain states and California, and that the vast mortality of the birds in this area must necessarily have had a direct effect in decreasing the supply for all the states involved."[27] The Biological Survey considered Bear River to be a "super refuge" and a key to supplying birds to other refuges throughout the western United States.[28]

By the early 1940s, the agency had medical means to treat sick waterfowl. Wildlife researchers tested an antitoxin for avian botulism at a research station established on the Bear River Refuge in Utah. Refuge personnel captured sick ducks, injected them with a small amount of the antitoxin, and allowed them to recover. This method was very successful, but it required many agency employees or volunteers to capture the ducks, administer the medicine, and release them back into the wild. Some refuge workers actually constructed "duck hospitals," where agency officials cared for the sick birds. Not surprisingly, dealing with such outbreaks was a major undertaking. Many refuge personnel were involved in not only capturing sick birds but burning dead ones. Although this work underscored the importance the agency placed on controlling disease, it also distracted refuge managers from other tasks.[29]

In effect, wildlife managers diligently collected sick birds, nursed them back to health, and released them back into the wild so hunters could kill them. Its actions exposed one of the ironies of the refuge system: wildlife managers did not save the birds from death. Agency personnel tried to prevent the *unintended* deaths of waterfowl by avian diseases so the *intended* deaths by hunters could continue. Wildlife officials mediated life and death on the refuges to meet management goals. Fulfilling these objectives proved difficult in an environment where natural threats such as botulism were just as challenging as human ones.

ADDING LINKS TO THE CHAIN

The project at Bear River was a success. Yet waterfowl numbers continued their steep decline during the early 1930s. Developing one refuge on the shores of the Great Salt Lake meant little if the wetlands the birds used elsewhere during the year were gone or drastically reduced. In the 1930s, the Biological Survey sought to cope with this problem by locating and purchasing additional lands for refuges in the Far West and throughout the nation. Finding usable habitat was only part of the criteria for a good refuge site. As the agency quickly learned, creating new refuges entailed carving out places within the grid of irrigated agriculture that had developed during the previous half-century. More often than not, the Biological Survey proved the weaker party as it tried to negotiate with farmers and irrigation districts to develop a chain of refuges along the Pacific Flyway.

Frederick Lincoln offered a powerful new framework for understanding bird migration with his flyway concept, but it was left to others in the Biological Survey to carry out the challenging task of selecting new refuge sites and securing properties. The person most responsible for this was J. Clark Salyer II, the architect of the federal wildlife refuge system. In 1934, Biological Survey head "Ding" Darling appointed Salyer the Chief of the Division of Wildlife Refuges—a post he held for nearly thirty years. In this position, Salyer played a key role in the selection and establishment of wildlife refuges. The geography of the refuge system reflects his understanding of the problems facing migratory waterfowl and how the Biological Survey could use ideas such as the flyway to develop a rationalized refuge system.

To sustain migratory waterfowl in the Far West, the Biological Survey needed additional refuges in the southern portion of the migration route: the Great Basin, the Imperial Valley, and most importantly, the Central Valley of California. But irrigation had taken a terrible toll on wetlands in all of these areas. The Central Valley, which was the most important wintering area for Pacific Flyway waterfowl, had lost 85 percent of its wetlands by 1939.[30] These figures hide a more complicated story. Water development did indeed destroy thousands of acres of wetlands in Oregon, Nevada, Utah, and California. But in some areas irrigated agriculture produced it, too. The irrigation disaster in the Imperial Valley created the Salton Sea, and ducks and other birds quickly began to use it. Waterfowl also adapted to the fields of crops that replaced the wetlands once spread across the Sacramento Valley, the northern portion of the Central Valley. The replacement of the wetlands with an agricultural landscape thus provided some opportunities for migratory birds. But the actions of farmers, sport hunters, and wildlife managers largely determined how migratory waterfowl could use this new landscape.

Salyer directed officials to survey areas throughout the nation as sites for new wildlife refuges. These officials included irrigation specialists from the Department of Agriculture. Since almost any potential refuge site in the West would be within irrigated landscapes, Salyer needed the expertise of irrigation engineers to advise him on the water available for refuges and the sorts of water control structures (dikes, canals, ponds) that the Biological Survey might need to construct. In addition to this on-the-ground knowledge, Salyer also

Lower Klamath Lake, 1907. (Record Group 115: Records of the Bureau of Reclamation, Box 63, #185, National Archives–College Park)

Tule Lake, 1916. By this time, the Reclamation Service had already dewatered part of the lake and opened it to homesteaders. (Record Group 115, Records of the Bureau of Reclamation, "Irrigation Projects, 1896–1935, Klamath Project, Oregon," JL291, National Archives–College Park)

(ABOVE) *"Here lay the land of my dreams . . ." William Finley and Herman Bohlman at Tule Lake marshes, 1905. (Oregon Historical Society, Finley Collection, A-1823)*

(FACING PAGE) *William Finley and Herman Bohlman studying cormorant eggs during their 1905 photographic expedition to the Klamath Basin. Through their photographs and writings, they portrayed the basin marshes as an enticing place for outdoor adventure and bird watching. (Oregon Historical Society, Finley Collection, A-1607)*

Anton Petrasek and his family on their Tule Lake homestead in 1916. Government photos such as this one depict the Tule Lake area as a landscape of agrarian opportunity, worked by hardy yeoman families on the dry lakebed. (Record Group 115, Records of the Bureau of Reclamation, "Irrigation Projects, 1896-1935, Klamath Project, Oregon," JL-304, National Archives–College Park)

ANTON PETRASEK
¼ MI. TO
KALINA STORE

The land beneath the Tule Lake marshes proved fertile. Here, two men take pride in a particularly bountiful crop of grain in 1916. (Record Group 115, Records of the Bureau of Reclamation, "Irrigation Projects, 1896–1935, Klamath Project, Oregon," JL-297, National Archives–College Park)

Klamath Straits, 1927. The Reclamation Service closed Klamath Straits in 1917 as part of an effort to starve Lower Klamath Lake of water and open the lakebed to homesteaders. Given the arid environment, it took only a few years for the shallow lake to evaporate in the high desert air. (Record Group 22, Records of the U.S. Fish and Wildlife Service, Box 27, B-32031, National Archives–College Park)

Lower Klamath Lakebed, 1929. The destruction of the Klamath Bird Reservation became a symbol among conservationists of short-sighted agricultural and irrigation development. "It doesn't even support a good crop of weeds," wrote government ornithologist Frederick Lincoln after a visit. "A jack-rabbit would starve on it." (Record Group 22, Box 27, B-35777, National Archives–College Park)

Ornithologist Frederick Lincoln at his desk with bird bands, 1939. Lincoln's flyway concept proved indispensable to the Bureau of Biological Survey in its efforts to create a viable network of refuges to sustain migratory birds, whose populations plummeted in the 1930s. (Record Group 22, Records of the U.S. Fish and Wildlife Service, Box 47 Administration, B-7631, National Archives–College Park)

Much of the Sacramento National Wildlife Refuge was barren before the Biological Survey bought the property. This photograph shows a part of the refuge in 1937 before the bureau flooded portions of it. (Record Group 22, Records of the U.S. Fish and Wildlife Service, Box 9 California, B-53130, National Archives–College Park)

The Biological Survey adopted new technologies to construct ponds, straighten creeks, and engineer other sorts of habitat for migratory waterfowl. This photo shows a dragline at work on the Sacramento National Wildlife Refuge in 1937. (Record Group 22, Records of the U.S. Fish and Wildlife Service, Box 9 California, B-52765, National Archives–College Park)

(FACING PAGE) *Ross and white-fronted geese in flooded units on the Sacramento National Wildlife Refuge, 1938. (Record Group 22, Records of the U.S. Fish and Wildlife Service, Box 9 California, B-64-X4, National Archives–College Park)*

(ABOVE) *Refuge managers adopted the tools of industrial agriculture in their quest to grow more feed for wintering waterfowl. Here, an airplane disperses rice seeds on the Sacramento National Wildlife Refuge in 1947. (Group 22, Records of the U.S. Fish and Wildlife Service, California, B-63364, National Archives–College Park)*

The arsenal of chemicals refuge managers employed to deal with unwanted pests included herbicides and insecticides such as DDT, which was widely used on western refuges in the 1940s and 1950s. This 1947 photo shows the experimental spraying of tules in the Sacramento National Wildlife Refuge with the herbicide 2,4-D. (Group 22, Records of the U.S. Fish and Wildlife Service, B-63361, National Archives–College Park)

used the flyway concept to assess what areas along each flyway might be essential for refuges. Yet as he quickly learned, purchasing land and securing water to sustain refuges in these vital areas of the Pacific Flyway was fraught with difficulties.

In selecting sites, the agency relied on ornithologists, game wardens, and sport hunters who were familiar with the habitats and movements of western waterfowl. In 1935, biologists and agricultural engineers scoured the Great Basin, Central Valley, and Imperial Valley for possible refuge sites. With many farmers and landowners suffering financially due to the Great Depression, the Biological Survey hoped to capitalize on these circumstances by finding suitable waterfowl habitat on land that owners were willing to part with at a reasonable price.

Water rights were just as important as land. At first glance, one of the most promising areas for a migratory waterfowl refuge in California was the Los Banos region of the San Joaquin Valley. However, much of the land and nearly all of the water rights were controlled by the Miller & Lux company, one of the largest landowners in the western United States. The Biological Survey learned that the company was unable to make payments on lands. Even so, it proved unwilling to sell land that was most useful for waterfowl. Many of the duck hunting clubs in the area were struggling, and they offered to sell their property to the agency. But the water rights for the clubs were controlled by Miller & Lux. Negotiations with the company broke down when it became clear the company would not part with its water rights to the land, or at least at a price the Biological Survey could accept.[31]

Agency biologists were not the only ones searching for refuge sites for the Biological Survey. Irrigation engineers with the Department of Agriculture's Bureau of Agricultural Engineering also played a key role in selecting and evaluating possible refuges. One such engineer, Luther Winsor, was one of the principal figures involved with evaluating and designing the water projects on the Bear River Refuge during the late 1920s. Using the experience gained during that assignment, Winsor went on reconnaissance missions throughout the Far West to evaluate locations. Not surprisingly, given his profession, Winsor was concerned with how the Biological Survey could construct dikes and canals to manage refuge water. The agency's fondness for devising engineering solutions to ecological problems was evident from the time the agency first surveyed potential western sites.

Biological and engineering considerations came together as the Biological Survey considered refuge sites in Nevada. For the most part, Nevada was bereft of large wetlands, but one site stood out: Ruby Lake, in the north central part of the state. Sustained by freshwater springs gushing from the eastern flanks of the Ruby Mountains, the lake served as a breeding area and migration stop for ducks and geese. Unlike other existing and potential refuge sites in the Far West, the water sustaining Ruby Lake was not wastewater from irrigated agriculture. The freshwater helped reduce the instances of duck sickness, a paramount concern for the Biological Survey. Agency biologists recognized the usefulness of the lake as a year-round site. Despite these obvious preexisting advantages, engineer Winsor saw even greater potential when he visited the lake in the summer of 1936. He wrote that this was "easily our outstanding project in Nevada," but dividing the lake with dikes would aid control of water and enable the agency to manage water more effectively. While surveying the lake and surrounding countryside on horseback in 1939, Winsor saw ways to put the water to better use. "The water that is being wasted in the production of this dense growth of bull rush and cat tails might better be utilized," he wrote in letter to the bureau chief. With careful planning and construction, the agency could develop "an extensive series of the most desirable kind of pools and marshes along the shore line."[32] As at the mouth of the Bear River in Utah, engineering could transform a site already used by breeding and migrating birds into an environment that could support greater numbers of waterfowl.[33]

The Biological Survey undertook similar reconnaissance missions in California's Central Valley, the key wintering area for Pacific Flyway waterfowl. The most promising place to establish a wildlife refuge in the valley was the Spalding Ranch, near Willows, California. Sport hunters considered the ranch to be one of the best places in California to hunt geese, and the ranch served as a private hunting reserve for the Spalding family and their business associates, such as bankers, lawyers, and officials of the Southern Pacific Railway. Although the ranch had poor soil, the Spalding Trust Company was able to grow rice on part of the property and graze sheep on the rest. As rice prices dropped in the early 1930s, the company opened more of the ranch to hunters willing to pay a fee. Even with the added revenue brought in by sport hunters, the ranch continued to lose money. By 1935, the company owed over two hundred thousand dollars to the Glenn-Colusa Irrigation District, which supplied the ranch with water, and to the local reclamation district, which was responsible for maintaining canals that carried water away from the fields. With the company unable to pay its debts, the Glenn-Colusa Irrigation District assumed title to the Spalding Ranch.[34]

The Biological Survey inspected the ranch in 1935 to determine whether it was suitable as a migratory waterfowl refuge and whether the agency could develop the property. The report the agency produced not only describes the condition of the land at that time, it also provides a valuable indication of how the land could fit into the Biological Survey's overall plans for the Pacific Flyway. Here, as elsewhere, the bureau thought of the potential refuge as a sanctuary where hunting would be prohibited. Although market hunting had decreased substantially in California since the turn of the century and sport hunting was more closely regulated, the bureau still believed that refuges should be protected areas where birds could find relief from shooting during the hunting season. Moreover, the proposed Spalding refuge could hold an important place in the Biological Survey's management of Pacific Flyway birds. The number of hunters in southern California was increasing as Los Angeles, San Diego, and other cities in the area grew. Without a substantial refuge in the Sacramento Valley, migratory waterfowl would continue to fly southward past an increasing gauntlet of California hunters. The bureau did not expect a Sacramento Valley refuge to stop further migration entirely, but it did hope that "further southern migration might to some degree be halted." It was confident that "with water and feed conditions made favorable, this expectation [was] not unreasonable."[35]

While the size of the Spalding Ranch attracted the interest of wildlife officials, they knew that the extent of a refuge mattered little without sufficient water to nourish wetlands. The early surveys of the Spalding Ranch devoted considerable attention to the water situation on the ranch and to how the agency could find enough water to make a refuge viable. To supply the refuge with water, the Biological Survey could buy water from the Glenn-Colusa Irrigation District, pump it from wells on the property, or divert drainage water flowing through the ranch into ponds constructed by the bureau. To conserve funds, the agency favored the last option. It hoped to divert water from Logan Creek, an ephemeral stream running through the property, for its ponds. The Glenn-Colusa Irrigation District maintained that the water belonged to them since farms using district water were the source of the creek's flow. Even if Glenn-Colusa had no right to the stream, the quality of water in Logan Creek was often poor. Sewage from the town of Willows to the north flowed into Logan Creek (the Biological Survey hoped the California State Board of Health would force the town to end this practice). Pumping water from creeks outside the property would be even more contentious. Buying water from the district was the least attractive choice financially, but legally the Biological Survey realized it might have no other option.[36]

Negotiations with the Glenn-Colusa Irrigation District revealed the Biological Survey's inexperience with land purchases. The agency demonstrated its interest in the Spalding Ranch throughout 1935 and 1936 by surveying the land and by sending high-level officials to visit the ranch. With only a cursory knowledge of the area and limited experience in purchasing real estate, the agency exposed itself to deception. As negotiations to buy the land proceeded in the summer of 1936, the Biological Survey learned that no provisions for water had been made in the preliminary contract with the Glenn-Colusa Irrigation District.

A representative from the Spalding Trust Company told the agency that without an agreement on water, the new refuge might not receive any water whatsoever or that the agency might be forced to buy it from the irrigation district at a premium rate. Federal attorneys working on negotiations for the Biological Survey were furious that the U.S. government had nearly purchased a wildlife refuge without water. Winsor, the irrigation engineer for the Department of Agriculture, believed that the Glenn-Colusa Irrigation District knew "perfectly well what that outcome of the transaction would be. They have water to sell and they realize perfectly well that there is no other adequate supply for the property." The agency renegotiated the contract and managed to secure water from the district at a reduced rate. The Biological Survey's enormous blunder demonstrated that even though it was part of the federal government, long-established, powerful interests could check the agency's power in the Sacramento Valley.[37]

Water was crucial to the development of the Sacramento Refuge. The agency was not attempting to restore lost wetlands so much as create new wetlands where few had existed before. The Spalding Ranch was a valuable addition to the federal refuge system, but not because it contained remnants of the Central Valley's lost marshes. Rather, the property was attractive for its low price and as a site where the bureau might develop new marshes using the lessons learned on the Bear River Refuge in Utah. The Biological Survey envisaged the property as a migratory waterfowl sanctuary amid an intensely managed agricultural countryside. Yet its plans would change over the decade to accommodate the interests of farmers, irrigation districts, and sport hunters. Like a weather vane, it was turned by shifts in the winds of local and national politics. Attempts by the Biological Survey to bolster its public image had material consequences on the ground as the bureau managed water, vegetation, birds, and other species to accommodate these political forces.

The refuge was not only a sanctuary from the guns of sport hunters; it was a space in which to segregate waterfowl from farmland. By acquiring the refuge, the Biological Survey became more deeply involved in conflicts over the depredations caused by waterfowl in the Sacramento Valley. One of the agency's surveyors, S. A. Young, wrote in 1935 that "with the development of the Spalding Ranch into a refuge, responsibility for whatever trespass exists will undoubtedly be placed on Bureau shoulders, and there will arise the demand that the refuge produce at least some of the meals [for waterfowl]."[38] Achieving this required the careful development of refuge lands. The debate over how to achieve these dual goals hinged on whether to grow suitable aquatic plants in the refuge's new ponds or to undertake a rice farming program to grow more feed in a limited area.

In the end, this debate was secondary. Above all, the refuge needed water. Conflicts between the Biological Survey and the Glenn-Colusa Irrigation District flared throughout the late 1930s and early 1940s. To reduce operating costs, the Biological Survey wanted to divert water from Logan Creek, which carried drainage water through the refuge.

The bureau realized that the creek would rarely contain enough water to supply all of the refuge's needs, but using water from the creek was preferable to buying all of it from Glenn-Colusa. It also realized that filing a legal claim on water in the creek would antagonize the irrigation district. Given the choice of either buying sums of water it could not afford or using water from Logan Creek, the bureau chose the latter.[39]

The Glenn-Colusa Irrigation District responded swiftly to the Biological Survey's water application in February 1938. Lawyers for the district argued that the Sacramento Refuge lay within the district's boundaries and was subject to its water use regulations. According to the district, water flowing through the refuge was not natural but artificially derived from fields irrigated with water the district pumped from the Sacramento River and diverted into the area. The lawyers urged the Biological Survey to proceed cautiously, and that pursuing this matter might jeopardize relations between the bureau and the district. The district was prepared to make things difficult for the Biological Survey if necessary. When the agency prepared to act on its filing and divert water from the creek into the refuges ponds, the irrigation district threatened to divert the water around the sanctuary to another creek, a move that would leave the refuge entirely dry.[40]

Postponing the delivery of water was another means by which the Glenn-Colusa Irrigation District could exercise its authority. In 1943, the U.S. Fish and Wildlife Service (FWS)[41] attempted to negotiate an agreement to purchase water for growing rice on the refuge to feed waterfowl. Despite an agreement in principle, the Glenn-Colusa board delayed signing the contract and called repeatedly for minor revisions. The district refused to grant requests for water even though the delay might mean the rice crop would not mature in time to feed the migratory waterfowl arriving in the fall. Recognizing that failure to secure the water and raise a rice crop would erode local support for the refuge and tarnish the agency's image, J. Clark Salyer II interpreted the district's recalcitrance as "a move to further embarrass us with the local farmers."[42]

For the FWS, the conflict over water supply on the Sacramento Refuge was also a struggle over space. Title to land in the semi-arid Sacramento Valley meant little without water. Managing the refuge required controlling the flow of water in and out of its borders. As long as the refuge lay within the Glenn-Colusa Irrigation District, it was subject to its dictates. These often ran counter to the conservation goals of the FWS. Like the refuges in the Klamath Basin and the Salton Sea Refuge in the Imperial Valley, the Sacramento Refuge was a unit in a much larger irrigation network. The service's ability to manage its refuges was made possible by these districts, which delivered the water that sustained the refuge marshes and crops. Creating the Sacramento Refuge on a dry plain that had never held extensive wetlands would have been impossible without the irrigation network maintained by the districts. As a consequence, the Sacramento Refuge and other refuges in California regularly found themselves subservient to the dictates of their water suppliers.[43]

As troubling as these disputes were, the FWS faced a more serious problem with duck and geese depredations in the Sacramento Valley. Even though rice production increased on the Sacramento Refuge, it failed to satisfy the needs of the waterfowl. The birds continued to feed in rice fields outside the refuge. The damage they inflicted on private lands varied each year. The depredation problems only worsened during the early 1940s. Rice production had remained more or less stagnant in the Sacramento Valley during the preceding decade. With America's entrance into World War II in 1941, however, rice acreage expanded dramatically, just as it had during World War I. In Glenn and Colusa counties, the heart of California's rice-growing district, rice acreage more than doubled between the mid-1930s and mid-1940s.[44] As rice production increased, complaints about bird depredation rose as well. Although the Sacramento Refuge grew rice, birds continued to feed on crops outside the refuge. As the original Biological Survey reports about the Spalding Ranch predicted, the federal government was held responsible for birds trespassing on private farmland. The increase in rice production throughout the Sacramento Valley had made growing feed for ducks on the refuge essential to prevent depredations.

Poor soil and an inadequate water supply limited the FWS's ability to convert more of the Sacramento Refuge to rice production. Yet rice farmers generally blamed FWS ineptitude for the continuing depredations by birds. These attitudes jeopardized the agency's plans to expand the refuge program in California. If the FWS could not develop the Sacramento Refuge, its premier sanctuary in the middle of the state, how could it competently create new refuges elsewhere? The FWS wanted to add further links to the chain of refuges throughout the wintering range of migratory waterfowl along the Pacific Flyway, but criticism of the way the service handled the Sacramento Refuge threatened to undermine its larger goals.

In the fall of 1943 the FWS attempted to enlarge the Sacramento Refuge by purchasing condemned land east of the sanctuary. The property lay within the Provident Irrigation District, which was also run by the head of the Glenn-Colusa Irrigation District, Charles Lambert. Although the service wanted to create refuges elsewhere in the state, some officials in the FWS believed that enlarging the refuge was essential. The FWS used the Sacramento Refuge essentially as a rice farm for waterfowl. Albert Day, assistant head of the FWS, wanted to change this. Adding lands in the Provident Irrigation District would allow the service to grow more aquatic plants in the Sacramento Valley. "The present Sacramento Refuge does not have the element of naturalness such as Provident would have," Day wrote to regional director Leo Laythe and regional biologist Dr. E. E. Horn. But this, Day argued, was a temporary circumstance. The FWS should develop the Provident lands with the marsh and aquatic plant needs of the waterfowl in mind. Bigger refuges (in the Sacramento Valley and elsewhere in California) would not only give waterfowl a large area in which to feed, they would provide a "sufficient area for them to be herded on during the crop season."[45]

Laythe and Horn disagreed strongly with the Provident purchase and with Day's plans for the post-war geography of Pacific Flyway refuges. Buying the property would only anger farmers and the Sacramento Refuge's water supplier, the Glenn-Colusa Irrigation District, even further. The district continued to accuse the FWS of stealing water pumped to the area by the district and of failing to contain the birds. In a letter to U.S. Senator Hiram Johnson of California, the district claimed that the rice the FWS planted only encouraged more birds to congregate in the rice-growing district. "Did these plantings [on the refuge] keep the birds home? NO, IT DID NOT . . . birds want to fly and roam to the hills, river and all over the country, or to any land that has any water standing on it." Sport hunters did not care about the farmers' legitimate grievances against the FWS and were interested in coming to the area "to hunt and have a good time." Although the FWS did not allow hunting on the refuge, sport hunters came to areas nearby and damaged fences, trampled crops, and shot farm animals. Purchasing the Provident property would also remove a large portion of land from county tax rolls, adding to that already removed when the federal government bought the Spalding Ranch in 1937.[46]

California sport hunters did not support enlarging the refuge either. Contrary to what the Glenn-Colusa Irrigation District said, most hunting groups acknowledged the damage the birds caused. They felt that the solution lay not in creating a large "super" refuge in the Sacramento Valley, but in establishing refuges throughout the valley and to the south in the San Joaquin Valley. Despite their differences, both farming and sport hunting groups agreed on the need to disperse migratory waterfowl throughout the state. By creating feeding areas in other parts of California, farmers could distribute the bird menace as much as possible. For sport hunters, the reasons for supporting a system of smaller refuges were more complex. Although they appreciated the protection offered by the Sacramento Refuge, they feared that too many ducks and geese would winter in the Sacramento Valley and fail to migrate farther south. Sport hunters in southern California believed that without a wider distribution of refuges, they would have few chances to hunt migratory waterfowl in their parts of the state. By law, lands bought with Duck Stamp revenue (the primary source of funds for purchasing federal wildlife refuges) were off-limits to hunting. Even so, the sanctuaries could serve as waterfowl magnets, attracting ducks and geese to areas where southern Californians could hunt the birds on private land nearby.[47]

The debate over the Provident purchase revolved around more than the pressures of interest groups. Officials within the FWS also differed on the types of environments the refuges should foster. Political necessity had pushed the service to emphasize rice cultivation on the Sacramento Refuge. Growing rice was the simplest and most efficient way to raise large amounts of food for waterfowl and lure waterfowl away from private cropland. Yet agency officials at FWS headquarters in Chicago[48] such as Albert Day and J. Clark Salyer II still hoped to grow natural aquatic plants for ducks and geese to eat rather than just grains like rice and barley. Regional biologist Horn was skeptical of this goal to grow natural plants on the Provident land if the FWS acquired it. "While Mr. Salyer refers to the naturalness of some of these units, I find that the ducks and geese concentrate in greatest numbers on areas that are thoroughly unnatural. The concentration of 100,000 ducks on several flooded rice fields, and their feeding upon 1,500 acres of adjacent rice . . . makes one wonder as to just what waterfowl prefer." Horn's experience in California had convinced him that grain fields in the Sacramento Valley would serve as irresistible attractions for migratory waterfowl. Developing a viable refuge for the birds meant growing what the ducks clearly preferred, not what FWS officials in Chicago might have liked.[49]

RESTORING THE KLAMATH BASIN

As the Biological Survey added new refuges in the Central Valley and throughout the nation, it also sought to restore long neglected refuges in the Klamath Basin, the bottleneck for migratory birds along the Pacific Flyway. During the New Deal years, the basin was the site of a wildlife and wetland restoration program that dwarfed those in the Sacramento and Imperial Valleys. This was one of the largest restoration programs in the country. Labor and federal funds poured into the basin as the Biological Survey strove to rehabilitate its damaged marshes. But the efforts did not mean that the Bureau of Reclamation ceased to dictate water use in the basin. Rather, the management of the basin's refuges proceeded only when they served the interests of the Bureau of Reclamation and the farmers to whom they supplied water. Like the refuges farther south in California, the Klamath Basin refuges lay within a shared space—hydrologically and politically. This simple reality frustrated attempts to develop sharp distinctions between different types of land.

In the 1920s, the Biological Survey had struggled to establish new refuges in the Klamath Basin to compensate for the drainage of Lower Klamath Lake. The federal government established Upper Klamath

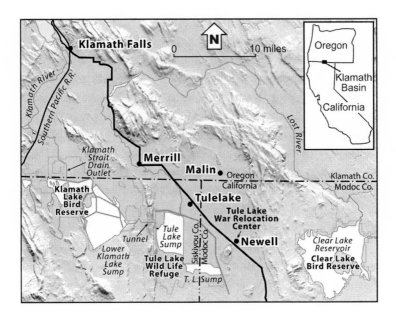

MAP 6 *Upper Klamath Basin, 1945*

Lake Refuge in 1928 with little opposition by sport hunters or business groups in Klamath Falls. The refuge encompassed the freshwater marshes where the Williamson River entered the northern part of the lake. Few sport hunters ventured there, and the refuge threatened no farms.

The Tule Lake Refuge was established to compensate for the loss of the Lower Klamath Lake Bird Reservation, but it fared no better. For most of the 1920s and the early 1930s, diversions by irrigators up river reduced Tule Lake to little more than a pond. In three decades it had shrunk from nearly 50,000 to only 2,000 acres. To be sure, the margins of the lake had fluctuated considerably before Euro-American settlement, but these natural adjustments had never reduced the lake surface so dramatically. Farmers leasing land surrounding the diminished lake and hunters along the shoreline claimed newly exposed land. Neither group accounted for the way precipitation and runoff varied in the basin or how sudden changes in rainfall could threaten the uses of the lakebed. When hydrologic conditions shifted during the mid-1930s, reclamation officials, wildlife managers, and sport hunters tried to adapt.

Despite claims by the Bureau of Reclamation that it controlled water in the basin completely, it was still learning how to deal with extreme weather events that affected water supply. In 1932, a flood sent water down the Lost River into Tule Lake. An even larger flood in 1937 overwhelmed a diversion dam constructed to direct excess water away from Tule Lake and into the Klamath River. The lake level rose quickly and breached the simple dikes surrounding the lake. Farmers and men from a CCC camp tried to contain the flooding with little success.[50]

Even without these floods, the Bureau of Reclamation would have had difficulty restricting Tule Lake to only 2,000 acres. Although the Lost River was the main source of water for Tule Lake before the reclamation project began, the development of irrigated farms brought in water through new, partly artificial routes. After farmers irrigated their fields, drainage canals carried excess water (known as return flow) to Tule Lake. Since the basin lacked a natural outlet, water collecting in the basin enlarged the lake and threatened the dikes surrounding it.

Together, the dewatering of Lower Klamath Lake and the flooding around Tule Lake had proved to be an unmitigated political disaster for the Bureau of Reclamation. Dust from the exposed Lower Klamath lakebed continued to plague residents within nearby towns such as Merrill, Malin, and Klamath Falls. Even the Tule Lake basin, which held rich soils and better prospects for homesteaders, was threatened by erratic water flows. Three decades of water development in the basin had destroyed two of the most important wildlife refuges in the nation.

As it had in the past, the Bureau of Reclamation tried to engineer its way out of the predicament. J. R. Iakisch, a bureau engineer, designed a solution to address the oversupply of water in Tule Lake and the lack of it in Lower Klamath Lake. Iakisch's plan included restoring the two lakes for migratory waterfowl, an outcome that sport hunters and bird protectionists had long requested. The centerpiece of the plan was a mile-long tunnel through Sheepy Ridge, which separated Tule Lake from Lower Klamath Lake. Excess water in Tule Lake would be pumped into the tunnel to flow into Lower Klamath Lake. Canals would then direct the water through a series of smaller ponds or units divided by dikes. After flowing through this system, the excess water would pass through a large canal into the Klamath River. By diverting its water into the Klamath River watershed, Tule Lake would have the outlet that the Bureau of Reclamation wanted. Work on the dikes in Lower Klamath Lake slowed during the early 1940s as funds and labor were diverted for the war effort, but shortly after the Second World War ended, the FWS and Bureau of Reclamation completed most of the key features of the project proposed by Iakisch.[51]

Engineering blurred the distinction between the natural hydrological regime of the basin and the constructed network of canals, dikes, and sumps built by the Bureau of Reclamation and the FWS. When possible, both agencies used preexisting features of the landscape, such as streams and lakes, as bases for their engineering. It was cheaper and more practical to build a dam that raised the level of Clear Lake or to channel the Lost River to allow water to pass quickly into canals. Yet the agencies also created entirely new structures to manage water. The tunnel through Sheepy Ridge connected basins that had remained separate since the end of the Pleistocene epoch, and the miles of dikes built on Lower Klamath Refuge introduced features never seen before on the lake. Each additional piece of engineering made it more difficult to distinguish between the natural and artificial within the Klamath Basin.[52]

The changing fortunes of Lower Klamath and Tule Lake refuges mirrored the newfound power of the FWS. By the 1940s, the agency had greater control over water within the refuges and the infrastructure to manage it more systematically. After disappearing for nearly twenty years, flocks of ducks and geese returned to the Lower Klamath Refuge in stunning numbers. In the coming years, the agency would undertake more ambitious schemes to curb the spread of avian diseases and to develop farming programs to provide food for migrating waterfowl. The beleaguered agency that had once seemed unable to save even itself, much less the wildlife under its care, was now emboldened to attempt large restoration programs throughout the country.[53]

However, there were serious limits to the agency's ambitions. It still held no water rights for any of the refuges. The FWS signed agreements with the Bureau of Reclamation to manage water in the project. Even so, Tule Lake and Lower Klamath refuges lay within the Bureau of Reclamation's Klamath Project, and the agency still managed water in the basin primarily for the needs of irrigators, not of refuges. In the coming decades, irrigators took control over more of the operation of the Klamath Project. The FWS would find that dealing with the irrigators was just as challenging as working with the Bureau of Reclamation.

A striking example of the FWS's still limited ability to manage its Klamath Basin refuges occurred during the Second World War. Labor and funding provided through New Deal programs quickly disappeared when the United States entered the conflict. The Tule Lake CCC camp shut down, and the refuges' staff shrank as personnel joined the armed forces. Agency officials in Washington, D.C., watched as Congress slashed FWS funding. The relocation of the agency's headquarters to Chicago in 1942 further hampered the ability of the FWS to manage refuges effectively and served as an example of how conservation could be quickly sidetracked in times of war.[54]

Budgetary and labor shortages were not the only problems. In April 1942, the newly formed War Relocation Authority (WRA) began constructing an internment camp for Japanese Americans on the eastern boundary of the Tule Lake Refuge. The camp was the largest of ten camps built by the federal government during the Second World War to detain Japanese Americans. Eventually it housed over 18,000 people. There is little indication that the WRA or the Department of the Interior consulted with the FWS before building the camp. J. Clark Salyer II was furious about the placement of the camp, saying that the agreement struck between the War Relocation Authority and the Bureau of Reclamation reduced the FWS to "the role of an innocent bystander."[55] Even though the camp was built a couple of miles away from the refuge, Salyer worried that hunters might lose access to areas near the camp on the refuge's public shooting grounds. There was also the possibility that the War Relocation Authority might build additions to the internment camp on the refuge itself.[56]

From the Bureau of Reclamation's perspective, the lands where the camp was located were not yet private property, but lands leased to farmers on the Klamath Project. The agency had little problem terminating the leases, since the WRA claimed these internment camps were needed for national security. To the WRA, the lands were an attractive location to place a camp for many reasons: they were relatively isolated, far from the Pacific Coast, and, crucially, already owned by the federal government. The WRA could use the lands to construct a camp without purchasing the property from private owners. The agreement between the bureau and the WRA showed almost a complete disregard for the refuge or the wildlife that depended on those lands.[57]

Although the WRA did not use the Tule Lake Refuge for the camp, it did start a farming program on the refuge. Salyer worried that FWS could not protect waterfowl that used the areas where internees grew crops, and that the birds would devour many of the grains and vegetables they planted. He accused the Japanese internees of harassing geese and ducks by driving trucks through flocks of waterfowl and of harvesting waterfowl illegally by using fishhooks baited with food. Salyer also felt that the WRA wasted much of the vegetables internees grew on the refuge by allowing potatoes and lettuce to freeze in the fields while boxcars of food were delivered to the Tule Lake camp.

In his letters to Ira Gabrielson and other FWS officials, Salyer revealed that his attitude toward the Japanese American internees was as distrustful as that expressed by many other Americans during the war. He considered the internment camp a menace to the migrating waterfowl and likened the Tule Lake Refuge to a group of American soldiers held captive by the Japanese military. He also claimed that the WRA had little control over the internees, who could easily obtain passes to leave the camp, and that while working in the fields, the internees pestered waterfowl and made bird management difficult. In Salyer's view, the credibility of the FWS would suffer among sportsmen if the internees were not more closely supervised.[58]

At the same time, the FWS also sought to use Japanese internees as laborers on refuge conservation projects. With the demise of the CCC shortly after the United States entered the war, the FWS was forced to scramble for manpower to complete construction projects begun in the 1930s. Japanese internees at WRA camps seemed like a convenient substitute for the departing CCC men. In the summer of 1942, Salyer urged the WRA to allow internees from the Tule Lake camp to work on refuge projects. Salyer also hoped to use internees to help develop a proposed refuge in Owens Valley, California, near the site of the Manzanar War Relocation Center. The WRA refused both requests, saying that internees were needed to work on camp farms and other projects directly associated with the relocation centers. Although unsuccessful, the FWS attempt to use internees for its own conservation objectives demonstrated a callous disregard for the plight of Japanese Americans during the war.[59]

Despite Salyer's concerns, the internment camp and its farming program caused no more damage to the Tule Lake Refuge than other farming operations during the war. Klamath Project farmers probably would have leased that land if the War Relocation Authority had not done so. It did show, however, the unwillingness of other federal agencies to consult with the FWS before it took action that might affect federal refuges. During the 1930s the FWS had established itself as a partner in the use of the basin's water, and it had argued for the needs of waterfowl. Once the war began, its views were disregarded as the War Relocation Authority and the Bureau of Reclamation developed the farming program for the Tule Lake camp.

After years of failure, the Fish and Wildlife Service developed viable refuges during the late 1930s within the grid of irrigated agriculture. In spite of its earlier haphazard management and its inability to stop the destruction of important bird sanctuaries by irrigators, the FWS was able to secure water supplies for its older refuges and establish new ones. The Klamath Basin refuges—long symbols among conservationists of misguided water development and ineffective management—were resurrected from the dust and ash on the dry lakebeds.

On maps, these refuges appeared separate from the surrounding countryside, but they were anything but that. Refuges were units within the irrigated landscape. Over the course of the early twentieth century, irrigators and the Bureau of Reclamation constructed an elaborate irrigation system to serve farms. The FWS succeeded in creating refuges by connecting them to this new plumbing system. As the early years of the Sacramento Refuges and the Klamath Basin Refuges showed, the FWS was most successful when its restoration programs complemented the water plans of existing groups. The ability of the FWS to restore some semblance of the Klamath Basin marshes was due less to agitation by conservationists than to flooding caused by poor planning on the part of the Bureau of Reclamation. If the Klamath irrigation project was to continue, the bureau needed a way to store and dispose of wastewater. The engineering scheme concocted by the FWS did this. This seemed like a win-win situation for irrigators and the FWS, but the outcome was that refuges now served as sumps for irrigation wastewater. If the quantity or quality of water changed, refuges would suffer.

Despite the differences between farmers and the FWS, and the years of conflict between the Bureau of Reclamation and the agency, all of the groups shared similar views toward the landscape and a fondness for engineering solutions. Both groups sought to radically simplify the landscape to produce a small number of products. For farmers, it was grain and other crops; for the FWS, it was ducks and geese. A carefully engineered landscape was easier to manipulate. From the perspective of FWS managers, the loss of wetlands to irrigated agriculture and the need to cope with avian diseases made worse by bird overcrowding in refuges gave them little choice but to engineer the landscape in this fashion.

These simplifications, which were so evident on the refuges, were also apparent at other scales of management. Frederick Lincoln's flyway maps were an important contribution to ornithologists' knowledge of bird migration. They also served as an essential tool for managing the habitats of migratory birds that crossed vast distances. Lincoln's flyway maps made the mysterious paths of migratory birds visible or "legible," to use a term by anthropologist James Scott.[60] FWS officials such as J. Clark Salyer II could use these maps to devise a continental refuge system in which each refuge would have a role within a larger migration system divided by flyways.

Mapping migration was a relatively simple matter compared to managing birds in the irrigated landscape. Migratory waterfowl crossed multiple borders in their journeys: national, state, and local. But international borders were not the most important ones ducks and geese crossed. The border between Canada and the United States was simply a political line with no ecological significance; the same was true for state and county borders. Yet the borders dividing private land from wildlife refuges were a different matter. Since they often divided wetlands from farmland, they had real ecological consequences. For some waterfowl these borders were sharply defined. Diving ducks such as northern shovelers and canvasbacks fed almost entirely on wetland plants and aquatic insects. For these species, farmland proved useless as habitat. With other waterfowl the situation was more complicated. Canada geese, snow geese, and pintails could devour grain on private farmland near refuges, showing that the land, at least in this respect, could serve as habitat. Yet in crossing the line from public refuges to individual farms the birds became trespassers in a private realm.

By the 1940s, Pacific Flyway waterfowl found themselves within a hybrid landscape where the boundaries between domesticated farmland and private wildlife spaces blurred. The grid of private property was supposed to divide individual plots of land from one another and private land from public refuges, but some species crossed these borders and used all spaces with impunity. In the coming years, these wayward birds would pose the greatest challenge to wildlife managers. Through their migrations, Pacific Flyway waterfowl showed that the Far West was a shared space.

4

DUCK FARMS

REFUGE MANAGEMENT INVOLVED MANY THINGS—building ponds, raising food, and regulating hunting. In the mid-1940s, it also entailed flying airplanes and lobbing hand grenades. As waterfowl returned in greater numbers to the Klamath Basin and Central Valley during their fall migration, the U. S. Fish and Wildlife Service was ready with this new arsenal to contend with flocks of ducks and geese feasting on private farms. Federal regulations prohibited farmers from shooting the "trespassers," so they called upon the FWS to move the waterfowl—a public resource—from the private farmland into the public space of the refuges. Using surplus military aircraft and equipment from the Second World War, agency pilots took to the sky to herd waterfowl into the refuges. Albert Day, the chief of the FWS, marveled at the pilots' skill. "It is fascinating to watch a good pilot swoop down on a flock of birds feeding in a rice field . . . circle back over them and drop a small but noisy hand grenade in their midst," he wrote. "Maneuvering back and forth in wide sweeps, he manages to keep the fleeing birds ahead of him and guides them to the refuge. As he pulls away they settle down and soon learn that they are welcome here even if they are not welcome elsewhere."[1]

Aerial herding was a common practice in the mid-1940s through the 1950s. It was one small part of the agency's response to a continuing challenge: how to manage mobile nature in the grid of private, irrigated landscapes in the Far West. Unlike other land management agencies in the western United States such as the U.S. Forest Service or the National Park Service, the FWS managed—to put it mildly—a very mobile resource. Not only did the birds breed and winter in different parts of the continent, they failed to heed the most important borders of all: the ones between private and public land. Aerial herding was a way for FWS to force birds to adhere to these borders. Managing waterfowl not only entailed providing adequate habitat for wintering birds; it also involved directing the flow of birds through the shifting human geography along the birds' migration route and wintering quarters.

Farmers were not the only groups concerned about the birds' movements. Sport hunters had a claim on the birds, too, and in the decades after the war, they exerted a growing influence on bird management and the geography of wildlife refuges in the wintering areas of the Pacific Flyway. For years, farmers had destroyed waterfowl habitat and harassed the remaining birds as they pleased. But after the war, this was no longer possible. Sport hunters from the West's growing urban regions—Los Angeles, San Francisco, and Portland—demanded places to practice their sport. Between 1945 and 1951, the number of waterfowl hunters in California rose from approximately 90,000 to 214,000.[2] They used their growing clout, and the FWS used funds from Duck Stamp sales and other sources, to acquire more refuges. Their power would ensure that waterfowl would have a place within the Far West's irrigated agricultural landscapes, a fact that farmers would grudgingly have to accept.

The flocks of birds feeding in Oregon and California grain fields showed that private farms—at least for some species—could serve as habitat. But refuges also became more like farms. The nascent refuge farming program begun during the late 1930s and early 1940s became a key component of refuges after the war. Lacking knowledge or experience with farming, FWS officials adopted the tools and practices of modern industrial agriculture to grow feed for hungry waterfowl. The tools included not only commercial seeds and farming machinery, but also the full arsenal of insecticides and herbicides that became common on American farms in the decades following the Second World War. In the name of conservation, the FWS sprayed grain fields with DDT, 2,4-D, and other pesticides. By the 1960s, the ecological costs of dependence on these chemicals would become all too apparent to the FWS. Until then, the chemicals would remain a staple of refuge management.

The FWS found itself in an uncomfortable predicament during this era. Irrigated, industrial agriculture had destroyed much of the waterfowl habitat in the Far West, but to save the birds and placate farmers, the agency felt it had little choice but to transform large portions of its refuges into mirrors of the agricultural landscape. This had positive results. Waterfowl populations recovered partially from their lows in the 1930s. Yet their recovery was based not on the restoration of lost wetlands, but the creation of duck farms.

FEEDING WATERFOWL

The roots of the conflicts over migratory waterfowl in the 1940s were found in the development of the Sacramento Valley rice landscape decades earlier. Unlike much of the Central Valley, the bottomlands of the Sacramento Valley were not reclaimed until the early twentieth century. The heavy, impermeable clays proved unsuitable for most types of farming but ideal for the cultivation of rice. Beginning in the 1910s, farmers began to grow rice on a limited scale, and during the First World War, rising prices for grains in general, and rice in particular, encouraged farmers to convert more of the bottomlands into rice paddies. With the development of the dikes along the Sacramento River, farmers could reclaim these lands without the fear that devastating floods would destroy their crops.

Some basic figures provide a sense of the transformation. By 1920, farmers had brought approximately 162,000 acres into production from less than 1,000 acres eight years earlier. Rice acreage plummeted during the rest of the decade and remained between 90,000 to 110,000 acres through the 1930s. Federal officials encouraged rice farmers to grow less rice during most of the Depression, but with the onset of the Second World War, conditions changed. Rice acreage increased dramatically, reaching 192,000 acres by 1942. To satisfy the demand for rice, farmers began cultivating marginal areas. Shortages of labor and machinery due to the war made it challenging to harvest all of the grain. Prices were high for rice, but growing it under the conditions imposed by the war put enormous pressures on farmers. With the cultivation of so much land for rice, conflicts between farmers and waterfowl intensified.[3]

The FWS originally considered protected areas such as the Sacramento National Wildlife Refuge as sanctuaries from overhunting, but increasingly they became holding pens to corral wayward ducks and geese. To attract larger numbers of waterfowl as well as different bird species, the FWS built ponds on the refuge. Even though the service spent most of the late 1930s constructing these ponds with CCC labor, it had developed only 1,800 acres by 1942. As waterfowl populations recovered from their collapse during the previous decade due to improved conditions in the birds' breeding grounds, the Sacramento Refuge had to accommodate more and more ducks and geese.[4] It was apparent that the Sacramento Refuge and other federal refuges in the valley did not provide enough aquatic vegetation or cultivated crops for the birds to eat. And without adequate food, the ducks and geese flew to private farms nearby in search of it.

The increased production of rice in the Sacramento Valley had a mixed impact on migratory waterfowl. For some ducks, such as mallards, pintails, and wood ducks, and for all of the geese that wintered in California, rice served as a much needed source of food in a part of the flyway that had once supported extensive wetlands. These birds proved their ability to adapt and utilize this new food source. However, farmers harassed birds that fed in rice fields with shotguns and flares. Sometimes they killed the birds, an illegal practice, but one that the FWS and California Department of Fish and Game found difficult to stop.[5]

Through their sheer numbers and persistence, waterfowl became a huge nuisance for California rice farmers. Moreover, some of the rice-growing practices contributed to the problem. Farmers flooded their fields early in the season and drained them before harvesting. In their rush to increase production, farmers often failed to level their fields each year, an expensive practice made even more so because of labor shortages and lack of farm machinery. On the margins of rice fields, depressions often formed between the rice paddies and the checks—small dikes surrounding the shallow water in the fields. The open water in such areas provided easy sites for ducks to land and eat rice. As the ducks consumed the grain, they created open water in their wake, which attracted yet more waterfowl. Some species were particularly troublesome in this regard. Farmers and FWS biologists noticed that wood ducks were among the most difficult species to frighten. Despite persistent harassment from shooting and explosives, wood ducks often refused to move. Even worse for farmers, wood ducks often left the refuge earlier than other waterfowl each morning to feed in the fields and attracted other ducks.[6]

The numerous private hunting clubs throughout the Sacramento Valley did little to improve the situation. Duck club clusters developed in areas where waterfowl congregated in the autumn and winter. Seven duck clubs formed one such cluster around the Sacramento Refuge.[7] Rice farmers also rented all or parts of these lands at other times of the year. During the hunting season, club operators partially flooded their land to attract waterfowl, but game regulations prohibited the dispersion of food for birds by club owners. Since the clubs only provided water for a few months of the year, these temporary ponds lacked the aquatic plants the birds once found in the marshes and riparian areas in the Sacramento Valley. Open water attracted birds, but once on the clubs, they found little or nothing to eat. Most clubs were either surrounded by rice fields or near them; some clubs even grew rice.[8]

Rice farmers grew resentful of the FWS and the game policies it enforced. "No attempt should be made to belittle the supreme contempt with which a duck's life is considered in Colusa and adjacent counties," wrote one FWS official in California. "When conditions come to the point where some rice farmers studiously hunt for and destroy all waterfowl nests found in their fields one has reached a climax in anticonservation."[9] Farmers complained that they provided feed for waterfowl that only wealthy sport hunters in duck clubs hunted. There was truth in their accusations. The Sacramento Refuge was not open to hunting, and as of 1942, the state and federal governments had established no public hunting grounds in the Central Valley. Unless they belonged to duck clubs, sport hunters had no place to hunt ducks and geese legally. One rice grower complained that the FWS "pasture their ducks on our rice fields night after night, lie there watching and waiting for market hunters while the ducks eat our rice crop."[10] FWS officials feared that without significant action, the entire waterfowl conservation program in California might collapse.

FWS officials in California urged the leaders of the agency to act quickly. They advocated creating more feeding areas for waterfowl, establishing public shooting grounds, and separating hunting clubs from commercial rice growing. Since the creation of the Sacramento Refuge in 1936, the FWS had prohibited hunting on the refuge. The development of ponds and marshes on the Sacramento Refuge successfully attracted more species of waterfowl than the land had previously. Yet the refuges did not provide enough food to prevent them from seeking out rice on private farms.[11]

In response to these concerns, the FWS began raising crops in the 1940s to lure waterfowl out of private farms and onto the refuges. The FWS had grown crops for waterfowl on the Tule Lake and Sacramento Refuges during the late 1930s, but the onset of the war prevented the service from expanding the program. FWS officials debated whether service personnel should grow the crops or whether the agency should hire farmers to sharecrop on the refuge.[12] Under the latter arrangement, farmers would harvest part of the crop for themselves and leave the remainder as feed for waterfowl. E. E. Horn doubted that many farmers would agree to sharecrop, since many of them were struggling to cope with waterfowl on their own lands. Ducks and geese might wipe out the farmers' share of the grain as well as the grain designated for the birds. Horn predicted that the service would have to undertake the program itself if it hoped to raise sufficient feed for birds. [13]

New refuges in the Central Valley were established primarily to serve as food-raising areas for waterfowl. In 1944, the FWS leased 800 acres near the town of Colusa and 420 acres in the Sutter By-Pass,

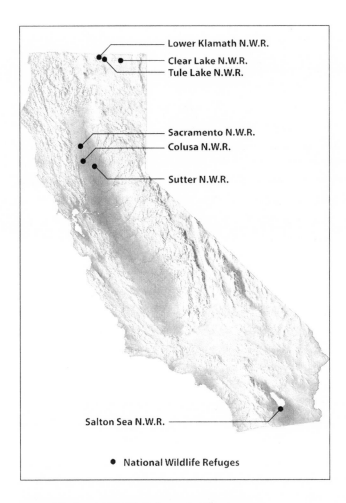

Lower Klamath N.W.R.
Clear Lake N.W.R.
Tule Lake N.W.R.

Sacramento N.W.R.
Colusa N.W.R.

Sutter N.W.R.

Salton Sea N.W.R.

● National Wildlife Refuges

MAP 7 *National Wildlife Refuges, California, 1955*

upon which the service raised over 24,000 bags of rice.[14] The following year the FWS purchased these properties (and other land nearby)
to create the Colusa and Sutter National Wildlife Refuges. The FWS
managed the Sacramento Refuge as a mixture of crops, ponds, and
natural vegetation. In 1945, it planted 335 acres of barley, 475 acres of
rice, and flooded 1,500 acres of ponds and marshes.

In 1948, the U.S. Congress passed the Lea Act, which provided

funds for the federal government and the State of California to purchase land for waterfowl. The goal was to create small feeding areas
throughout the agricultural regions of California to disperse waterfowl. Using funds from the federal and state governments, the California Department of Fish and Game also created refuges (called
Waterfowl Management Areas) to raise food for waterfowl. Most of
these federal and state refuges were between 2,500 and 8,000 acres.
(All of these refuges, except the Sacramento Refuge, were open to
hunters.) These refuges were equivalent to islands within the Central
Valley agricultural landscape.[15]

At the same time, the FWS enlarged its farming program in the
Klamath Basin. The service started planting barley for waterfowl in
the late 1930s and increased the acreage under cultivation throughout the war. As on the refuges in the Sacramento Valley, the service
farmed some of the land itself and leased refuge land in a sharecropping arrangement with farmers to raise grain. By 1948, the Lower
Klamath Lake and Tule Lake refuges produced over 100,000 bushels
of grain for waterfowl, of which 45 percent was grown by the service.[16]
Crops grown on the Tule Lake and Lower Klamath Lake refuges not
only supported birds in the Klamath Basin, but throughout California as well. The farming operation was so successful that the service
also shipped grain to other wildlife refuges in the Sacramento, San
Joaquin, and Imperial Valleys to supplement the feed grown there for
waterfowl.[17] It was possible for ducks and geese to pass through the
state while feeding on Klamath Basin grain at each refuge.

The FWS relied on the farming program more and more, not only
because it needed to feed the growing numbers of waterfowl using
Pacific Flyway refuges, but also because of farmers' complaints about
depredations. Refuges served a dual function as protected areas and as
bait to lure waterfowl away from crops and to hold them until farmers
completed their harvest on farms nearby. But segregating the birds
from nearby farms proved a challenging task. FWS chief Albert Day
got a sense of the circumstances faced by Pacific Flyway waterfowl
during a flight over the Sacramento Valley in 1947:

The situation from the air was startling. We could see mile after mile of rice
fields pointed up by the irrigation ditches and rice checks which wove intricate

patterns on the landscape below. But those were privately owned rice fields. Where was a duck to go if he wanted to get an honest bite without encroaching upon someone's $4.00 per hundred rice? . . . In more than three hours of flying over this whole section, we saw mighty little for the birds. There were tiny spots of green vegetation on the Colusa and Sutter Federal Refuges, a larger patch as we flew over the Sacramento Refuge, and another small one to the eastward on the state's Grey Lodge Refuge. Interspersed throughout the general area we spotted a few duck clubs where water had been spread in anticipation of the forthcoming hunting season. These represented the sum total of all the places available for birds in the vast level stretch of productive farmland. Everywhere else ducks were about as welcome as grasshoppers.[18]

Day's comments point to one of the contradictions created by the destruction of wetlands and the development of grain farming in California. Irrigated agriculture and flood control had eliminated most of the marshes on which geese and ducks depended. Yet this new landscape was not necessarily inhospitable to waterfowl. The challenge was to direct waterfowl to grain on refuges while keeping them out of private farms. In order for waterfowl to find the refuges, someone needed to point the way.

To do this, refuge staff and farmers experimented with a number of methods. Some farmers used shotguns or flares to scare the birds from their fields. During the early 1940s in the Klamath Basin, they stationed laborers in the fields at night to prevent ducks and geese from devouring crops. To aid the farmers, the FWS developed mortars that projected small explosives into the air above flocks of feeding waterfowl. More often then not, the explosions and harassment shifted the birds to move to someone else's farm. Over time, the birds grew accustomed to the harassment and stopped moving very far. In the Klamath Basin and Imperial Valley, farmers and refuge officials were moderately successful using antiaircraft searchlights to prevent waterfowl from landing in their fields at night. When farmers were vigilant, they could keep birds from destroying at least part of their crops, but if they let their guard down, ducks and geese could wipe out acres of rice, barley, or lettuce in a matter of hours.[19] Aerial herding was the most dramatic—and one of the most successful—methods for directing birds into refuges.

But even with aerial herding, depredations remained a serious problem through the 1950s. The numbers of migratory waterfowl was still high at the time. In the Klamath Basin, for instance, up to four million waterfowl rested and fed on the Tule Lake Refuge during the peak of the fall migration. It was nearly inevitable that the birds would come into conflict with farmers who farmed lands on or near the refuges in the Klamath Basin and Sacramento Valley.[20]

By the late 1940s, depredation control was becoming the primary purpose of new refuges. FWS flyway biologist E. E. Horn oversaw the Pacific Flyway refuges and played the most important role in influencing the service's views on mitigating waterfowl crop damage, establishing new refuges, and deciding how the service should develop them. In a report sent to the FWS regional director in Portland, Horn outlined his vision for existing and future refuges in California. All refuges needed to have a balance between ponds, marshes, and cultivated areas. Unless the service was willing to undertake farming programs on the refuges, Horn insisted, there was no point in establishing additional refuges in the Central Valley. "Any creation of ponds without adequate quantity and quality of waterfowl foods to compete with adjacent agricultural crops is most certain to create a worse crop depredation situation than now exists," Horn wrote. "Such an area would only concentrate more birds there without providing adequate food at the critical seasons."[21] Horn believed that the state's agricultural industry was too well-organized and profitable to tolerate "crop losses, be they caused by rodent, predation, insect, plant disease, or by migratory birds."[22] Without adequate food to feed waterfowl, Horn feared that complaints by farmers losing crops to waterfowl would lead to the demise of the refuge program in California. At the very least, further acquisition of refuges in the state depended on, if not the support of farmers, at least their assent.

To create a successful farming program, the service adopted the full spectrum of tools employed in mid-century industrial agriculture. To reduce costs and dependence on transient labor, rice farming in the state became highly mechanized during the 1940s. Instead of paying a large number of laborers to plant, tend, and harvest rice, farmers employed a smaller number of skilled laborers to operate farm machinery. Farmers used tractors to prepare fields for planting and large-capacity grain combines to harvest mature rice. One of the most important innovations was the use of airplanes to spread fertilizer and rice seeds. Airplanes dispersed ammonium sulphate fertilizer over the rice fields, and after spreading the fertilizer, farmers flooded the fields with two to four inches of water before airplanes spread the seeds. The FWS and sharecroppers employed all these techniques and tools on the Sacramento Valley refuges to cultivate rice, barley, and millet.[23]

Over the 1950s and 1960s, the farming program hijacked refuge management. Instead of providing habitat and food for a number of species, the FWS concentrated on growing food for a relatively small number of duck and geese species. In a 1964 report, one refuge official at the Sacramento Refuge stated the situation in stark terms:

Our importance in preventing crop depredations by waterfowl has caused us to place extra heavy emphasis on habitat requirements for the "problem species," particularly pintail and mallard. In recent years, much work has gone into "marsh rehabilitation"—converting marsh areas of little waterfowl food production (i.e., bulrush-cattail marsh, deep open water areas, etc.) into high production millet pools. This has been necessary and justifiable, but we are fast approaching the point of having almost a monotypic refuge with food and cover for a few species but with nothing left over for many others. Diving ducks, cinnamon teal, wood ducks, and other waterfowl need something besides rice and millet. Herons, egrets, shorebirds, and many land species find their preferred habitats shrinking each year. We should be able to keep these species and still do our job as a depredation unit, but we must start planning now before we find ourselves on a 10,000 acre rice and millet farm, rather than on a wildlife refuge.[24]

Clearly some refuge staff realized that the rice and other crops being grown did not benefit all species. Indeed, wading birds like herons and egrets ate only aquatic insects, crustaceans, and fish, not grains. Referring to the Sacramento Refuge as a "depredation unit" reveals that even the FWS saw the refuge primarily as a place to prevent damage to private farms rather than as a sanctuary for a variety of birds. Questioning of the farming program would intensify over the coming decades and would force the FWS to alter its management to benefit more species than just waterfowl.

SPRAYING, TRAPPING, AND MEDICATING

By building ponds, digging canals, and planting crops, refuge managers sought to create an ideal habitat for waterfowl. They could not bring back the splendor of the marshes that Finley saw in the Klamath Basin or the seasonal inland sea in the Sacramento Valley, but they did try to foster an environment where waterfowl could thrive. Yet refuge managers could not escape the fact that refuges were part of the irrigated landscape that surrounded them. They depended on water supplied by the same network of canals that nourished nearby farms. Since the refuges were now part of this landscape, they contributed to, and were affected by, a biological exchange of organisms. To achieve their management objectives, refuge managers attempted to control this exchange for their own benefit, as did farmers, who also tried to limit the movement of species to protect their crops. They often saw the refuges as the source of dangerous outbreaks of insect and weed pests. When necessary, they pressured the FWS to use pesticides and herbicides to control these outbreaks, and the agency also used these chemicals to help sustain its farming program.

Developing a farming program based on the template offered by industrial agriculture helped foster conditions aiding the spread of pests. Monocrops of rice, barley, and other grains were highly vulnerable to insects and weeds. A more diverse landscape and food sources for birds might have lessened the refuges' exposure to these organisms. Yet the desire to boost production of food for waterfowl coupled with pressures on refuge managers by farmers and agricultural agencies to prevent the spread of insects and weeds from refuges to private farmland convinced the FWS to use pesticides extensively.

The environmental historian Mark Fiege has coined the term *ecological commons* to describe the space created when organisms cross human boundaries, such as those between refuges and privately owned farmland, and the collective response to these transgressions. Many types of plants and animals moved unimpeded across these borders. Often the solution to such transgressions lay in developing ways to contain plants and animals within designated spaces. It also meant refuge managers and farmers uniting to deal with insects, weeds, and waterfowl. In the case of waterfowl, the birds were both a pest (for farmers) and a resource (for sport hunters). Weeds could easily spread from the refuges to nearby fields and vice versa. Also, coyotes that hunted for prey in the refuges sometimes moved into farms and attacked livestock. In addition to being an architect of refuge lands and water, the FWS also acted as a gatekeeper, trying to keep the movement of unwanted organisms within this ecological commons to a tolerable level.[25]

Insects and weeds found in irrigated fields thrived on the refuges, and physical structures in the refuges aided their spread. Weeds such as Russian thistle or wild mustard proved a troubling problem. The miles of dikes constructed in the Sacramento Valley and Klamath Basin refuges proved ideal environments for their dispersal. Weeds thrived on the dry, disturbed soil on the edge of the dikes. In a similar way, canals that distributed water throughout the refuges were often filled with cattails that inhibited the flow of water. The growth and spread of such plants were more than nuisances; together they undermined the agency's capacity to manage the refuges. Prior to World War II, clearing weeds from these canals was a laborious task. During the 1930s, the Bureau of Biological Survey used machinery such as draglines to remove cattails from irrigation canals, although sometimes this work was done by hand, a labor-intensive and time-consuming process, only feasible during the years when workers from the CCC were available.[26]

The agency had already experimented with chemical agents. During the 1920s, the Bureau of Biological Survey, in conjunction with the U.S. Chemical Warfare Service, tested chemicals such as mustard gas, chlorine, and chloropicrin (all of which were used in combat during the First World War) on small birds, such as blackbirds, which farmers considered pests.[27] At that time, the Biological Survey was also involved in research to determine the utility of birds for controlling insects. When the Biological Survey did poison animals, it was usually predators, such as coyotes and wolves in the western United States.[28] The agency believed that it could use these "war gases" to prevent the destruction of crops by blackbirds in California's Imperial Valley.

Despite its hopes for using such chemical weapons against birds, the researchers found that birds quickly escaped from the poisons before they could take effect.[29]

By the late 1940s, a new generation of herbicides was available, which the FWS enthusiastically adopted. The agency routinely applied the herbicide 2,4-D on refuges throughout the nation, including ones along the Pacific Flyway in the Sacramento Valley, Klamath Basin, and the Harney Basin of eastern Oregon. The herbicide was commonly used by farmers on private lands in these areas and throughout the country. On the Sacramento Refuge, for instance, refuge managers started applying 2,4-D on an experimental basis to waterways and plots of land in 1947.[30] The agency quickly found that the herbicide was an effective tool for controlling the spread of weeds such as Russian thistle and mustard, especially along the miles of dikes built by the CCC and FWS.[31] Even when herbicides killed weeds, they often grew back very quickly. Herbicides had little effect on cattails, one of the most virulent weeds on the refuge. Wildlife officials also worried that herbicides might kill plants eaten by waterfowl.[32]

Many of the lands within the refuges were marginal and already infested with weeds. In a memo distributed in 1949 by the FWS Section of Habitat Improvement, FWS researcher Warren S. Bourn argued that herbicides were needed to bring these lands into crop production for waterfowl feed and to limit the spread of weeds from refuges to private farms. He recognized that such spraying might spark controversy and stated that "in no case is the use of 2,4-D or similar chemicals on refuge areas to be publicized." He feared that a botched spraying of herbicides on refuges might damage private crops and lead to lawsuits against the agency. "The loss of a crop from blight, insects or other causes may conceivably be blamed on 2,4-D use in the vicinity. Therefore, appropriate secrecy should attend its application on refuge areas." Even at this early date, the FWS realized that new chemicals like 2,4-D could spread beyond the refuges and lead to complaints against the agency.[33]

Weeds were a nuisance but did no real damage to dikes. Animals such as muskrats, however, were a more serious problem. Muskrats were common in western marshes before reclamation destroyed the wetlands, and they returned in abundance as the FWS undertook its restoration program. Muskrats benefited waterfowl in some ways. (Canada geese, for instance, build nests on top of muskrat houses.) However, when muskrat populations grew too high, they consumed large amounts of marsh vegetation—food intended for ducks. A more pressing concern was the damage they inflicted burrowing into dikes, creating cavities, and, in the words of one refuge report, causing "no end of cave-ins and washed-out dikes."[34] Sections with dense networks of tunnels could fail and send water flooding into other units. Repairing dikes diverted valuable personnel and machinery toward dealing with this problem rather than other tasks. Although a time consuming chore, maintaining dikes was vital, since they were necessary to manage refuge water and because the tops of dikes also served as roads to access the interior of refuges.[35]

The FWS tried to keep the muskrat populations in check through an ambitious trapping program. Beginning in the 1930s, the FWS issued permits to trappers to capture muskrats in the Tule Lake and Lower Klamath refuges. The take was commonly 8,000 to 10,000 muskrats per year, though in the 1937–38 season, trappers killed more than 16,000 muskrats on the Tule Lake Refuge alone. During the five-and-a-half-month-long trapping season, up to twenty trappers and skinners worked on that refuge and sold the pelts to the Seattle Fur Exchange. The challenge was finding enough trappers to work on the refuges, since the agency required them to pay one-quarter of the price they obtained for the pelts to the FWS.[36]

To control insect pests, the FWS used the insecticide DDT, a chemical that would have lasting consequences for the refuges and for the surrounding environment. Like the herbicides the agency used, DDT was one of a number of pest-fighting chemicals developed during the 1930s and employed by the U.S. military in the Second World War.[37] During the Pacific campaign, the military found the insecticide an effective tool for controlling lice and in killing mosquitoes, which carried malaria. By the end of the war, farmers and municipalities were already beginning to use DDT to kill insects that damaged crops or trees in parks, part of a move to bring the war against insects from the battlefield to the United States. Although DDT was the most well-known of the new insecticides, other chemicals belonging to a group of insecticides known as chlorinated hydrocarbons and organophosphates were also widely used by farmers, and eventually, the FWS.[38]

The eagerness of the FWS to spray DDT on the refuges is somewhat surprising given that the agency was one of the first institutions to study the effects of the insecticide on birds and mammals. Analyses conducted during the late 1940s showed that when incorrectly applied, DDT could lead to the immediate deaths of mammals and fish. Such studies suggested that problems with DDT were a consequence of applying incorrect dosages rather than with the chemical itself. Investigators looked for unintended mortalities due to poisoning, not for deaths caused by long-term exposure to the chemical. Researchers at the agency's Patuxent Wildlife Research Center in Maryland discovered that DDT could affect the reproduction of birds exposed to the chemicals, even in very small quantities. Other scientists not affiliated with the FWS would later argue that the insecticide had environmental consequences far beyond the insects targeted by spraying programs.[39]

Farmers continued to use DDT and other chemical insecticides during the early 1950s, and the FWS followed their lead. Both groups considered the new insecticides a cheap and efficient way to control insects that harmed crops. The agency believed that using the chemicals would help boost production of grain for waterfowl. However, pressure to use the chemicals also came from farmers, state agricultural agencies, and the U.S. Department of Agriculture, all of whom saw the refuges as sources of insect outbreaks. On a number of occasions, regional insect control programs affected the refuges. In 1953, an outbreak of rice leaf miners spread through the rice growing districts in the Sacramento Valley. To bring the outbreak under control, farmers spent $1,200,000 to spray over 200,000 acres with dieldrin, a chlorinated hydrocarbon pesticide similar to DDT. Farmers sprayed rice fields at the refuge edge, and mists from the insecticide drifted on to refuge fields and waterways.[40] The FWS also signed agreements with the Department of Agriculture to deal with insect problems in agricultural areas. In 1956, the FWS and the Plant Control Branch of the Department of Agriculture agreed to use DDT and other insecticides to control a grasshopper infestation on the Tule Lake Refuge.

The agencies argued that if left unchecked, the insects would cause "serious damage to such croplands as well as to adjacent crops on lands leased to private individuals."[41]

Although in the 1950s scientists did not fully understand the long-term consequences of exposure to DDT and other insecticides, there were already clear signs that the chemicals could have serious effects on species not targeted by the spraying. The use of insecticides to deal with rice leaf miners on farms in the Sacramento Valley killed wading birds such as snowy egrets, black-crowned night-herons, and great blue herons on the Sacramento Refuge; refuge staff estimated that up to 10 percent of these birds died, as well as some ducks and upland birds.[42] Richard E. Griffith, chief of the FWS's Section of Habitat Improvement, wrote that this was probably unavoidable given the need to grow rice for ducks and geese:

Such losses are a calculated risk in the treatment for crop protection. In the case of the refuge rice fields, we will have to accept some slight losses if we are to produce the large amount of grain needed for waterfowl management during the critical harvest season.[43]

Even worse die-offs occurred on the Tule Lake Refuge. In 1960, refuge personnel noticed hundreds of dead grebes, pelicans, gulls, and egrets—all fish-eating birds—within the Lower Klamath and Tule Lake refuges. Analysis of the carcasses revealed that many of the birds contained high levels of the chlorinated hydrocarbon insecticides toxaphene, DDT, and DDD. Of the nearly 360 dead birds refuge staff found, over 200 were white pelicans. FWS scientists suspected that the greater mortality of white pelicans was due to the type of fish they ate. Larger fish tested in the area had much higher concentrations of pesticides than smaller fish. Even more startling was the concentration of pesticides found in the developing eggs of one of the cormorants tested. The female had 2.6 parts per million of the pesticides. But the developing eggs contained 44 parts per million—nearly seventeen times more than an adult cormorant.[44]

Such a large die-off of birds on a wildlife refuge was bound to garner attention. Rachel Carson, a former editor and scientist for the FWS, discussed the death of the birds in her indictment of pesticides, *Silent*

Spring. In her rendering, the birds' deaths were the result of insecticides finding their way into canals that carried wastewater from private farms into the refuges, not from the application of pesticides by the FWS.[45] The omission is puzzling. As a former employee of the FWS she was well aware of how refuges were managed throughout the United States. While working for the agency, Carson wrote a series of information booklets, called *Conservation in Action,* about important federal refuges in the country. She must have been aware that the FWS used insecticides and herbicides. Yet throughout *Silent Spring,* Carson portrays the FWS as the investigator of pesticide effects on wildlife and not as a pesticide user.[46]

During the postwar period, the FWS was a leading investigator of the ecological effects of insecticides and herbicides *as well as* a frequent user of DDT, 2,4-D, and other pesticides. For the FWS, the spraying of pesticides and herbicides was an important way to achieve its conservation objectives. In order to increase waterfowl production on the refuges, the agency needed to combat anything that interfered with that goal. Insecticides and herbicides seemed the most effective tools for eliminating pests and weeds that could damage crops intended as feed for waterfowl. The agency's actions shows that the "war against insects" was a tactic of conservation.

The FWS responded to the death of fish-eating birds on the Tule Lake Refuge by applying yet more pesticides. The agency did stop using DDT on the Lower Klamath and Tule Lake refuges, but immediately searched for less harmful pesticides. Refuge managers recognized the potentially devastating consequences of DDT, though not enough to abandon the use of pesticides altogether. In 1963, as in previous years, scores of water birds perished on the refuges, and the agency suspected pesticides as the cause. Yet that same year the agency sprayed over a thousand acres on the Tule Lake Refuge with Sevin to control a grasshopper outbreak. It also began testing the effects of other pesticides, including Dylox, on captive waterfowl and pheasants. Although aware of the potential consequences of some pesticides on wildlife, the agency still needed to control insects that might damage refuge crops or spread to farms beyond.[47]

The corpses of western grebe and white pelican in the marshes of Tule and Lower Klamath refuges vividly demonstrated that modern pesticides could turn sanctuaries into death traps. But natural maladies could take a heavy toll on birds as well. Although DDT might kill a few hundred birds a season, avian diseases could kill thousands of waterfowl in a matter of weeks. Such diseases continued to afflict migratory waterfowl on western refuges in the 1950s and 1960s. In addition to botulism, which had long affected migratory birds in the region, a new disease, avian cholera, also began claiming birds. Avian cholera fist appeared among waterfowl during the winter of 1943–44 on the Muleshoe National Wildlife Refuge in Texas and spread to California soon after. In some ways, avian cholera was more insidious than avian botulism, though the latter killed many more birds. Infected birds usually exhibited no symptoms before suddenly dying, thus making it difficult for managers to cope with the disease before many hundreds—and sometimes thousands—of birds died.

As was the case with botulism, changes in wintering areas promoted conditions suitable for the spread of cholera. Large flocks of waterfowl on Pacific Flyway refuges coupled with warm, shallow water in the early fall made an ideal situation for the diseases to spread. Migrating birds could easily transport the pathogenic agents hundreds of miles, from one refuge to another. Refuge management, in part, contributed to the problem. The overriding goal of refuge management was to provide ample food and resting space on its small refuges. Working together, farmers and the FWS harassed and herded birds out of private farms where they were dispersed and concentrated them in refuges. There ducks and geese found respite from harassment, but they were left highly vulnerable to pathogens in crowded spaces within the refuges. Collectively, these measures brought birds together in massive numbers, and when the conditions were right, avian diseases felled ducks and geese by the tens of thousands.[48]

By the early 1940s, the FWS had the medical means to treat sick waterfowl. Wildlife researchers tested an antitoxin for avian botulism at a research station established on the Bear River Migratory Bird Refuge in Utah. Refuge personnel captured sick ducks, injected them with a small amount of the antitoxin, and allowed them to recover. This method was very successful, but it required many FWS employees or volunteers to capture the ducks, administer the medicine, and release them back into the wild. Some refuges actually constructed "duck hospitals," where FWS officials cared for the sick birds. Not surprisingly, dealing with such outbreaks was a major undertaking. Many refuge personnel were involved in capturing sick birds and burning dead ones. All of this distracted refuge managers from other tasks and underscored the importance the FWS placed on controlling the disease.[49]

PUBLIC HUNTING

The beneficiaries of these efforts to protect waterfowl from disease and to grow crops to feed them were not just ducks and geese. Such efforts were designed to ensure high numbers of prey (or "game') for hunters. In the decades after the Second World War, the FWS found itself under increasing pressure to ensure adequate hunting areas for the region's growing number of hunters. The elimination of bird habitat coupled with the proliferation of private duck-hunting clubs left few places for those unaffiliated with clubs to pursue waterfowl. This enclosure of the hunting commons became a central issue for the FWS as it tried to provide viable habitat and food for waterfowl while satisfying the desires of waterfowl hunters, its main constituency.[50]

The number of hunters rose dramatically in West Coast states after the war as they did elsewhere across the country. During the war, government ammunition restrictions and gasoline rations made it difficult for hunters to seek waterfowl, not to mention the drafting of many men into the military meant fewer hunters. After the war ended, hunters returned to the Klamath Basin and Sacramento Valley in record numbers; in 1946, two to three times as many hunters visited the Klamath Basin refuges as had come the previous year. Freed from wartime restrictions, and with greater leisure time and disposable incomes, more people were able to make the trip from coastal cities to these interior hunting grounds. Having survived the war on limited budgets and reduced staff, the FWS was unprepared for the mass of hunters that descended on the refuges.[51]

The growing number of hunters had important ramifications for the Klamath Basin refuges, which collectively formed the largest public waterfowl hunting area in the West Coast states. Two thousand hunters visited the basin refuges for the opening weekend of hunting season in 1948, and the following year the number of hunters increased to nearly 4,500. Almost half of the hunters came from northern California, but 20 percent traveled from central California and 29 percent from southern California. The distance these visitors traveled is some indication of the value of the Klamath Basin refuges to sport hunters—particularly those who did not have access to hunting on private land elsewhere in California. Despite the reflooding of Lower Klamath Lake, most of these visitors still hunted on the Tule Lake Refuge, though this would change over the next decade.[52] In reports from this time, refuge staff noted that they felt overwhelmed by the number of people coming to the basin. A 1955 report depicts the pandemonium of opening day on the Tule Lake Refuge:

1,100 were in the marsh and 900 in the fields. . . . As these modern Hiawathas stealthily stalked their game they got in each others way, shot high, shot early and turned birds back in before they came over the line, squabbled, bickered, drove cars up to the blinds and parked them there, wandered all over the place, drove back and forth across the firing line, refused to honor others' shots and kills. . . . One enterprising nimrod drove the front wheels of his convertible up on the embankment . . . let down the top, broke open a case of beer, lit his stogie, and scanned the sky for geese.[53]

Refuge staff described a similar scene on Lower Klamath Lake Refuge, where hunters chased waterfowl from one grain field to another. Hunters at a firing line, which divided open and closed areas to hunting, shot indiscriminately at passing birds. "The crippling loss was staggering as the birds circled overhead just within gun range. Unable to cross the borrow ditch because of it being too deep or poorly equipped for waterfowl hunting, hunters shot to be killing. Others just as kill crazy were too lazy to walk to places where the ditch could be crossed." All told, the 19,111 hunters on the two refuges killed more than 20,000 geese and nearly 60,000 ducks.[54]

Increasingly in the 1950s and 1960s, hunters expected the FWS and the California Department of Fish and Game to serve their needs. Most of the hunters using the Klamath Basin refuges were unaffiliated with gun clubs; they were, as wildlife agencies called them, "unattached hunters." Even though federal and state government refuges established during this time all allowed hunting (as required by the 1948 Lea Act), hunters continued to demand more areas for public shooting. The only protected area that did not allow hunting was the Sacramento Refuge. Bird protection groups, such as the National Audubon Society, had long insisted that this refuge served as a valuable sanctuary where birds could retreat from the guns of hunters and that it should remain this way. Many California sport hunters, however, expected federal and state agencies not only to sustain waterfowl numbers but also to open the greatest number of areas to hunters unaffiliated with private clubs.

As pressure to open the Sacramento Refuge intensified in the early 1960s, FWS refuge managers, regional agency officials, and agency leaders in Washington, D.C., debated what stand to take. The California Department of Fish and Game was an enthusiastic proponent of opening the refuge, saying that the need for public shooting areas in the state was "very great."[55] Federal FWS officials in Washington were sympathetic to this argument, but they worried about a nationwide response by conservationists. "In the interest of the national waterfowl program we cannot disregard the fact that the Sacramento is a symbol of waterfowl preservation in the minds of conservationists throughout the United States," wrote Lansing A. Parker, the agency's acting director. Opening the refuge might hurt relations with national conservation organizations on whose support the FWS depended if it hoped to prevent homesteading on the Klamath Basin refuges. Although opening the Sacramento Refuge might help the waterfowl refuge program in California, it jeopardized support for FWS efforts in the Klamath Basin and elsewhere.[56]

The FWS regional headquarters in Portland concurred with the California Department of Fish and Game. Regional Director Paul T. Quick urged the FWS to reconsider its opposition. Public hunting opportunities were disappearing throughout the state, leading to diminishing interest in duck and goose hunting. "We are rapidly losing public support for the Bureau's land acquisition program because of decreasing opportunities for public participation in waterfowl hunting," said Quick. "There is inescapable evidence that the majority of waterfowl hunters are old-timers and there is an obvious shortage

of new recruits. Duck hunting is definitely a specialized and compara-
tively costly sport and unless there is a reasonable opportunity for a
man to hunt with some degree of satisfaction, the incentive for purchasing a duck stamp is lacking."[57] Since Duck Stamp revenues were
still one of the primary ways the FWS funded refuge acquisition, the
long-term consequences of declining numbers of hunters was clear.
Maintaining support for more refuges depended on satisfying the
needs of sport hunters.

Not all waterfowl hunters shared the views of the California wildlife agency or FWS's regional officials. Owners of private duck clubs
near the refuge were generally against the opening. Hunting clubs
were common in the Central Valley; over 200 clubs were found within
fifty miles of the Sacramento Refuge.[58] Club owners feared that hunters on the Sacramento Refuge would scare birds away from the vicinity and reduce the number of birds flying over club lands. In a letter
to J. Clark Salyer II (by then a wildlife consultant for the FWS), Dr.
Everett D. Ivey, a physician and club owner from Oakland, expressed
his concerns about the proposal:

I hope to at least indicate to some degree the great personal damage which
will incur to my large investments and that to other neighboring clubs as
well, if there is adjacent public shooting. And I am sure you know, after a few
shots, and with public shooters running wild, wildfowl will largely disappear.
At least that is our experience, on our property, despite the fact that our hunters have blinds, and also despite the fact that we quickly eliminate shooters
who are uncontrolled in manner of hunting.[59]

Ivey's comments suggest that he saw "unattached hunters" as disor-
derly sportsmen who would lower the value of his land and compromise the hunting experiences of club members. Other landowners
who hunted on their land or leased it to others for the same purpose
also worried that permitting shooting on the refuge would reduce the
number of birds crossing their land. It was precisely such an arrangement (a wildlife sanctuary surrounded by private hunting lands)
that the California Department of Fish and Game and its supporters
wanted to disrupt by pressuring the FWS to allow hunting on the Sacramento Refuge.[60]

Bird protectionist groups such as the National Audubon Society and even the Wildlife Management Institute, a conservation group often supportive of hunting, opposed opening the refuge. They still saw the Sacramento Refuge as a sanctuary to which birds could retreat from a hostile countryside where hunters abounded. Former FWS chief and institute president Ira Gabrielson felt that the service was going "over board" to provide more public shooting areas for California hunters when it was under no obligation to do so. The FWS was required to protect waterfowl under the provisions of the Migratory Bird Treaty Act, and nothing more. In the view of Carl Buchheister, president of the National Audubon Society, the FWS was capitulating to the demands of the California Department of Fish and Game. Abandoning the sanctuary ideal was not the answer. Public shooting was allowed on the Sutter and Colusa federal refuges as well as on the Delevan National Wildlife Refuge, a new area acquired near the Sacramento Refuge in 1963. In the view of the Audubon Society, the FWS and California Department of Fish and Game had provided enough hunting places for people who were unaffiliated with shooting clubs.[61]

The opposition of these organizations and other groups did not sway the FWS or Secretary of the Interior Stewart Udall. In September 1964, Udall approved the opening of 40 percent of the refuge to hunting, the maximum percentage allowed under the amended Migratory Bird Hunting Stamp Act.[62] The act came just in time to enable hunters to use the refuge in the fall of 1964. Over 8,500 shooters hunted on the refuge during the first season. Hunters along the refuge's western edge shot at waterfowl flying into the refuge, often disrupting traffic as they chased wounded and dead ducks and geese that fell in the highway bordering the refuge. With the opening, the Sacramento Refuge became a public hunting ground like the other federal and state refuges in California, thus ending the sanctuary ideal in California.[63]

California's hunters, and the landscapes they hunted in, were divided among class lines. They were a vital constituency for the FWS, but they were not homogenous. The agency depended on the support of hunters to purchase Duck Stamps, which the service used to acquire and maintain refuges. It also needed hunters' support from the constant threat of farmers who still complained about the refuges near their farms. In pushing to open the refuges, these unattached hunters voiced what geographers Paul Robbins and April Luginbuhl call "gun-populism."[64] Privatization of hunting landscapes exposed class divisions, as unattached hunters argued that access to public hunting lands was essential to perpetuate the sport. In voicing such concerns, unattached hunters expressed a sentiment that ecologist Aldo Leopold would have found familiar. Leopold believed waterfowl were a public resource. Yet the enclosure of common lands, especially habitat for ducks and geese, had almost led to the de facto privatization of ostensibly publically owned waterfowl. The sanctuary ideal that early refuges embodied assumed waterfowl needed a retreat amid a landscape of rapacious hunters. In the postwar years, although hunters proved the leading advocates for establishing and maintaining refuges in California, their support was contingent on the opening of new hunting grounds. Amid this pressure, the sanctuary ideal treasured by an older generation of FWS officials such as Ira Gabrielson could not endure. The FWS would need the support of unattached hunters to fight the Bureau of Reclamation, which sought to open the Tule Lake Refuge in the Klamath Basin to homesteaders in the 1960s.

THE KLAMATH BASIN REFUGES AND THE KUCHEL ACT

By the 1950s, the Klamath Basin refuges had become the West's most highly prized public waterfowl hunting area. The development of the area as a landscape of recreation masked the fact that the Bureau of Reclamation, and the farmers it served, still considered the area as primarily for agriculture. Farmers continued to lease land on the Lower Klamath and Tule Lake refuges to grow crops, and the refuges still depended on water supplied through Bureau of Reclamation canals and tunnels to sustain marshes and crops used for waterfowl. Hunters and the FWS came into increasing conflict with irrigators and the Bureau of Reclamation as both groups tried to define the highest use of refuge lands. Ironically, one of the FWS's greatest supporters was not just the California hunting community, but rice farmers in the Central Valley, who feared changes in the Klamath Basin would affect the pace of waterfowl migration to their detriment.

On all Bureau of Reclamation projects, the agency expected homesteaders to form private irrigation districts once it completed the major water structures. In 1956, control over the irrigation structures and management of the water supply within the Tule Lake area passed to the Tulelake Irrigation District (TID). The district charged the farmers fees to deliver water, and in turn the district used these funds to maintain dams, canals, and pumps. As the TID assumed control of water delivery, managers on Tule Lake Refuge soon learned that district officials could be just as difficult to deal with as the Bureau of Reclamation.

The FWS realized that it needed assurances that the TID would still provide the water it needed to manage the refuge for migratory waterfowl. When signing the agreement to form the irrigation district, the Department of the Interior insisted that the TID maintain water levels requested by the FWS in the Tule Lake Refuge sumps. There were a number of reasons for doing this. During the summer, the FWS wanted levels to remain low enough to avoid flooding goose and duck nests. In the autumn, the FWS needed higher water levels so hunters could easily reach the sumps with their boats and so that hunters' dogs could retrieve birds that fell into the water. Throughout the late summer and early fall, the FWS also wanted to ensure that enough water was in the sump to prevent the spread of botulism.[65]

The TID failed to abide by the agreement. In 1959, the water levels were too high during the summer, and waterfowl nests were flooded. The previous winter, the TID lowered the level of the sump two feet below what the FWS had requested, which may have contributed to the spread of an outbreak of avian cholera, which killed more than four hundred birds. Furthermore, low water levels in the fall of 1959 created vast mudflats on the margins of the shrinking sump, making it impossible for hunters to launch their boats or retrieve birds shot from shore. Hunters were unwilling to venture into the quagmire, and they also killed fewer birds that year. A huge outcry from the region's hunters followed, and they made their voices heard in FWS refuge headquarters, regional newspapers, and congressional offices. Hunters alleged that the TID was destroying the best public hunting grounds in the state.[66]

The Tule Lake Refuge faced other threats besides poor water management. During the late 1950s, the Bureau of Reclamation renewed its effort to open the Tule Lake Refuge for homesteading. Why it tried to do so is unclear. Farmers were permitted to lease much of the refuge; establishing homesteads within it would bring no new land into production. Although the Bureau of Reclamation had little success persuading Congress to allow homesteading on the refuge, it did manage to raise the attention of sport hunters and other bird enthusiasts, who saw it as another threat to the important refuge.

In 1963, Senator Thomas H. Kuchel of California responded to hunters' concerns and introduced a bill to protect the Klamath Basin refuges from homesteading while allowing the lease-farming arrangement to continue. It ensured that farmers could continue leasing land within the refuge, defined the areas they could lease, and established water levels for the Tule Lake sumps. In some respects, the bill simply restated what the Bureau of Reclamation, the FWS, and the Tulelake Irrigation District had agreed to in 1956. But it went further by assigning specific acreages to agricultural areas and to the Tule Lake sumps.[67]

By this time, the TID realized that it had to alter its management of the sumps within the Tule Lake Refuge. At the hearings regarding the bill, representatives from the district worried that the needs of farmers were not being considered. Lester M. Cushman, vice president of the TID, said, "The conflict which has arisen is caused by the fact that those who want to protect the migratory waterfowl intend to do so without regard to the cost to the farmers and people of the area."[68] Migratory waterfowl used private farmland, too, he said, and agricultural areas provided important habitat and feed for the birds. Since the sumps served as a place to divert excess irrigation water, he worried that the water levels established by the act might limit the ability of irrigators to handle floods. A flood in 1962, for instance, nearly breached the dikes surrounding the two sumps before the TID could release water into an uncultivated area of the district. The TID feared that managing the refuges primarily for migratory waterfowl might undermine the district's ability to sustain an agricultural economy in the Tule Lake area.[69]

Throughout the hearings, members from the Klamath Basin's agricultural community insisted on the primacy of farming within the region. The states of Oregon and California had given lands within the area to the federal government for reclamation, and during the past half century, the Bureau of Reclamation had transformed the hydrology of the basin. The executive orders establishing the basin refuges recognized that the lands within the basin were to be used primarily for agriculture. At every opportunity, the TID and its supporters pointed out the need to place agricultural interests first.[70]

Not surprisingly, conservationists stressed the importance of the Klamath Basin for waterfowl along the Pacific Flyway. But they also emphasized that the further diminishment of the basin's waterfowl habitat and crops would mean the earlier arrival of ducks and geese in the agricultural areas of the Sacramento and Imperial valleys. Losing the refuges of the Klamath Basin would worsen depredations in other parts of California, which by the early 1960s was largely under control. In effect, the Klamath Basin served as a temporary holding pen for ducks and geese until farmers completed their harvests elsewhere in California.[71]

Congress passed the Kuchel Act in 1964, which ended the threat of homesteading by allowing farmers to continue leasing land on the refuges under the condition that farming not interfere with waterfowl management.[72] The attempt by the Bureau of Reclamation and farmers to allow further homesteading failed, but not just because of opposition by sport hunters and bird enthusiasts concerned about the welfare of migratory waterfowl. Famers farther south along the flyway lobbied for passage of the Kuchel Act, as they feared that the actions of the TID or homesteading refuge lands would compromise the ability of the basin's refuges to sequester birds in the basin before rice farmers in the Sacramento Valley harvested their crops. These conflicts over migratory waterfowl in California during the mid-twentieth century demonstrate that wildlife managers were not the only ones using the flyway concept. Once conservationists and California farmers realized that ducks and geese traveled along an identifiable route, they tried to adjust the rhythm of migration for their own benefit. Sport hunters and bird protectionists supported these efforts, since it helped to sustain the birds they enjoyed hunting or viewing, and Sacramento Valley farmers used their clout to protect their crops from the earlier arrival of hungry waterfowl. The fate of the birds lay between these groups, as the FWS and state wildlife agencies manipulated the habitat that birds depended on for survival.

TERMINATION AND KLAMATH FOREST REFUGE

In the 1950s and 1960s, sport hunters, farmers, the FWS, and state wildlife agencies were key players in the debates over refuges. Their concerns largely shaped the parameters of discussions about, and ultimately the geography of, refuges in the Far West. Yet in the 1950s, changes in federal policy relating to Indians also affected Pacific Flyway refuges. A crucial episode in the Klamath Basin during this period illustrates how the FWS quested to acquire new refuges even at the expense of Native peoples.

Although they had played virtually no direct role in the management of the area's wildlife refuges, the Klamath Tribes played an important role in other aspects of life in the basin. Most Klamath peoples lived on or near the Klamath Indian Reservation, located about fifteen miles north of Klamath Falls. Numbering about 2,100 in 1950, the Klamath Indians lived on a reservation comprised of thousands of acres of ponderosa pine. In addition to being surrounded by this bounty of timber, another resource lay at the heart of the reservation: the Klamath Marsh.

Even among Indian reservations in the western United States, the Klamath Reservation was quite large, though it had diminished in size over the years. Once comprising 1.9 million acres, various surveying errors, grants to transportation companies, and the sale of land to non-Indians whittled the reservation down to only 1 million acres by the 1940s. The rich stands of ponderosa and sugar pine supported a robust timber industry. This timber harvesting generated annual payments for the tribe. The Klamath continued to trap beaver and river otter and to collect wetland plants such as wocus on Klamath Marsh.[73]

Although federal Indian policy had always emphasized the assimilation of Native peoples, this trend intensified during the late 1940s and early 1950s with the move for termination. Supporters of termination sought to dissolve reservations and federal support for Indian tribes. Numerous earlier acts and programs had sought to undermine Indian sovereignty and banish Native customs, but the goal of termination was to push Indians into mainstream American society. The Klamaths were one of a number of tribes chosen to lose their reservation and tribal status under this movement.[74]

As Congress pushed for the termination of the tribe and its reservation, other federal land management agencies sought to claim the natural resources left behind. The U.S. Forest Service acquired the bulk of the reservation's forest lands, which became the Winema National Forest; the U.S. Fish and Wildlife Service sought the Klamath Marsh. Refuge officials saw acquiring the marsh as a way to bolster its holdings within the Klamath Basin, especially since the future of its prime refuges elsewhere in the basin, such as Lower Klamath and Tule Lake, seemed to be in jeopardy in the 1950s. Bird migration studies during this time confirmed the Klamath Basin's vital role in sustaining Pacific Flyway birds. J. Clark Salyer II stated that the Klamath Marsh was the "greatest residual piece of marshland left in our Nation." Not only did it provide valuable habitat for migrating birds, he believed it served as one of the few remaining large breeding areas for diving ducks, such as redheads and canvasbacks. Creating another refuge along this pivotal section of the flyway seemed a shrewd move by the FWS. Salyer also thought time was of the essence. He feared a number of consequences if the agency did not act quickly. First, he worried that the Klamath tribes or the management specialists working on their behalf could sell the marsh to a private interest that might decide to alter or drain the wetland. Second, he feared that the Bureau of Reclamation might appropriate the marsh and convert the area into a reservoir for irrigators farther south in the basin. Either way, the marsh's usefulness for waterfowl, particularly diving ducks, would be diminished.[75]

The efforts of the FWS to acquire the marsh were further complicated after April 1958 when members of the Klamath Tribes voted on whether to remain in the tribe and allow its remaining assets to be managed by a trust or to renounce their membership and receive a payment from the government for the reservation's assets (namely, the sale of the reservation's timber lands). This was a very difficult vote for the Klamath Indians to make—one that would have repercussions for tribal members for decades to come. Within a month after the vote, it became clear that at least some of those who chose to remain in the tribe did so because they believed the Klamath Marsh, or at least Wocus Bay (one part of the marsh), would remain under tribal control. After an intense meeting with remaining tribal members in May 1958, T. B. Watters, a management consultant for the tribes, told Salyer that "the members in attendance were very bitter in their denunciation of the efforts that have been made to acquire this property as a Wildlife Refuge. Further, they were firmly convinced that the value of this property, if converted to grazing purposes, will far exceed its value for wildlife."[76] Watters told the group that sale of the land was clearly in the best interests of the remaining members, since "in view of the record which the Tribe has made to date in its management of its own affairs, it is necessary for the Secretary of the Interior to assure proper management of the resources retained by these people by having a qualified trustee assume the primary responsibilities for management."[77]

Salyer had little faith that Klamath Marsh would survive as a viable place for waterfowl if the remaining tribal members continued to own and use the marsh. In a memo titled "Wocus Bay Indian Problem—Klamath Marsh," Salyer wrote that if Klamath tribal members retained control of the bay, it would be a threat to the rest of the proposed refuge. The agency sought to construct the sorts of shallow units it had developed on refuges elsewhere along the Pacific Flyway. Impatient with the tribe, Salyer wrote, "We still believe our original offer to the tribe is best. I say this because we have had one or more similar arrangements with various Indian tribes and find that they invariably fail to hold up their end of the bargain and, moreover, lose interest in the project they earlier insisted upon." To Salyer, the tribe's position was an attempt by a group of self-interested members to enrich themselves at the expense of wildlife as well as others in the tribe. "If the decision is made to chop off Wocus Bay and turn it over to the tribe," Salyer continued, "it is my recommendation that we get out . . . because such action would greatly complicate our development and management of the area and also seriously reduce its service to waterfowl and other forms of wildlife. We have been in this type of a situation before and it simply doesn't work out, recognizing the changeable and impractical actions of these people."[78]

In spite of its difficulty negotiating with the Klamath Tribes, the FWS did acquire the area in 1958 and created the Klamath Forest National Wildlife Refuge (it was later renamed the Klamath Marsh National Wildlife Refuge). The acquisition seemed a clear victory for FWS and for those conservationists who hoped to retain public ownership of some of the few remaining large marshes along the Pacific Flyway. With time, however, the Klamath peoples came to see the termination of their reservation and the division of its natural resources between the U.S. Forest Service and the Fish and Wildlife Service as a crime. Two decades later, after much work, the federal government renewed the Klamath peoples status as a tribe. Thus far, their effort to reestablish their reservation has not succeeded. The divide between the FWS and the Klamath peoples about Klamath Marsh highlighted the contrasting ways the groups viewed the landscape. For the FWS, the refuge was yet another unit in a migratory route that also served as a breeding habitat for flyway birds. Yet for the Klamath Indians, the Klamath Marsh was a vital part of their ancestral homeland, acquired in an underhanded manner due to a misguided federal policy. By the 1990s, the Klamaths and other Indian tribes in the lower basin began to assert their treaty rights to water and fish. In the process, they affected the management of refuges throughout the basin.[79]

During the postwar years, the FWS performed a delicate dance. It sought to sustain abundant ducks and geese for thousands of sport hunters while minimizing the damages wrought by birds on private crops. It did so by cultivating rice, barley, and other grains for famished birds to eat, and when necessary, bombing recalcitrant birds and guiding them into refuges. More than anything else, the geography of Pacific Flyway refuges was designed to produce game for hunters. Refuges were distributed throughout the Klamath Basin, Central Valley, and Imperial Valley to provide birds with habitat and food in areas they had always used. Yet pressure by farmers ensured that these refuges were limited in size and distributed throughout the region to reduce the threat of depredations.

Such refuges existed within an irrigated, agricultural landscape *and* a private landscape. As habitat disappeared and private duck hunting clubs proliferated, hunters unaffiliated with such clubs put pressure on federal and state wildlife agencies to provide the necessary access to continue their sport. The dispute over permitting hunting on former sanctuaries such as the Sacramento Refuge showed that differences among hunters mattered. Although waterfowl hunting was by no means a poor person's sport, there were class divisions among the hunters. To ensure support for their agencies, the California Department of Fish and Game and the FWS catered to "unattached" hunters who bought the hunting licenses and Duck Stamps that funded the agencies and the acquisition of new refuges. This support proved crucial as the FWS successfully fought back efforts to open the Klamath Basin refuges to homesteading in the 1950s and early 1960s.

Yet a closer look at refuges reveals that managers held a narrow view of the refuges' purposes. Refuges were depredation control units within the agricultural landscape that provided opportunities for men (and they were almost always men) of modest means to hunt Pacific Flyway ducks and geese. The agency had made space for waterfowl amid this radically altered landscape, but at a cost to other species. As the death of grebes and pelicans showed, applying pesticides to control pests attacking waterfowl crops had unintended consequences. Simplifying refuge landscapes into duck farms left many other species out of the picture. Other birds that depended on refuges, such as egrets, herons, and red-winged blackbirds, and non-avian species, such as amphibians, fish, and mammals, received little attention. Muskrats were an exception, but only because the FWS considered them a pest. They became the focus of an aggressive trapping campaign in order to reduce the damage they caused to vital refuge dikes. Such actions show that the FWS lacked a broader vision of the refuges as landscapes that included game and non-game animals. Individual FWS employees may have cared about other species, but this concern rarely appeared in refuge management. As refuge officials noted in their own reports, the single-minded pursuit of raising feed for a few species of ducks and geese left many other animals out of the picture. What was good for waterfowl was not necessarily good for other species.

5

REFUGES IN CONFLICT

BY THE MID-1960S, the Fish and Wildlife Service had secured a place for refuges amid the Far West's irrigated landscapes and had successfully fended off attempts to open its premier refuges in the Klamath Basin to homesteading. The splendor of the West's marshes, which had once cloaked many of the region's larger valleys and basins, was long gone. But amid this destruction, the agency had constructed a network of refuges to sustain migratory birds within an otherwise forbidding landscape for waterfowl. Such gains came at a cost that became all too apparent in later decades. Refuges needed water to function, and for the most part, the FWS relied to a large degree on agricultural drain water flowing from nearby farms. The agency proved adept at turning this waste from agriculture into verdant fields to feed waterfowl and into marshes and ponds for loafing birds. Trouble loomed, however, if the drain water was toxic or if other groups sought to divert irrigation water for other purposes.

The FWS and its supporters were more or less united in their conviction that the primary function of these refuges was to support the millions of waterfowl that migrated through the Far West and to ensure that West Coast duck and goose hunters could continue to enjoy their sport. In her book *Where Land and Water Meet*, a study of the management of riparian areas and wildlife refuges in the Malheur Basin of eastern Oregon, Nancy Langston writes that refuge officials in the 1940s and 1950s sought to build "an empire of nature, a world aimed at increasing waterfowl production."[1] Refuge officials elsewhere along the flyway shared this attitude. Langston does not see this as a consequence of blind faith in engineering, but as a response to crashing waterfowl populations during the 1930s. In the midst of this disaster, refuge staff needed to devise creative ways to supply refuges with water. The numbers of ducks and geese increased in the 1940s, and this seemed to confirm that the FWS's management approach was effective (the FWS counted over 3.5 million waterfowl during the 1950s and 1960s).[2]

This consensus began unraveling in the 1970s. Like other federal areas in the western United States, wildlife refuges became contentious sites that were drawn into the wider debate over the purpose of public lands.[3] Disputes between refuge officials and their supporters on the one hand and irrigators on the other became multifaceted conflicts among the FWS, the Bureau of Reclamation, farmers, environmentalists, and Indian tribes. The environmental movement fractured the consensus over the purpose of the wildlife refuges and challenged the heavy-handed approach that had characterized refuge management for decades. Native groups such as the Klamath Tribes—whom the Bureau of Reclamation and the FWS had never consulted when managing the lakes and marshes within their territory—now used their growing legal power to pressure the federal government to manage water in the Klamath Basin with their interests in mind. The claims made on the refuges by these various groups forced the FWS to reconsider its practices as management became more challenging and contentious.

Refuges existed within the physical context of the irrigated landscape. They also existed within political and cultural contexts, and as those contexts changed, so did the refuges. The 1970s witnessed the growth of the environmental movement and a new set of laws, such as the Endangered Species Act and Clean Water Act, which had serious repercussions for refuges in the Far West and the Pacific Flyway.

Environmentalists and hunters, the FWS's primary constituencies, saw the refuges differently. Unlike hunters, who expected refuges to produce or sustain high numbers of waterfowl, environmentalists wanted the FWS to protect other species, even at the expense of raising feed for ducks and geese. Refuge managers, too, came to value other aspects of the refuges that had received scant attention from earlier generations of agency officials.

The rise of broader interests in the refuges occurred during a time when there were fewer hunters each year. The number of hunters in California dwindled from a postwar high of more than 200,000 to 72,000 in 2003, even though the population of the state rose dramatically from 11 million to 35 million. The number of waterfowl hunters in Oregon also dropped by half during the same period.[4]

The breakdown in consensus, the implementation of the Endangered Species Act, and changing water policies in Oregon and California all had severe ramifications for Pacific Flyway refuges. Wildlife refuges were also affected as irrigators' power waned and municipalities sought farmers' water. Farmers dependent on federally subsidized irrigation water faced a number of regulatory and political changes. Legislation to protect endangered species meant that more water had to remain in the rivers of California and Oregon for salmon and other fish. Closer to the present, cities such as San Diego and municipalities in northern California increasingly sought to transfer water used for agricultural purposes to urban areas. Farmers dependent on this water have fought this reallocation to ensure the profitability (sometimes the survival) of their operations. But in some cases, such as in the Imperial Valley, irrigators struck deals with urban water districts to conserve irrigation water and transfer it to West Coast cities. Lost in most of these debates over the protection of endangered species or the transfer of water to metropolitan areas was the fact that the Pacific Flyway refuges were part of the irrigated landscape. For more than half a century, wildlife refuges had depended on water supplied through irrigation systems set up for farmers. Keeping water in rivers or directing it to metropolitan areas, even in the name of conservation, threatened water for refuges as well as farmers. In this changing political landscape, migratory waterfowl faced an uncertain future.

A CHANGING REGULATORY ENVIRONMENT

The burgeoning environmental movement of the 1960s and 1970s led to the passage of a host of new laws to protect America's water, air, land, and wildlife. Among the most sweeping of them was the Endangered Species Act of 1973 (ESA). It required refuge managers, farmers, and other land users to consider the effects of their activities on all threatened species, not just those of interest to sport hunters or those with economic significance. Some species—mostly conspicuous, so-called "charismatic" animals such as migratory waterfowl, the bald eagle, and the bison—were the focus of protection campaigns.[5] The ESA differed from earlier legislation to protect species in that it applied not only to well-known animals, but also to obscure species, such as the snail darter, northern spotted owl, and sucker fish.[6] The act forced the FWS to broaden its mission and to alter the way it managed waterfowl refuges.

Earlier versions of the act (in 1966 and 1969) lacked the scope and conferred less power than the 1973 act, which required all federal departments to ensure that their activities did not threaten the survival of endangered or threatened species and mandated that the agencies take measures to restore endangered populations.[7] It required these agencies to consider how their programs would affect the habitats of endangered species. Given the scope of the legislation, the ESA had the potential to affect American land use in significant ways.[8]

In practice, the ESA had the greatest impact on federal public lands. Since most of them were in the western United States, the act affected that region more than other parts of the country. It applied not only to waterfowl, which the FWS had managed for decades, but also to amphibians and to fish in the marshes, canals, and open water of the refuges. Since the FWS did not monitor most of these species, it had a limited knowledge of their numbers and their vulnerability to extinction. As for plant species, the FWS had viewed vegetation on the refuges solely in terms of its utility for waterfowl. Staff managed the water on refuges to facilitate the growth of natural plants that ducks consumed as well as to cultivate rice, barley, and other crops that the agency grew for the birds. They also cut willows, sprayed cattails with herbicides, and attacked other plants that interfered with the goal of improving waterfowl habitat.

Although the ESA hampered some of the traditional roles of the FWS *within* refuges, it dramatically increased the ability of the agency to influence land use *outside* refuges. Until the ESA, the staff of the FWS was largely unable to shape land use beyond refuge boundaries. The FWS could educate landowners about the role their lands played in perpetuating wildlife, and with the help of state wildlife agencies it could also enforce hunting regulations. Otherwise, the FWS had little say in the use of private lands. This changed with the passage of the ESA, for Congress gave the FWS primary responsibility for its implementation.[9] The FWS had the power to list species, determine whether they were threatened or endangered, and propose recovery plans on public as well as private land. In effect, this meant that the FWS was partially responsible for determining the environmental suitability of projects carried out by other federal agencies, including the U.S. Forest Service and the Bureau of Reclamation. For an agency that had once been relatively powerless in the face of actions by other federal agencies that negated their conservation programs, this new authority was extraordinary.

THE SHORT, UNHAPPY LIFE OF THE KESTERSON REFUGE

Changes in water allocation also had major consequences for the Central and Imperial Valley refuges. In the 1960s, Californians increasingly questioned the unrestricted development of the state's rivers and the continued loss of wetlands. Previously, such concerns had rarely stopped projects. Owens Valley residents, for instance, futilely opposed the diversion of water from the valley to supply Los Angeles in the early twentieth century not because of the ecological consequences of the action, but because it limited their own ability to utilize the water in irrigating farms and grazing lands. More than forty years later, conservationists were emboldened by successfully stopping plans by the Department of the Interior to construct Echo Park Dam in the late

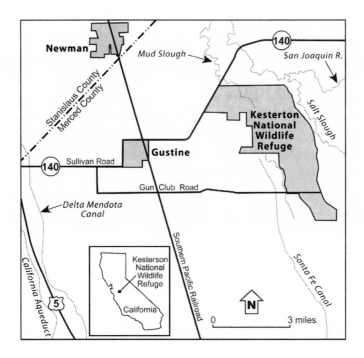

MAP 8 *Kesterson National Wildlife Refuge*

1950s (which would have flooded many of the valleys in Dinosaur National Monument in Colorado). The conservationists turned their attention to other water projects throughout the West. Federal agencies such as the Bureau of Reclamation and the U.S. Army Corps of Engineers that had once faced little opposition to their water projects now had to justify their actions economically and to reckon with the deleterious environmental effects of water development.[10]

The refuges established in the Central Valley after the 1960s were usually add-ons to new irrigation projects. One of these, the Kesterson National Wildlife Refuge on the west side of the San Joaquin Valley, was a sump for agricultural drainage flowing from the Westlands Water District. Encompassing nearly 600,000 acres, the district was the largest irrigated land holding in the United States. Prior to the 1960s, the district used groundwater for irrigation, but beginning in 1968, district farmers received their water from the Bureau of Reclamation's Central Valley Project, which had played a key role in building dams and canals to service irrigators throughout the valley. The district was one of the last areas serviced by the project. Critics objected to its creation because of the poorly drained soils.[11] Impervious layers of clay within three to ten meters of the surface prevented water from percolating deeply through the ground. Without adequate drainage, salts and other minerals could accumulate, eventually rendering the land unfit for agriculture.[12]

To solve the problem, the Bureau of Reclamation started constructing the San Luis Drain, a canal that would carry excess water from district lands north through the San Joaquin Valley and divert it into the Sacramento–San Joaquin River Delta. Farmers began widespread irrigation of lands in the district during the late 1960s before the drain was finished. While the Bureau of Reclamation was completing the project, the agency diverted water via canal into the Kesterson Reservoir, a sump approximately thirty-five miles northwest of the district. The FWS saw an opportunity to use this water for wildlife and successfully lobbied to have Kesterson designated a national wildlife refuge in 1970. Like the Lower Klamath, Tule Lake, and Clear Lake refuges in the Klamath Basin, Kesterson was superimposed on a Bureau of Reclamation water project. From the bureau's perspective, Kesterson was little more than a temporary sump for wastewater. In the 1970s, the Bureau of Reclamation tried to complete construction of the San Luis Drain, but strenuous public opposition forced it to abandon the plan. Environmentalists and state leaders worried that agricultural runoff carried by the drain would further degrade the already polluted delta from which many California municipalities derived drinking water. During most of the 1970s, Kesterson received surface water from local sources outside the district, but beginning in 1979, the principal source of water for the refuge became agricultural wastewater from the Westlands Water District.[13]

Environmentalists worried that pesticides and other pollutants would harm migratory birds. Since the Bureau of Reclamation intended the reservoir to serve its needs as a sump, the FWS had little choice but to accept the water. The agency followed the water management model it had developed for other western refuges and carved the sump into units of managed wetlands. Distributing the water facilitated evaporation. The potential for water quality problems was high, since the sumps were a "mechanism of waste disposal by design and a wildlife refuge only by coincidence."[14]

Troubles began to emerge in the early 1980s when the California State Water Resources Control Board refused the request by the Bureau of Reclamation to complete the San Luis Drain to the delta. Without an outlet for the drain water, polluted water continued to flow into the Kesterson Refuge. Selenium accumulated in the marshes and, ultimately, in the bodies of refuge wildlife. Scientists and refuge staff noticed a decline in the number of carp, catfish, and largemouth and striped bass living in refuge ponds. By 1982, all of the fish were dead, and fewer birds hatched. When scientists examined bird eggs from the refuge, they found embryos with hideous deformities. Many were missing eyes or feet; some had brains protruding from their skulls. All the embryos, as well as many mature birds using the refuge, had elevated levels of selenium, a naturally occurring mineral common in the soils on the western side of the San Joaquin Valley. Irrigation water leached selenium from soils in the Westlands Water District, and subsurface drains then carried the wastewater into the main canals that emptied into the Kesterson Refuge. As the irrigation water evaporated, salts and selenium were left behind and accumulated in the refuge marshes and ponds. Like DDT, selenium built up in the tissues of fish and birds in toxic concentrations, which caused deformities and death.[15]

The bird deaths at Kesterson quickly became a national controversy. Initially, the Bureau of Reclamation denied the problem, but then moved to cut off water to the refuge. The next step—a far less appealing one for the bureau—was to stop delivering water to the approximately 40,000 acres of Westlands district farmland, which were the primary source of the selenium. Opposition from the district forced the Department of the Interior to devise another solution. Instead of ending water deliveries to the Westlands district, the department filled the former refuge wetlands and covered them with soil imported from areas without high levels of selenium. Wildlife advocates lost an important (albeit highly polluted) refuge. Irrigators in the Westlands

Water District lost the sump for the water drained from their lands.[16] Without adequate drainage, the district was forced to find methods to reduce the build-up of salts in the soil.[17]

For a few years, the controversy at the Kesterson Refuge brought national attention to water quality problems facing other refuges in the United States. Reports from the Department of the Interior showed that many refuges depended on polluted water coming from agricultural areas. Although contaminants affected refuges outside the West, refuges in the region were particularly susceptible to contamination since they relied on irrigation water to support ponds and marshes. The Department of the Interior denied that water quality problems on these other refuges were as severe as the problems afflicting the Kesterson Refuge. But they could not refute that a suite of pollutants, including insecticides, fertilizers, and herbicides, were finding their way into many of the nation's waterfowl refuges. Pollution did not make the Kesterson Refuge unique. Selenium did, and it produced particularly grotesque results in bird embryos. The pollutants draining into other refuges did not cause such dramatic problems, but over time they progressively degraded the quality of refuge waters.[18]

A DYING REFUGE?

Although the Klamath Basin refuges were fortunately spared the horrors at Kesterson, conditions at some of the area's refuges deteriorated for other reasons. After the passage of the Kuchel Act in 1964, the Klamath Basin Refuge staff was pleased with their success. With the help of sport hunters, conservation organizations, and farmers in other parts of California, the FWS prevented further homesteading of the Tule Lake Refuge. The Kuchel Act also signaled a truce between the FWS and the Tulelake Irrigation District, two groups that had fought throughout the 1950s over water levels in the sumps, which formed the heart of the refuge. In 1952, the Tulelake Irrigation District had agreed to maintain the sump at water levels set by the district and the Bureau of Reclamation. Farmers could continue to lease lands on the refuge as long as farming did not interfere with waterfowl management. Despite its opposition to the irrigation district's water management practices and to the Bureau of Reclamation's plans to homestead part of the refuge, the FWS was not opposed to farming per se. The number of waterfowl using the Tule Lake Refuge was still high in the 1960s, and the agency needed to provide food for the birds. By continuing its own farming program and allowing leasing to continue, it ensured that there would be enough food for the waterfowl.

The Kuchel Act protected the Tule Lake Refuge from immediate threats, but it also constrained the FWS's management. The agency managed the Lower Klamath, Sacramento, and many other refuges along the Pacific Flyway principally by manipulating water. Extensive diking and canal systems enabled the agency to move water throughout the refuges and to adjust water levels to maintain wetland productivity and cope with avian disease. The temporary draining or drying of marshes from drought exposed the substrate to oxygen, allowing vegetation to decompose. Without periodic disturbances, such as draining and flooding, or the burning of dried vegetation, marshes steadily became less productive and the marsh habitats less diverse. There were other problems. The Lost River carried sediment to the Tule Lake Refuge sumps, and over time, this reduced the water depth and diminished their capacity.[19]

Collectively, these processes affected the diversity of the Tule Lake marshes. Prior to the construction of the Klamath Project, the water level and extent of Tule Lake fluctuated considerably between spring and late summer and during long-term wet-dry cycles. The area of the lake changed, too, ranging from an estimated 53,000 acres in 1846 to more than 100,000 acres in 1890.[20] This dynamic hydrologic regime was largely responsible for the high biological productivity of Tule Lake, and the diverse habitats made the lake attractive for many species of waterfowl. After the completion of the Klamath Project, dams moderated the flow of the Lost River, dikes fixed the borders of the Tule Lake sumps, and the Kuchel Act mandated specific water levels in the sumps.[21] As a consequence, the productivity of the Tule Lake marshes declined, as did the numbers of ducks and geese using the refuge. By contrast, the number of ducks and geese using the Lower Klamath Refuge increased, although the population of waterfowl along the Pacific Flyway had declined over the previous forty years. (In fact, more waterfowl used the refuge in the late 1990s than did in the 1960s.) The many small units on the Lower Klamath Refuge allowed the FWS to manipulate water levels, and such disturbances enabled the marshes to retain their productivity. Ducks such as redheads and gadwalls, which are more dependent on the aquatic plant species and invertebrates common in seasonal marshes, were particularly hard-hit by the ecological changes on the Tule Lake Refuge. Mallards, pintails, Canada geese, and other waterfowl that could consume grain fared better, but even their use of Tule Lake declined. The decrease in water depths also affected native fish—especially Lost River suckers—that lived in the sumps. The fish preferred deeper waters, yet with each passing year, the lake became shallower. Since sedimentation continued to affect the capacity of the sumps, the steady decline in wetland productivity and in the use of the Tule Lake Refuge by waterfowl seemed likely to continue.[22]

To stem further decline of the Tule Lake Refuge, in the 1990s the FWS proposed a creative solution. Recognizing that the Kuchel Act required that farming be allowed to continue under the condition that it not interfere with waterfowl management, the FWS sought to diversify habitat. This meant converting existing fields into new sumps and existing sumps into new fields. Wetland plants would colonize these recently flooded lands, creating emergent marshes. Farmers would continue leasing refuge land, but in areas that had once been sumps. Over the years, the FWS would drain and flood different parts of the refuge to maintain the disturbance regimes common in Tule Lake before the development of the Klamath Project. This proposal would allow the refuge staff to maintain a variety of habitats throughout the refuge, including seasonal marshes, permanently flooded wetlands, and deeper water areas. As an added benefit, flooding would kill agricultural pests, such as parasitic nematodes, and some plant diseases within the soil. If implemented, the plan would enable the uneasy relationship between farming and wildlife to continue on the Tule Lake Refuge by converting that area into a giant jigsaw of marshes, ponds, and fields of crops reordered periodically to maintain the productivity of wetlands and farms.[23]

As imaginative as this solution was, in many ways it simply maintained the status quo. Although the plan made sense as a way to reintroduce particular ecological factors (such as disturbance) to the Tule Lake Refuge, it also perpetuated commercial farming. The FWS said, justifiably, that it had limited options under the Kuchel Act. If it could devise a way to improve the waterfowl habitat on the Tule Lake Refuge while farming continued, it was obliged to do so. The act clearly stated that refuge officials must manage the refuges with full consideration of the needs of commercial agriculture.

Environmentalists saw things quite differently. They viewed farming on the Tule Lake Refuge as a blatant violation of the National Wildlife Refuge Improvement Act of 1997, which made conservation the highest priority on national wildlife refuges. The Lower Klamath and Tule Lake refuges were the only ones in the federal system where the FWS permitted commercial farming. Refuges were for wild species, environmentalists insisted, not agricultural monocultures. Even worse, in their view, was that water that should have supported marshes and ponds on the two refuges irrigated crops subsidized by the U.S. government, such as barley, potato, and onion. And, like other farmers throughout the West, farmers leasing refuge lands also used pesticides and fertilizers that made their way into refuge waterways and marshes. In response to these criticisms, refuge staff insisted that they had limited options. "We inherited a compromised situation and we're managing a compromised situation," said Fran Maiss, assistant manager for the Klamath Basin National Wildlife Refuges. "If you're going to raise crops on a commercial scale, you're going to need some chemicals. If we tried to promote [organic farming], it wouldn't work. You can't make a conventional farmer into an organic farmer."[24]

Such arguments did not persuade environmentalists, who wanted the FWS to curtail commercial farming. In 1997, a coalition of regional and national environmental organizations filed a lawsuit against the Department of the Interior and the Tulelake Irrigation District, arguing against commercial farming on the refuge on a number of grounds.[25] They insisted that the row crops (e.g., onions, potatoes, and sugar beets) that farmers grew on some of the leased lands were of little use to waterfowl and that farmers were increasingly dependent on pesticides and fertilizers. They cited the accumulation of pesticides in refuge sumps as a primary reason for the decline in Klamath Basin bird populations.[26]

Environmentalists correctly noted that farmers continued to use pesticides on Tule Lake Refuge lease lands. Yet this did not mean that farmers used them indiscriminately. The FWS had adopted an Integrated Pest Management program (IPM) in the 1990s, which limited the types, amounts, and places where farmers could apply pesticides. They sought a middle ground between industrial models of agriculture, which required frequent and widespread applications of pesticides, and organic agriculture, which avoided using pesticides altogether. Under the IPM program, farmers strove to use smaller amounts of pesticides by applying them only when conditions warranted and to use nonchemical methods to control weeds and insects whenever possible. The goal was to reduce wildlife exposure to pesticides, but not to eliminate them. Advocates of IPM hoped that fewer pesticides would lower production costs.[27]

According to the FWS, after DDT was banned there was no evidence, except in a few isolated cases, that pesticides caused bird deaths. FWS officials argued that since pesticides were expensive, farmers rarely applied more than was necessary to control pests. Also, to protect refuge marshes, the FWS prohibited the use of pesticides within fifty feet of waterways and sumps. Farmers leasing lands on the refuge faced greater restrictions on pesticide use than farmers on other lands within the Klamath Project. Thus, the FWS argued that few, if any, pesticides reached the Tule Lake marshes.

The pesticide issue was part of the environmentalists' broader criticism of the farming program. "The basic quandary before the agencies and national public is not so much whether pesticide use on the refuges is in the public interest (clearly, it's not), but whether the lease-land farming system itself should be continued," wrote William Kittredge, a well-known writer who grew up in the area and once farmed in southeastern Oregon.[28] Wendell Wood, the Klamath Falls representative for the Oregon Natural Resources Council (ONRC), an influential Portland-based environmental group, stated the problem in stark terms: "We view the continued and sanctioned use of pesticides on

Wildlife Refuges as but a symptom of the greater problem. Refuges must be managed for wildlife first."[29] In this view, the continued use of pesticides was an affront to the primary purpose of wildlife refuges. The refuges were supposed to be places where wildlife could flourish, not yet another place for growing potatoes or alfalfa. The point was not the amount of pesticides used. Rather, it was the continuance of modern commercial agriculture on what was once one of North America's premier wildlife refuges.

As appealing as the "wildlife refuges for wildlife" argument might have been, it denied the uncomfortable but real connections between irrigated agriculture and the Lower Klamath and Tule Lake refuges. Since the refuges had no water rights, the FWS depended on water supplied by Klamath Project farms to sustain the refuges. The Tule Lake Refuge is the last stop for water that has flowed from the outskirts of Klamath Falls twenty-five miles to the northwest, through project farms, and finally into the Tule Lake Refuge sumps. Environmentalists argue that the refuges would be better off if the FWS eliminated the lease-land farming program. But if the refuge farming program ended immediately, the refuges probably would not receive any more water than they do already. The water used by farmers who lease land on the refuge would go instead to farmers upstream, who have senior water rights. Some of the return flow from that irrigation would make its way into the Tule Lake Refuge sumps, but it is unclear whether the refuge would gain water overall.

Eliminating lease-land farming on the Tule Lake Refuge would solve the problem of pesticide use in the immediate vicinity, but stopping pesticide use on the refuges would do nothing to prevent the use of pesticides upstream. The refuges cannot escape their dependence on irrigation water. Environmentalists might argue that ending the application of pesticides (particularly in the immediate proximity of refuge marshes) is preferable to continuing to spray insecticides and herbicides on refuge lands. Yet the poor water quality of Klamath Basin lakes, canals, and marshes reflects decisions made throughout the basin, not just contamination from Tule Lake Refuge lease-lands. Water—which divided so many groups in the basin—connects them all through the natural and constructed waterways of the Klamath Project.

The turn of the twenty-first century brought a new water conflict to the fore in the Klamath Basin. This time the Tule Lake and Lower Klamath Lake refuges were not at the center of the conflict. Rather, they suffered from federal government decisions to provide water for endangered fish species at the expense of irrigators. In the midst of one of the worst droughts in a century, the U.S. Fish and Wildlife Service and the National Marine Fisheries Service recommended in the spring of 2001 that the Bureau of Reclamation curtail the water supply to the 1,200 farms within the Klamath Project. Irrigators had coped with dry years before. Typically, those with senior water rights could restrict their water use and still receive water. For those with junior water rights, a dry year might mean that they receive no water whatsoever. Typically, however, most farmers were able to get enough water to irrigate their alfalfa fields or rows of potatoes and garlic.

For most of the previous half-century, the refuges had received water whenever irrigators did. Usually there was enough return flow from irrigators to support refuge marshes. During droughts, irrigators and refuges suffered together (though in severe droughts, the refuges suffered more because they received only residual water from farming operations). Beginning in the 1990s, the FWS attempted to rectify this situation by claiming water rights as part of the Klamath Basin adjudication held by the State of Oregon. The adjudication process was designed to grant water rights to individuals, groups, and organizations that used water within the basin prior to 1909, the year the State of Oregon assumed responsibility for regulating surface water use within the state.[30]

Up until the 1990s, under the doctrine of prior appropriation, those who claimed water rights first were entitled to first rights to water ("First in time, first in right"). Those with senior water holdings had the right to use their allotment before those with junior rights. This meant that water went to non-Indian settlers, especially to farmers served by the Klamath Project. By virtue of the treaties they signed with the U.S. federal government, Indian tribes such as the Klamath and Modoc should have had superior rights to the non-Indian users, but in practice, the federal government did not recognize their rights in the early twentieth century (though, as discussed below, this began to change after the 1970s). Fish, waterfowl, and other animals and plants that depended on the basin's water had no right to water either.[31]

The institutional landscape had changed in the Klamath Basin since the last major drought in the early 1990s. The Bureau of Reclamation and farmers still managed the waters of the Klamath Project primarily for irrigation. They saw the basin's lakes and rivers as components of a plumbing system, not as elements of ecosystems. In effect, the Lower Klamath and Tule Lake refuges depended mostly on water left over from upstream irrigators after it had flowed through the project's canals, pumps, and sumps.[32] Water passed from irrigators into the Tule Lake Refuge, then through a tunnel into Lower Klamath Refuge, and then by canal into the Klamath River.[33]

Environmentalists and Indian tribes had a different view of the Klamath Basin waterscape. Environmental organizations such as the Oregon Natural Resources Council, the Klamath Forest Alliance, and the Wilderness Society saw the Klamath Basin as a landscape of loss.[34] To them, irrigators and the Bureau of Reclamation had destroyed the primal marshlands that existed nearly a century before. In its place, the bureau and farmers had constructed an artificial network of canals and sumps that supported a destructive form of chemically dependent agriculture. Its casualties were the wild inhabitants of the basin: migratory birds, sucker fish, salmon, bald eagles, and other animals. The destruction of the basin's marshes was a tragedy, the leasing of refuge lands to farmers an abomination.[35]

Indians also lamented the transformation wrought by irrigators, but for different reasons. Klamath and Modoc Indians had long caught suckerfish in the marshes, lakes, and rivers of their traditional territories. The many structures built by irrigators had destroyed riparian habitat and made much of the basin's water inhospitable to suckerfish and other native fish. Unlike the Indians, farmers saw the suckerfish as junk fish. When they irrigated their fields, water sometimes carried suckerfish across the land, where the fish flopped on the ground and died.[36] After a series of lawsuits during the 1970s and 1980s, federal district courts recognized that the Treaty of 1864 signed by the Klamath Indians entitled the tribes to water rights that superceded those of other users in the basin. The basis for the decision was the clause in the treaty ensuring the tribes' right to use the resources of the reservation in exchange for ceding much of their former territory to the federal government. However, having rights to resources such as suckerfish and salmon meant little unless there was sufficient water to support them. The courts recognized this, and in later rulings decided that the Klamath Tribes were entitled to enough water to protect the resources they traditionally hunted and fished—including suckerfish. The implications of this ruling were enormous. In effect, it overturned a century of water allocation in the Klamath Basin. The tribes, who had long been marginalized socially and economically in basin affairs, now had priority rights to the most valuable natural resource in the Klamath Basin.[37]

Enforcement of the Endangered Species Act also had implications for water allocation. In the 1980s, the once abundant shortnose sucker (*Chasmistes brevirostris*) and Lost River sucker (*Deltistes luxants*) populations in the Klamath Basin declined precipitously. In 1988, both species were classified as endangered under the ESA. The fish lived in Upper Klamath Lake, Tule Lake, and the Lost River (but not in Lower Klamath Lake). The draining of lakes and marshes by the Bureau of Reclamation was partly responsible for the populations' decline, but other factors contributed to it, including poor water quality, which made it difficult for the suckers to survive. In the summer and fall, algal blooms raised the pH levels of Upper Klamath Lake, and when the algae died, it removed oxygen from the water as it decomposed. Algal blooms were associated with major die-offs of suckers in 1971 and 1986. In June 1992, the pH level where Upper Klamath Lake emptied into the A-Canal (one the main Klamath Project irrigation channels) was 10.5—only slightly less than the pH of ammonia. Although scientists believe that eutrophic conditions were common in Upper Klamath Lake before the twentieth century, the changing water conditions created by the Klamath Project have likely made the situation even worse. Nitrogen and phosphorous used in farm fertilizer and carried into basin lakes contributed to algal blooms and led to the worsening conditions for shortnose and Lost River suckers. After droughts in 1992, the Fish and Wildlife Service stated in a biological opinion that both species would likely become extinct unless the Bureau of Reclamation altered its management of the Klamath Project.[38]

The populations of coho salmon that spawned in the Klamath River also declined in the 1990s. Unlike the shortnose and Lost River suckers, coho are not restricted to the Klamath Basin. Coho once lived in rivers and streams between northern California and Alaska, but their numbers had declined greatly due to overfishing and the destruction of river habitat. The coho spawning in the Klamath River watershed are genetically distinct from coho populations that use other watercourses along the West Coast. Dams built on the Klamath River during the later 1950s and early 1960s impeded access to spawning areas upstream. Landscape changes affecting salmon habitat contributed to the species' decline. Logging and road construction on hill slopes above salmon-bearing streams led to greater erosion, which eliminated spawning areas or reduced their quality. Hatchery-raised coho also competed with wild coho for the remaining spawning areas. In addition to these threats, coho had to contend with reduced water flows, as irrigators in the upper reaches of the Klamath Basin used water for irrigation. Along the Trinity River, one of the main tributaries of the Klamath River, the Bureau of Reclamation diverted water outside the watershed and into the Central Valley. From there, canals and pumps conveyed the water hundreds of miles to farmers in the Westlands Water District in the San Joaquin Valley. Declining populations of coho salmon led the National Marine Fisheries Service to list the fish as threatened under the ESA in 1997.[39]

Together, the ESA and Indian reserved water rights were powerful legal tools for changing water allocation in the basin—tools that would have significant consequences for the basin's wildlife refuges. The FWS and National Marine Fisheries Service argued that more water was needed in basin lakes and rivers to support endangered fish species. Since they harvested these species, members of the Klamath, Yurok, and Hoopa tribes also had a stake in the survival of suckerfish and coho salmon. Until the 1990s, the Bureau of Reclamation operated the Klamath Project with little regard for these species and the water rights of Indian tribes. As the number of sucker fish and coho salmon dwindled, the bureau came under increasing pressure from the agencies responsible for enforcing the ESA, from Indian tribes, and from environmentalists to do more to protect these species. The Bureau of Reclamation was able to fend off critics for several years by promising to protect fish. But severe drought changed the situation. The bureau could keep these critics at bay only so long as severe drought did not affect the basin. When it did, the bureau had to decide whether to shut off water to irrigators, and in so doing, stop the flow of water to refuges lying at the end of the Klamath Project's irrigation canals.[40]

This was the situation in the spring of 2001. The winter of 2000–2001 was the driest on record in the Klamath Basin. By late spring, most of the snow pack had melted, leaving water levels in Upper Klamath Lake and Clear Lake (which were also reservoirs for the Klamath Project) much lower than normal. Under the ESA, the Bureau of Reclamation was required to consult with the FWS and National Marine Fisheries Service to determine the minimum lake levels in Upper Klamath Lake and the minimum flows in the Klamath River needed to support endangered fish. The Bureau of Reclamation wanted to lower the level of Upper Klamath Lake to 4,136.8 feet in summer, but the FWS insisted on a minimum of 4,140 feet. Since Upper Klamath Lake is shallow even in wet years, this amounted to a difference of roughly 200,000 acre feet of water. Not only did the Bureau of Reclamation need to keep more water in Upper Klamath Lake to protect endangered shortnose and Lost River suckers, it also had to release some of the remaining water into the Klamath River to support threatened coho salmon.[41]

In April 2001, the Bureau of Reclamation announced that it would not release water from Upper Klamath Lake to Klamath Project farmers. Farmers who had wells or access to other lakes and streams could irrigate their fields, but for most, the closure meant they would receive no water. For most of the spring and summer of 2001, the Tule Lake and Lower Klamath refuges received no water either. Refuge staff had been able to divert water into both refuges early in the winter of 2000–2001, so there was some water on the refuges after the cutoff. On the Lower Klamath Refuge, the FWS began the grim task of triage by selecting some ponds and marshes as sacrifice areas. Refuge staff diverted water from these units into other marshes deemed more important. As the summer progressed and the residual water in the drained units evaporated, the refuge began to resemble the dry Lower Klamath lakebed of the 1920s.[42]

For the FWS, this was a remarkable and disturbing turn of events. As one of the two agencies in charge of enforcing the ESA, the FWS had the power to list species as endangered and to issue biological opinions on whether the actions of other federal agencies might adversely affect endangered species. Based on the statements of FWS and National Marine Fisheries Service scientists, the Bureau of Reclamation shut off water to the irrigators in the Klamath Project. An agency that had once been fully at the mercy of the Bureau of Reclamation at various times during the twentieth century was now able to compel the bureau to manage water with the needs of endangered species in mind. Yet the new power was a devil's bargain. Since the FWS wildlife refuges depended on water from the Klamath Project and had junior water rights in relation to project irrigators, they also suffered when irrigators went without water. Unless the FWS could demonstrate that endangered species were on the refuges and that low water conditions harmed them (or their habitat), the refuges, like the farms of the Klamath Project, would have to go without water. The FWS was faced with ordering more water to remain in the Upper Klamath Lake and the Klamath River at the expense of refuges to the south. The result was that the agency's Lower Klamath and Tule refuges went without water for much of the hot, dry summer of 2001.[43]

Farmers' protests over the water cutoff drowned out concerns over the dire situation facing the refuges. The cutoff affected more than 1,200 Klamath Project farms. Initially, the loss of water stunned the farmers, but as they realized the full consequences of having to survive financially for a year without crops, their disbelief turned to rage. "We're real people here, and we're being annihilated," said Rob Crawford, a farmer dependent on Klamath Project water. He and other farmers blamed environmentalists for their plight, saying that the water shutoff was part of a systematic effort by environmentalists and the FWS to engage in "rural cleansing." Although it might appear unseemly to compare the effect of environmental protection on rural communities to genocide, comments like these demonstrated the depth of farmers' anger. Such comments became common after the Oregon Natural Resources Council proposed that the federal government purchase land and water rights from willing sellers in order to ease pressure on water supplies in the Klamath Basin.[44]

To bring national attention to their plight, farmers and their supporters launched a series of protests that demonstrated both their capacity to unite many in the Klamath Basin behind their cause and to garner media attention. During the spring and summer of 2001, stories about protests in the Klamath Basin against the actions of the federal government were common in regional newspapers and on television news programs, and occasionally, in national news outlets.[45] In May 2001, over ten thousand farmers and their supporters rallied in Klamath Falls to protest the water cutoff and to call for amendments to the ESA. In a gesture designed to exemplify their plight to the media, protesters passed buckets of water drawn from Upper Klamath Lake through the Main Street of Klamath Falls and then dumped the water into the main canal of the Klamath Project. U.S. Congressmen Wally Herger (R-California) and Greg Walden (R-Oregon) and Senator Gordon Smith (R-Oregon) participated in the protest as well. "Urban people, people from the northeast, they just don't understand because they've never been affected by the ESA," said Congressman Walden.[46] Paul Christy, a World War II veteran and Klamath Project homesteader, also placed the blame for the water crisis with urban environmentalists, saying, "We have some pretty nutty people—we call 'em the green people—over the hill. It's hard to believe that it could all be wrecked."[47] During the summer, smaller groups of protesters took measures beyond simply marching in the streets. On the Fourth of July protesters cut off the lock to the head gates of the Klamath Project's main canal and released water from Upper Klamath Lake. The Bureau of Reclamation closed the gates, but protesters returned to open them repeatedly during the next two weeks. Since the local sheriff refused to intervene and the district attorney refused to prosecute the perpetrators if arrested, the Bureau of Reclamation eventually called in U.S. federal marshals to protect the head gates from further vandalism and prevent the release of more water from Upper Klamath Lake.[48]

Signs erected along highways and back roads within the Klamath Basin also made the farmers' points in stark terms. Farmers were victims of callous environmentalists and of government regulations designed to protect endangered species over the needs of hardworking people. Farmers and their supporters argued that irrigation water was an entitlement promised by the federal government. By failing to continue the supply of water at levels prevailing in the previous century, the federal government was seen to have turned on the people. Supporters of the irrigators claimed that Lost River and shortnose suckers were not worth the protection afforded under the ESA. Betrayed and frustrated, the farmers continued to make their case with the media and through the courts during the rest of the summer.

Given that the Fish and Wildlife Service's Tule Lake and Lower Klamath Lake refuges were mostly dry that summer, the agency might have expected to gain some sympathy from the farming community. On the contrary, the agency became one of the main objects of the farmers' discontent. Indeed, the fact that FWS decisions to protect endangered fish had led to water shortages on the agency's refuges clearly illustrated that the FWS was inept, insensitive to the needs of people and wildlife. In a striking departure from earlier depictions of farmlands as places for crops rather than wildlife, farmers now emphasized the role their lands played in supporting waterfowl, deer, and other wild animals. Wildlife became unwitting allies in the rhetorical strategy of those protesting against the decisions of the FWS.[49]

In making their case, basin residents opposing environmentalists and the federal government adopted a populist discourse based on the primacy of labor. In contrast to environmentalists, whom they depicted as radicals living in urban areas far from the basin, farmers and their supporters depicted themselves as true Americans fighting to protect rural livelihoods. "People in rural America, by and large, are true patriots," said an eighty-five-year-old resident of Klamath Falls and the owner of a fertilizer business. "But we're not too patriotic here anymore. . . . We just can't believe that a great country would do this to our own people."[50] In their view, the withdrawal of irrigation water was not just an economic hardship, it was an assault by the federal government on the American family farm and the hardworking men and women who tilled the soil. Many of the original Klamath Project homesteaders were also veterans of the First or Second World Wars, and some of them participated in the bucket brigade protest.

It was, they said, an insult that the federal government was willing to endanger the livelihood of veterans and their descendents for the benefit of ugly and worthless fish.[51]

At the end of the summer, Secretary of the Interior Gale Norton ordered the Bureau of Reclamation to release 70,000 acre feet of water to irrigators, but this was "too little, too late" for most farmers. The growing season was almost over, and since farmers had been told not to expect any water during the year, they had not maintained distributary canals for their fields. Environmentalists sued the Department of the Interior, claiming that the biological opinion filed by the FWS in March 2001 stated that any extra water must go to the wildlife refuges to protect the bald eagles using the Lower Klamath Refuge.[52] Eventually, the Bureau of Reclamation released water to the refuges, too, though the water levels in both the Tule Lake and Lower Klamath Lake refuges were far below average. Despite the worst fears of environmentalists, sport hunters, and the FWS, there was no major die-off of waterfowl during the fall migrations. The birds were able to withstand one year of drought. Since the Klamath Basin serves primarily as a staging area rather than a wintering ground, migratory waterfowl could accommodate the loss of some habitat in the basin for one season. The cumulative effect of multiple dry years and reduced water deliveries to the refuges might have a more pronounced effect.[53]

In response to the controversy generated by the water cutoff, Secretary Norton asked the National Academy of Sciences to organize a panel of scientific experts to review the biological opinions issued by the FWS and the National Marine Fisheries Service, investigate the validity of the government scientists' findings, and publish them in a preliminary report by the spring of 2002.[54] Convening the panel of experts seemed to be an effort by Norton to answer critics who charged that the scientists based their biological opinions on weak and inconclusive evidence. "We should base our decisions on the best available science," Norton said. She hoped that an independent review of the science would ease tensions and serve as proof of the government's attempts to make fair decisions. Farmers and their supporters worried that the committee would simply affirm the agencies' views. Environmentalists and groups representing commercial fishers were enthusiastic. "We're by no means afraid," said Glen Spain, northwest director for the Pacific Coast Federation of Fishermen's Association. "The science is bulletproof. This will demonstrate what we all know: Fish need water to exist."[55]

Ultimately, the committee did not rubber-stamp the biological opinions, and it strongly criticized the assessments of the federal scientists.[56] It said that there was no conclusive evidence that linked water levels in Upper Klamath Lake with sucker mortality. In fact, many suckers had died during years when lake levels were high. There was no reason, in the view of the committee, to keep the lake at levels requested by the FWS and National Marine Fisheries Service. Furthermore, the release of water from Upper Klamath Lake into the Klamath River to aid coho salmon might actually have harmed the fish, since the water coming from the lake was warmer than the salmon could tolerate. Rather than blaming excessive irrigation as the main reason for the decline of the coho, the committee identified the diversion of water from the main tributary of the Klamath River, the Trinity River, as a more important factor influencing the survival of coho (during the summer months, water from the Trinity River is typically cooler than water flowing from Upper Klamath Lake).[57] Farmers were elated. Norton and the Bush administration were pleased, since it gave them justification to release more water for irrigators. The reputations of the FWS and National Marine Fisheries Service—already badly tarnished by the previous summer's controversy—were damaged even further in the eyes of many basin residents.[58]

Farmers and their supporters had only a few months to savor their victory. Basing their decision on the committee's findings, the Bureau of Reclamation released far less water from the Upper Klamath Lake into the Klamath River than it did the previous year. When chinook salmon began their run up the Klamath River in August and September, thousands of the fish began to die only a few miles from the river's mouth. The immediate cause was unknown, but as the number of dead fish rose, commercial fishermen, Indian tribes, and environmental groups laid the blame with the decision to provide more water to irrigators. By early October, over 30,000 salmon were dead. In protest, tribal leaders shipped tons of rotting salmon and dumped them on the steps of the Department of the Interior in Washington, D.C. Norton and officials with the Department of the Interior said there was no scientific basis for the critics' accusations. Even so, the fish kill contributed further to the mistrust and acrimony among the various interest groups concerned with water allocation in the Klamath Basin.[59]

The basin's water crisis had a lasting influence on the management of the Tule Lake and Lower Klamath Lake refuges. The crisis increased the bitterness farmers and some basin residents already felt toward the FWS. Farmers believed that the agency used poor science in formulating the biological opinion that led the Bureau of Reclamation not to release water to irrigators, and they felt that the report from the National Academy of Sciences' committee vindicated their position. Certainly, the report emboldened basin residents to fight further enforcement of the ESA. With its scientific expertise called into question, the FWS faced more opposition to any serious changes in the way it managed refuges or endangered species. Support did not come from officials with the Department of Interior or from the administration of George W. Bush, which sought to weaken the ESA and to reduce the economic impact of other environmental regulations.[60] But the death of thousands of salmon the following year only seemed to confirm fears by environmentalists, Indian tribes, and federal scientists that reduced flows in the Klamath River would lead to increased salmon mortality. The National Academy of Sciences' committee was supposed to render the final scientific judgment on the water crisis. Instead, it only contributed to the animosity among the various stakeholders in the basin.[61]

Yet the FWS had little choice but to continue working with Klamath Basin farmers. Its refuges were still dependent on water from irrigators, particularly in dry years when refuge staff scrambled to find water to support the marshes. The FWS faced just such a situation in 2002. Although the basin received more precipitation than it had the previous year, Upper Klamath Lake was still low from the drought of 2001. To sustain refuge marshes at acceptable levels, the FWS requested water from the Tulelake Irrigation District. In the midst of this, environmentalists launched another lawsuit to eliminate farming from the Tule Lake and Upper Klamath Lake refuges. The refuge staff in the Klamath Basin saw lack of water, not lease farming, as the main threat to the future of the refuges. In their view, alienating

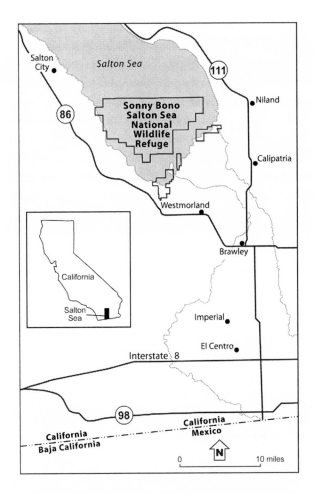

MAP 9 *Sonny Bono Salton Sea National Wildlife Refuge*

farmers would make their job only more difficult and make finding a solution to the basin's water problems more challenging. "I feel like we're in a boat swept down the river with no oars and no rudder," said Phil Norton, the chief refuge manager for the Klamath Basin refuges. "And instead of doing anything about it, we're in the boat, fighting like hell."[62]

Unless the U.S. Congress rewrites the ESA and weakens its provisions, water conflicts like the one that shook Klamath Basin in 2001 will likely reoccur. By reserving more water for fish in basin lakes and rivers, there will be less water available for wildlife refuges. The FWS predicts that in future dry years the Tule Lake and Lower Klamath Lake refuges will be short of water. Legally, the needs of endangered species, Indian tribes, and the water rights of Klamath Project irrigators who have senior water rights come before the water demands of refuges. The refuge will remain at the "end of the line" for water, though the agency continues to press the State of Oregon to grant them a more senior water right. But there is no indication when the state will finish the adjudication (the process began over twenty-five years ago), and when it is completed, there is no guarantee the FWS will receive all the water it claimed.[63]

After the salmon die-off on the Klamath River in the fall of 2002, Sue Marsten, chairwoman of the Yurok Tribe, wryly noted that water management within the Klamath watershed had come down to "who has the best political connections."[64] Tribes, farmers, environmental groups, the FWS, and others are all using legal and political means to gain a greater share of Klamath Basin water. Refuge managers are faced with the same water supply and quality problems as in the past, but in a more volatile political environment.

THE SUMP AT THE END OF THE WEST

As bad as environmental problems were in the Klamath, they paled in scale and scope to the ones surrounding the Salton Sea. During the century since its creation, the Salton Sea had served as a crucial wintering and stopover area for Pacific Flyway birds. The Imperial Irrigation District and the Coachella Valley Water District sustained the Salton Sea through the agricultural drain water they emptied into it. Although the continued influx of water kept the sea from evaporating completely, it contributed to the sea's radical transformation. As irrigation water passed through farms, it dissolved salts in the soil and carried them into the sea, steadily increasing its salinity. By the late 1990s, the salinity of the sea reached 45,000 parts per million—about 10,000 parts per million greater than ocean water. Scientists predicted that the Salton Sea would become hypersaline by 2020, making it inhospitable to most life except for brine shrimp, which are able to tolerate the extreme environment.[65]

Despite its high salinity, the Salton Sea supported multitudes of birds, including year-round residents, winter migrants, and flyway birds resting there while en route to wintering or breeding areas. During the 1990s, up to 30,000 snow geese and 60,000 ducks wintered at the refuge each year. The lake was even better known for the thousands of white and brown pelicans, grebes, and other fish-eating birds that fed on the sea's abundant tilapia fish. To call the sea an oasis may sound trite, but in this case the comparison is apt, since the sea lies in one of the hottest deserts in North America (over one hundred days above one hundred degrees Fahrenheit per year). After the loss of most of the Colorado River Delta in the 1930s, the sea became the only major open-water site in southern California and northwestern Mexico. However, the Salton Sea was not a one-to-one substitute for the lost delta lagoons and marshes. Although the sea supported some of the same types of wintering birds that used the delta, it also attracted birds such as pelicans and grebes in far greater numbers than the delta would have. The Salton Sea was a unique ecosystem made possible by large quantities of irrigation water carrying fertilizers, which allowed fish to thrive in the lake.[66]

By the 1990s, the lake was also a deathtrap for many species. The species most seriously affected were the fish-eating birds, particularly eared grebes and pelicans. When refuge staff discovered a few hundred dead eared grebes washed up on the south shore of the lake in 1992, they assumed that the birds died from avian cholera. Tests were inconclusive. Some suspected pesticides or selenium as the culprits, and indeed, the birds showed elevated concentrations of DDT, selenium, and other toxic substances. None of the concentrations seemed high enough to cause the death of so many birds, and the FWS never determined the reasons for the die-off. Grebes continued to perish by the thousands, their carcasses washing ashore, where refuge staff retrieved them. Eventually they collected 46,040 birds out of an estimated 150,000 that died. "It's not like I am managing a refuge now," said Charles Bloom, the manager of the Sonny Bono Salton Sea National Wildlife Refuge. "It's more like a battlefield."[67]

Four years later, there was another die-off of birds, this time among brown and white pelicans and ruddy ducks. The killer in this case was botulism, a common and serious threat to Pacific Flyway birds. Pelicans contracted the disease from tilapia (a small fish that was common in the sea). After the pelicans died, maggots consumed the carcasses. The carcasses were in turn eaten by ducks, which then died as well. This is the disease cycle so often repeated on the Sacramento and Klamath Basin refuges. The death toll was less severe this time (only 20,000 birds dead), but the 8,500 white pelicans and 1,100 brown pelicans that died constituted 15 and 10 percent, respectively, of the North American populations of those species. Like at Kesterson a decade earlier, the dead birds attracted national media attention. Most commentators saw the pelican die-off as an isolated natural disaster or a sad wildlife spectacle. Rarely, however, did the media note that the diseases killing Salton Sea birds were symptoms of a larger problem with refuges along the Pacific Flyway.[68]

These wildlife disasters in the 1990s are but a prelude to more severe problems that may occur in the future. Only four species of fish live in the Salton Sea: orange-mouth corvina, croaker, sargo, and tilapia. In time the salinity of the lake will rise to such a level that even these hardy species will die. Fish die-offs are more common than the epidemics that kill pelicans and grebes, but attract less attention. When the salinity finally becomes too much for these fish to tolerate and the last of them die, the pelicans, grebes, and other birds that feed on them will disappear, too. Waterfowl and some sea birds could thrive in the brine shrimp-dominated ecosystem that would likely replace the fish that now live in the sea. In the meantime, the Salton Sea would become a sump filled with rotting fish carcasses, making it an unpleasant place to visit, although it would produce food for animal scavengers near the area.[69]

The fate of the Salton Sea was intertwined with major changes in water politics in southern California. For decades, the state of California had withdrawn more than its share of water from the Colorado River. Along with other states along the river, California signed the Colorado River Compact in 1922, which assigned each an annual allotment of water.[70] California was allowed to take 4.4 million acre feet of water a year, but for the past half-century it has used more. The other states pressured the federal government to intercede, and in 1993, the

Department of the Interior told the State of California that it had to devise a plan to lower its take of Colorado River water substantially by 2010 or face the immediate cut-off of 800,000 acre feet effective January 1, 2003. The greatest user of the Colorado River in California was the Imperial Irrigation District. It used 70 percent of the state's allotment (in fact, the district had rights to one-fifth of the *entire* river's flow). To meet the demands of the federal government, the state had developed a water transfer program that involved the district reducing its water use overall as well as passing on some of its water to San Diego 120 miles to the west.[71] The state could compel the Imperial Irrigation District to transfer water because 1.1 million acre feet of water annually flowed off farmers' fields and into the Salton Sea, which helped sustain the sea, though critics cited it as evidence that the district wasted water. San Diego and other southern California cities saw the transfer as fitting and just (800,000 acre feet of water could supply three million people with water for municipal uses). But the transfer meant that even less water would enter the Salton Sea, thus exacerbating the rising salinity levels and hastening its demise as a stopover area for migrating birds.[72]

In the last decade, some have tried to prevent this fate. The Salton Sea Authority, a consortium of state and federal agencies, environmental groups, and concerned citizens, was formed in 1992 to devise possible solutions to the salinity crisis. Some proposed constructing two pipelines from the Salton Sea to the Gulf of California, one to carry water from the Salton Sea to the ocean, the other to carry ocean water to the sea. Over time this would lower the salinity level of the sea to a level approaching that of the ocean. The expense and engineering challenges involved in such a plan were formidable. A number of plans involved sacrificing part of the lake by constructing dikes. The area inside the dike would still receive waste water from the Imperial Irrigation District; the area isolated on the other side would eventually become hypersaline. All of the options would require massive funding. Estimates ranged from $300 million to $35 billion. Compared to the staggering problems facing the Salton Sea, the challenges in the Klamath Basin seemed rather benign.[73]

Prospects are grim for the Salton Sea and for the Pacific Flyway birds depending on this desert oasis. The demise of the sea might be inevitable were it not for the sustained media attention that its death throes would receive. Images of thousands of birds dying each year in the fetid waters might eventually lead to a sustained outcry to save the Salton Sea from annihilation, though by that point, it would likely be too late to resurrect it or the species that once used it.

For over sixty years, the sea has served as a partial substitute for the Colorado River Delta, which was destroyed by dams and water diversions upriver. Although there were important hydrological differences between the former delta marshes and the Salton Sea, it still supports thousands of migratory birds each year. If the Salton Sea became hypersaline, migrating birds would lose the most important wintering area in this part of the Pacific Flyway. For brown and white pelicans, this change would be catastrophic. Reversing or even slowing the increasing salinity of the sea would be very expensive. Such a program would rival the cost of the Florida Everglades restoration, one of the most ambitious ecological restoration programs in U.S. history. It is unlikely whether Californians and Americans in general would be willing to finance the restoration of a body of water that most people consider polluted and unappealing to begin with. A less costly but politically more challenging solution would be to allow more water to reach the Colorado River Delta. Even a relatively small amount of water could support many wetlands. Over the past two decades, wastewater from agricultural fields in northern Mexico has enabled marshes to develop in the former delta of the Colorado River.[74] Although the marshes are relatively small and constitute only a fraction of the wetlands once found within the delta, their presence is compelling evidence that if water is available, marsh vegetation and animals will return. Restoring the Colorado River Delta would certainly be less formidable than an expensive and technologically daunting attempt to save the Salton Sea.

In the early twenty-first century, birds along the Pacific Flyway have faced an uncertain future. One of the main staging areas for the migrating birds, the Klamath Basin, was the site of an intense and bitter conflict between farmers who have benefited from a government irrigation project and those supporting greater protection for endangered fish. In the process, wildlife refuges became collateral damage in this struggle. At the other end of the state, the main water supply for the Salton Sea is threatened. If the sea becomes hypersaline, it would be of little use to many migrating birds.

In spite of all of this, there was cause for hope in the Central Valley. During the 1990s, rice farmers came under increasing pressure from municipalities to restrict their water use and change their farming practices. The rice-growing industry had earned a bad reputation for its widespread use of pesticides and profligate use of water. The most serious criticism, however, involved the way that it disposed of rice stubble each year. In many countries, rice stubble was recycled for other uses, but in the Sacramento Valley, farmers burned it before planting a new crop of rice in the spring. Smoke from this burning often drifted out of the rice-growing districts and over the state capital of Sacramento to the south. In 1991, the state government passed the Rice Straw Burning Reduction Act, which required the industry to phase out rice burning over ten years. Farmers protested the act, saying that it would substantially increase their costs to dispose of the rice stubble. Faced with critics on all sides, the industry had little choice but to change its operations and to devise a solution.

The solution the industry found not only dealt with the rice straw, it also improved the public image of rice farmers in California. Normally, farmers kept their fields unflooded throughout the winter.[75] Farmers discovered if they flooded the fields, much of the rice stubble decomposed by the start of the growing season. Not surprisingly, the acres of water also attracted ducks, which fed on rice leftover from harvesting and on the invertebrates that thrived in the flooded areas. Now, when metropolitan residents complain about the high water use by the rice industry, farmers can point to the waterfowl benefits their industry provides. Although city people might care little about the rice industry, they do like ducks and geese. Without the water necessary for rice growing operations, waterfowl would lose important habitat.[76]

Whether winter flooding will remain a viable solution to the rice stubble problem is unclear. Farmers and agricultural scientists do not know the long-term consequences of keeping their fields flooded year-round. Leaving rice stubble in the fields may alter soil chemistry in detrimental ways. Also, if farmers can find a market for rice straw, they may harvest it and stop winter flooding altogether. In the mean-time, waterfowl have become allies in a public relations effort by rice farmers to retain their share of subsidized California water. Instead of devising methods to repel waterfowl from rice fields—as they did in the mid-twentieth century—rice farmers now welcome them.

Despite the degraded marshes and lakes in California, water-fowl and other birds continue to migrate. Their annual movements up and down the continent continue despite all of the changes along the flyway. Water development has destroyed most of the wetlands in the wintering range, and pollution has damaged refuge marshes. Although their numbers have shrunk, the birds have demonstrated surprising resiliency in spite of these changes to their habitat.

EPILOGUE

IN THE SPRING OF 2003, the U.S. Fish and Wildlife Service observed the one hundredth anniversary of the national wildlife refuge system. It was a muted celebration. While the agency praised the growth of the system since the creation of the first federal wildlife refuge on three acres of mangrove swamp in Florida by President Theodore Roosevelt in 1903, commentators noted that most of the agency's 540 refuges were underfunded and poorly maintained. As the FWS celebrated the past, Interior Secretary Gale Norton threatened the future by lobbying strenuously for the U.S. Congress to open Alaska's Arctic National Wildlife Refuge to oil drilling. Environmentalists worried that oil development would threaten the calving grounds of the porcupine caribou herd, which migrate annually within the refuge between the Brooks Range and the Beaufort Sea. This coastal plain is also the breeding area for many different species of Pacific Flyway birds, including snow geese and tundra swans. After a century of incursions into, adaptations of, and threats to wintering habitat of Pacific Flyway waterfowl in southern Canada, the continental United States, and western Mexico, this proposal threatened to bring industrial development to the birds' northern breeding grounds.[1] Up until now, the major threats to the habitat of Pacific Flyway birds were largely restricted to developments in the birds' wintering range. Now birds were threatened by developments not only in the agricultural areas of the Klamath Basin or the Central Valley, but on the Arctic plains of northern Alaska.

In the early twenty-first century, the problems facing migratory waterfowl and the refuges in the wintering range were only growing. The large coastal metropolitan areas in California demanded water claimed by agriculture in the Central and Imperial valleys. Such transfers would have major ramifications for agriculture and for the wildlife refuges in the midst of irrigated landscapes. In the Klamath Basin, environmentalists and Indian tribes were using the Endangered Species Act to pressure the Bureau of Reclamation to provide more water for threatened fish species. Refuges in the basin had survived by using agricultural drain water from farming operations, so if irrigators lost their water, refuges would suffer, too. Water conservation in the Imperial Valley had similar consequences for the Salton Sea and the birds that depend on it since excess water for farming within the Imperial Irrigation District had helped sustain the sea. Yet as famers used this water more efficiently and the saved water flowed to coastal cities, the Salton Sea diminished, leaving migratory waterfowl and other birds with less habitat in this part of the flyway.

These stories and others like them in the Far West illustrate the deep and complicated relationship between the irrigated landscape and wildlife refuges along the Pacific Flyway. Irrigators and agencies such as the Bureau of Reclamation had played a pivotal role in draining wetlands and diverting the water that once flowed into them. To perpetuate this landscape, irrigators needed sumps to hold excess drain water from their operations. Many, though not all, of the refuges within the wintering range of the Pacific Flyway were also sumps for excess irrigation water. Most refuges had limited water rights and some had none at all. Out of desperation, the FWS had relied largely on wastewater to support marshes and crops for migratory birds. These polluted sumps, which seemed so unappealing to the casual visitor, were the lifeline for the Pacific Flyway. The wastewater of agriculture helped sustain one of the great wildlife migrations on Earth.

This study complicates recent analyses of the state's role in environmental protection. In his book *Seeing Like a State*, James Scott argues that government conservation agencies were prone to a "high-modernist ideology" that saw the natural world as a set of resources capable of manipulation and simplification. Using the development of scientific forestry as his chief example, Scott shows how foresters attempted to regulate the forest in order to facilitate its conversion into commodities. Often this meant clearing the indigenous forest composed of many species and multi-aged stands of trees and replacing it with single-species and even-aged tree farms. Foresters attempted to eliminate everything that might damage merchantable timber (such as fire and insect pests). The goal was to manage the environment to maximize the output of a small set of commodities.[2]

In a similar fashion, the Fish and Wildlife Service tried to support more waterfowl through its management of the refuges. Although it never attempted to produce waterfowl artificially, it did try to manipulate the environment to support as many ducks and geese as possible. Along the Pacific Flyway, the FWS carried out most of its land management programs in the birds' wintering range. Farming and wetland restoration programs were designed to increase the availability of foods eaten by ducks and geese so that they could survive the winter and return to their summer breeding grounds. Although restoring and creating wetlands aided many plants and animals besides waterfowl, only the few species of ducks and geese that fed on wheat, barley, and rice benefited from refuge crops. By the late twentieth century, however, wildlife biologists understood that waterfowl needed a wider range of food than simply grains. Ducks and geese needed the plants and invertebrates found in wetlands as part of their diet.

Sport hunters were the intended beneficiaries of these programs. Hunters bought the duck stamps that enabled the FWS and state wildlife agencies to acquire more refuges. They also supported increased funding for the agency in times of need. Over much of its history, the FWS had struggled to decide whom it serves and, therefore, the purposes of the refuges. In the mid-twentieth century, sportsmen considered the refuges as places where hunters unaffiliated with private sporting clubs could hunt. The agency responded to this pressure and opened most of the Pacific Flyway refuges to hunters. Even there, ducks and geese faced the gauntlet of shooters that followed waterfowl throughout their annual migrations.

The FWS may have seen the wetlands and refuges along the flyway as a vast duck producing machine, but it faced serious constraints in its management. American and Canadian wildlife officials successfully developed methods to survey waterfowl populations in their breeding and wintering areas, and on the basis of such data, formulated hunting regulations. The real challenge with management, however, came at the local level. The FWS has never had as much control over its refuges as the U.S. Forest Service has over national forests or the National Park Service has over its parks. FWS refuges were too small and too much at the mercy of irrigators (and in some places, the Bureau of Reclamation). Indeed, many of the management programs the FWS attempted were responses to the agency's *lack* of control over water rather than its mastery of it. Since water supplies were limited on most Pacific Flyway refuges, refuge staff felt compelled to manage this vital resource closely by building dikes and canals to keep marshes and ponds at optimum water levels.

The environmental historian Donald Pisani argues persuasively that the U.S. conservation program was carried out by a fragmented collection of different federal and state agencies.[3] The Department of the Interior and the Department of Agriculture battled for funding; the Bureau of Biological Survey (and later the FWS) and the Bureau of Reclamation struggled over the use of water in the western United States. As conservationist and Bureau of Biological Survey head Ding Darling observed in the mid-1930s, "Conservation as a national principle has no stance or co-ordination. . . . Fourteen agencies in the Federal Government and forty-eight states with some semblance of an official organization in charge of conservation! But they are like so many trains running on single-track roads, often in opposite directions and without any train dispatcher or block system. Collisions are frequent, wrecks are a daily occurrence, and the destruction is greater than the freight delivered at the specified destination."[4] Bureaucratic fragmentation prevented the imposition of the unified conservation agenda, such that James Scott depicts in *Seeing Like a State*. There was not one state. Rather, many state agencies competed against one another, and often within the same federal department.

In the Klamath Basin, the federal government pursued two radically different agendas through the Bureau of Reclamation and the FWS. A relatively weak agency like the FWS could not impose its vision on the landscape; rather, it had to carve relatively small refuges within a landscape designed for other purposes.[5]

Yet there were commonalities with the way the Bureau of Reclamation and the FWS saw the landscape. For instance, Scott shows that one of the main pursuits of central planners was to make populations "legible" and easier to control. This was precisely what Frederick Lincoln and the Biological Survey tried to do with bird migration studies in the 1920s. Lincoln's flyway concept provided the Biological Survey with a simple, cartographic view of bird migration at a time when the agency was enlarging the refuge system. It provided a better basis for migratory waterfowl management than managing the refuges as individual, unconnected units. After the Second World War, the FWS and its Canadian counterparts surveyed the waterfowl breeding and wintering areas. With the results of these surveys and the concept of the flyway, wildlife agencies developed a rational basis for the scientific management of migratory waterfowl. Yet local conditions on or near the refuges impinged on the FWS's ability to act on its knowledge or on its capacity to manage the flyway as a system. Making birds "legible" did not necessarily make them simple to manage.

Over the past decade, the FWS has moved away from managing wildlife refuges solely for waterfowl to protecting biodiversity. Given the troubles the FWS had managing a handful of species, it seems doubtful that it will succeed in managing hundreds of them over more than 500 refuges in the federal system. Most federal refuges outside Alaska are simply too small to protect most species or preserve habitats at the landscape level. Yet this broadening of the FWS's vision is a welcome change from the narrow focus on migratory waterfowl characteristic of the agency's approach to refuge management in the past. In this way, the FWS is responding to Americans' growing appreciation of nongame species that have little direct economic use. So far, this appreciation has not translated into funding that will allow the FWS to achieve its new mandate.[6]

Society must decide how much it values migratory waterfowl and the wetlands that sustain them. For the past century, it has tried to protect waterfowl and wetlands as cheaply and easily as possible. By managing the sumps and wastewater from irrigated agriculture, the FWS has sustained migratory waterfowl on a shoestring budget. But relying on agricultural drain water to support the refuges has proved to be a mixed blessing. This system supported refuge marshes and farming programs, but the quality of water was often poor. For some refuges, such as Kesterson, the dependence on drain water proved lethal. Pesticide use near the refuges continues to be a problem. Although pesticides may not kill birds as widely as DDT did in the 1960s, the long-term consequences of their build up cannot be good. Yet, as poor as the quality of water often was, refuge managers could at least count on sufficient quantities to sustain refuge ponds and marshes. With the changes in water policy discussed above, even this now seems doubtful.

The future promises an even more challenging situation for migratory waterfowl as global warming alters climates and landscapes all along the Pacific Flyway. In California, for instance, climate models predict a radical diminishment of snowpacks in the Sierra Nevada Mountains with warmer temperatures. This will only aggravate the water conflicts downstream among municipal and agricultural water users. Since wildlife agencies and their supporters struggled throughout the twentieth century to secure adequate water for refuges, it is doubtful this will get any easier in the twenty-first century as the amount of available water for all uses decreases in a warmer world. Moreover, they will do so in a state where the population is expected to increase from 35 to 50 million people by 2025.[7] The Arctic and subarctic areas where many Pacific Flyway birds breed are already experiencing major warming, and climate models show this trend as continuing in the coming decades. This could lead to the disappearance of wetlands in some areas and the creation of new wetlands in others. Although the ultimate impact on migratory birds is difficult to predict, such change could alter the distribution of birds that use the Arctic and subarctic during the warmer months. Certainly, waterfowl have adapted to changing climatic conditions over the long span of geologic time. One might hope that they will continue to do so during this current period of warming. Yet in the wintering range of the birds, people have already claimed much of the water for other uses.

The survival of migratory waterfowl, at least in current numbers, will depend on wildlife officials securing stable water supplies on refuges and private land as this resource diminishes throughout the region.[8]

At the very least, federal refuges need more senior water rights than they now have. The long-standing arrangement to obtain water from irrigators is increasingly precarious. Wildlife refuges will suffer if irrigators lose water due to transfers from agricultural regions to urban areas or if more water remains in rivers and lakes to support endangered fish. FWS officials recognize this problem, and in the Klamath Basin, at least, they have filed water claims as part of the Klamath adjudication process. Until the adjudication is settled, however, refuges must continue to depend on irrigators for water. Environmentalists, with the support of some basin farmers, have proposed buying water rights from willing sellers to reduce the collective demand of irrigators on the waters of the Klamath Basin. Although this makes sense in principle, in practice it is politically dangerous. The perception among many farmers and their allies is that the water buy-out is a concerted effort by environmentalists and the federal government to remove people from the land. Environmentalists counter that farmers are suffering more from low crop prices than from endangered species legislation. Although that may be true, the policy makes environmentalists look like vultures waiting for farmers to go bankrupt so they can buy their water rights.

The challenge is to find a way to protect migratory waterfowl without sacrificing social justice. A number of recent works in environmental history and geography have shown how conservation initiatives often hurt rural people.[9] In the name of environmental protection, many rural people lost access to their land and resources. From this perspective, the proposal to purchase water rights from farmers in the Klamath Basin or use the Endangered Species Act to limit water deliveries is just another chapter in the conservation and environmental movements' history of insensitivity to rural concerns. However, the situation is more complicated in the Klamath Basin. There, the Klamath Tribes and the Yurok lost most of their access to water and fish in the wake of white settlement and the development of irrigation projects. Restoring salmon and sucker fish populations to healthy levels is part of the process of redressing past injustices, even though in the short term this may harm the mostly non-Indian farmers in the basin. A fair solution to the basin's water problems must provide for the needs of human communities as well as for the animals that have lost most of their habitat due to water development.

Migratory waterfowl and salmon, though very different species, share one thing in common. Both are migratory animals who have fared poorly over the past century. Decades of development have altered the rivers that salmon and waterfowl depend upon almost beyond recognition. Given their long migratory journeys, salmon and waterfowl must contend with numerous threats.[10] Our solution has been to open much of the landscape to development and parcel out small parts for wild creatures to use. Worse still, the needed water for both salmon and waterfowl was often too limited or of too poor quality to benefit these species.

Pacific Flyway waterfowl vividly demonstrate that the landscapes of the Far West are a shared space. Through their migratory journeys, these birds connect seemingly disparate places, since for them, the wetlands along the flyway serve as one habitat. If waterfowl and other birds are to have a future, society must cultivate and support the spaces they need to survive. Yet as this history demonstrates, this does not mean creating separate places apart from society or trying to restore landscapes to pristine conditions. Migratory waterfowl have survived in some of the most intensely transformed landscapes in North America. But if they are to thrive, rather than merely endure in small numbers, they need more than marginal land and waste water from agriculture. Having claimed the habitat of migratory waterfowl to build our farms and cities, it is time to give some of that space back. The Pacific Flyway—tattered and frayed as it is—can still endure, but it will require more generosity than we have offered in the past.

CITATION ABBREVIATIONS

KBNWR-HQ   Klamath Basin National Wildlife Refuges Headquarters, Tulelake, California.

NR-KBNWR   Annual Narrarive Reports, Klamath Basin National Wildlife Refuge.

NR-KBNWR   Annual Narrative Reports. Klamath Basin National Basin National Wildlife Refuge.

NR-SNWR   Annual Narrative Reports, Sacramento National Wildlife Refuge Complex.

RG 22, NA-CP   Record Group 22. U.S. Fish and Wildlife Service Records, National Archives and Records Administration, College Park, Maryland.

RG 22, NA-S   Record Group 22. U.S. Fish and Wildlife
Service Records, National Archives and Records
Administration, Pacific Alaska Region, Seattle,
Washington.

SNWR-HQ   Sacramento National Wildlife Refuge Complex
Headquarters, Willows, California.

WFP   William L. Finley Papers, Oregon State University,
Corvallis, Oregon.

NOTES

INTRODUCTION

1   The other flyways are the Central, Mississippi, and Atlantic.

2   Guy A. Baldassarre and Eric G. Bolen, *Waterfowl Ecology and Management*, 2nd ed. (Malabar, Fla.: Krieger Publishing Company, 2006), 373.

3   Richard Walker, *The Conquest of Bread: 150 Years of Agribusiness in California* (New York: The New Press, 2004), 1.

4   Samuel P. Hays, *Conservation and the Gospel of Efficiency: The Progressive Conservation Movement, 1890–1920* (Cambridge, Mass.: Harvard University Press, 1959); Paul W. Hirt, *A Conspiracy of Optimism: Management of the National Forests since World War II* (Lincoln: University of Nebraska Press, 1994); Donald J. Pisani, *To Reclaim a Divided West: Water, Law, and Public Policy, 1848–1902* (Albuquerque: University of New Mexico Press, 1992), "Federal Water Policy and the Rural West," in *The Rural West since World War II*, ed. R. Douglas Hurt (Lawrence: University Press of Kansas, 1998), and *Water and American Government: The Reclamation Bureau, National Water Policy, and the West, 1902–1935* (Berkeley: University of California Press, 2002); Nancy Langston, *Where Land and Water Meet: A Western Landscape Transformed* (Seattle: University of Washington Press, 2003); Hal Rothman, *America's National Monuments: The Politics of Preservation* (Lawrence: University Press of

Kansas, 1989); Alfred Runte, *National Parks: The American Experience,* 3rd ed. (Lincoln: University of Nebraska Press, 1997); Richard West Sellars, *Preserving Nature in the National Parks: A History* (New Haven, Conn: Yale University Press, 1997); Donald Worster, *Rivers of Empire: Water, Aridity, and the Growth of the American West* (New York: Pantheon Books, 1985).

5   Mark Fiege, *Irrigated Eden: The Making of an Agricultural Landscape in the American West* (Seattle: University of Washington Press, 1999), 60–61, 69–73, and "Private Property and Ecological Commons in the American West," in *Everyday America: Cultural Landscape Studies after J. B. Jackson,* ed. Chris Wilson and Paul Groth (Berkeley: University of California Press, 2003), 219–31; and Ted Steinberg, *Down to Earth: Nature's Role in American History* (New York: Oxford University Press, 2002), x, 59–61.

6   Julia Haggerty and William Travis, "Out of Administrative Control: Absentee Owners, Resident Elk and the Shifting Nature of Wildlife Management in Southwestern Montana," *Geoforum* 37, no. 5 (2006): 816–30.

7   Mark Fiege, "The Weedy West: Mobile Nature, Boundaries, and Common Space in the Montana Landscape," *Western Historical Quarterly* 36, no. 1 (2005).

8   "Interview with William Cronon," *Scapes,* 5 (Fall 2006): 37.

9   Kurkpatrick Dorsey discusses the Migratory Bird Treaty as well as other environmental protection agreements of the time in *The Dawn of Conservation Diplomacy: U.S.-Canadian Wildlife Protection Treaties in the Progressive Era* (Seattle: University of Washington Press, 1998), 165–237. See also Janet Foster, *Working for Wildlife: The Beginnings of Preservation in Canada,* 2nd ed. (Toronto: University of Toronto Press, 1998).

10 On legibility, see James C. Scott, *Seeing Like a State: How Certain Schemes to Improve the Human Condition Have Failed* (New Haven, Conn.: Yale University Press, 1998), 1–24.

11 Given the importance of the U.S. Fish and Wildlife Service in protecting endangered and threatened species, it has received remarkably little attention from historians or geographers. An administrative history of the U.S. Fish and Wildlife Service has yet to be written, but for a brief overview, see Mark Madison's entry on the agency in *The Encyclopedia of World Environmental History,* ed. Shepard Krech III, John R. McNeill, and Carolyn Merchant (New York: Routledge, 2004). See also Steve Chase and Mark Madison, "The Expanding Ark: 100 Years

of Wildlife Refuges," *Wild Earth*, Winter 2003–2004, 18–27; Langston, *Where Land and Water Meet*; Mark Madison, "Conserving Conservation: Field Notes from an Animal Archive," *The Public Historian* (2004): 145–56; Nathan F. Sayre, *Ranching, Endangered Species, and Urbanization in the Southwest: Species of Capital* (Tucson: University of Arizona Press, 2002); and Thomas R. Vale, *The American Wilderness: Reflections on Nature Protection in the United States* (Charlottesville: University of Virginia Press, 2005), 140–59.

12 W. E. Frayer, Dennis D. Peters, and H. Ross Pywell, "Wetlands of the Central Valley: Status and Trends, 1939 to Mid-1980s" (Portland, Ore.: United States Fish and Wildlife Service, 1989).

13 Nancy Langston discuses the rationale for and consequences of simplifying complex ecosystems to produce more commodities in *Forest Dreams, Forest Nightmares: The Paradox of Old Growth in the Inland West* (Seattle: University of Washington Press, 1995).

14 On hybrid nature, see Fiege, *Irrigated Eden*; Bruno Latour, *We Have Never Been Modern* (Cambridge, Mass.: Harvard University Press, 1993); Richard White, *The Organic Machine: The Remaking of the Columbia River* (New York: Hill and Wang, 1995). California's agricultural landscape has received a great deal of critical attention from geographers. See George L. Henderson, *California and the Fictions of Capital* (New York: Oxford University Press, 2000); Don Mitchell, *The Lie of the Land: Migrant Workers and the California Landscape* (Minneapolis: University of Minnesota Press, 1996); Walker, *Conquest of Bread*. Walker's work in particular has informed my thinking about agribusiness, industrial agriculture, and wildlife refuges.

15 On the history of hunting, see Matt Cartmill, *A View to a Death in the Morning: Hunting and Nature through History* (Cambridge, Mass.: Harvard University Press, 1993); Karl Jacoby, *Crimes Against Nature: Squatters, Poachers, Thieves, and the Hidden History of American Conservation* (Berkeley: University of California Press, 2001); Tina Loo, *States of Nature: Conserving Canada's Wildlife in the Twentieth Century* (Vancouver: UBC Press, 2006); John F. Reiger, *American Sportsmen and the Origins of Conservation*, 3rd ed. (Corvallis: Oregon State University Press, 2001); James Tober, *Who Owns the Wildlife? The Political Economy of Conservation in Nineteenth-Century America* (Westport, Conn.: Greenwood Press, 1981); Louis S. Warren, *The Hunter's Game: Poachers and Conservationists in Twentieth-Century America* (New Haven, Conn.: Yale University Press, 1997).

16 For overviews of the landscape idea in geography, see Don Mitchell, *Cultural Geography: A Critical Introduction* (Oxford: Blackwell Publishers Ltd., 2000), 1–34, 89–144, and John Wylie, *Landscape* (New York: Routledge, 2007). See also Carl Sauer, "The Morphology of Landscape," in *Land and Life: A Selection from the Writings of Carl Ortwin Sauer*, ed. John Leighly (Berkeley: University of California Press, 1965), and Donald W. Meinig, ed., *The Interpretation of Ordinary Landscapes* (Oxford: Oxford University Press, 1979).

17 Mitchell, *Lie of the Land*; Dennis E. Cosgrove, *Social Formation and Symbolic Landscape* (Madison: University of Wisconsin Press, 1984).

18 Mark V. Barrow Jr., *A Passion for Birds: American Ornithology after Audubon* (Princeton, N.J.: Princeton University Press, 1998), 102–25, 150–82, and Jennifer Price, *Flight Maps: Adventures with Nature in Modern America* (New York: Basic Books, 1999), 101–9.

1 · THE WETLAND ARCHIPELAGO

1 Tupper Ansel Blake and Peter Steinhart, *Tracks in the Sky: Wildlife and Wetlands of the Pacific Flyway* (San Francisco: Chronicle Books, 1987), 28.

2 Noble S. Proctor and Patrick J. Lynch, *Manual of Ornithology: Avian Structure and Function* (New Haven, Conn.: Yale University Press, 1993), 270–73.

3 Of course, the way they use these wetlands varies. In the summer, waterfowl need wetlands for molting and nesting, and during the winter they use them for food, rest, and cover.

4 Native people did have an impact on other aspects of the environment. However, they had a limited impact on the *hydrology* of wetlands. For discussions of the significant ways that Native groups in western North America affected wildlife populations and transformed landscapes, see Joseph Taylor III, *Making Salmon: An Environmental History of the Northwest Fisheries Crisis* (Seattle: University of Washington Press, 1999), 13–38; William Preston, "Serpent in the Garden: Environmental Change in Colonial California," in *Contested Eden: California Before the Gold Rush*, ed. Ramón A. Gutiérrez and Richard J. Orsi (Berkeley: University of California Press, 1998), 260–98; Stephen J. Pyne, *Fire in America: A Cultural History of Wildland and Rural Fire* (Princeton, N.J.: Princeton University Press, 1982), 71–83; William Robbins, *Landscapes of Promise: The Oregon Story, 1800–1940* (Seattle: University of Washington Press, 1997), 23–49.

5   Thomas Alerstam, *Bird Migration* (Cambridge: Cambridge University Press, 1990), 226. George Cox discusses the different theories explaining the development of bird migration in "The Evolution of Avian Migration Systems between the Temperate and Tropical Regions of the New World," *The American Naturalist* 126, no. 4 (1985): 451–56.

6   For an overview of the threats facing birds and other migratory species, see David S. Wilcove, *No Way Home: The Decline of the World's Great Animal Migrations* (Washington, D.C.: Island Press, 2007).

7   Baldassarre and Bolen, *Waterfowl Ecology and Management*, 390–91; Robert H. Smith, Frank Dufresne, and Henry A. Hansen, "Northern Watersheds and Deltas," in *Waterfowl Tomorrow*, ed. Joseph P. Linduska, (Washington, D.C.: United States Department of the Interior, Bureau of Sport Fisheries and Wildlife, Fish and Wildlife Service, 1964), 61–63; Blake and Steinhart, *Tracks in the Sky*, 4, 26; Frank C. Bellrose, *Ducks, Geese, and Swans of North America* (Harrisburg, Pa.: Stackpole Books, 1980), 114–15.

8   Baldassarre and Bolen, *Waterfowl Ecology and Management*, 390; Smith, Dufresne, and Hansen, "Northern Watersheds and Deltas," 57–59.

9   Baldassarre and Bolen, *Waterfowl Ecology and Management*, 388–89; Smith, Dufresne, and Hansen, "Northern Watersheds and Deltas," 51–52, 65–66.

10 Bruce D. J. Batt, Michael G. Anderson, C. Diane Anderson, and F. Dale Caswell, "The Use of Prairie Potholes by North American Ducks," in *Northern Prairie Wetlands*, ed. Arnold van der Valk (Ames: Iowa State University Press, 1989), 204–25; George A. Swanson and Harold F. Duebbert, "Wetland Habitats of Waterfowl in the Prairie Pothole Region," in ibid., 228–67.

11 Allen G. Smith, Jerome H. Stoudt, and J. Bernard Gollop, "Prairie Potholes and Marshes," in *Waterfowl Tomorrow*, ed. Joseph P. Linduska (Washington, D.C.: United States Department of the Interior, Bureau of Sport Fisheries and Wildlife, Fish and Wildlife Service, 1964), 39–50.

12 Henry R. Murkin and Patrick J. Caldwell, "Avian Use of Prairie Wetlands," in *Prairie Wetland Ecology: the Contribution of the Marsh Ecology Research Program*, ed. Henry R. Murkin, Arnold G. van der Valk, and William R. Clark (Ames: Iowa State University Press, 2000), 274–75; William J. Mitsch and James G. Gosselink, *Wetlands*, 3rd ed. (New York: John Wiley & Sons, Inc., 2000), 96–97.

13 The terms "breeding" and "wintering" areas should be seen as existing in a continuum rather than at two poles. In general, if food and open water were available during the colder months, waterfowl could winter in areas

that were primarily used for breeding. Waterfowl also used some important wintering areas, such as the Central Valley, for breeding. However, these areas did not support breeding waterfowl in the numbers that the Prairie Pothole region or the river deltas in the North did.

14   R. Wayne Campbell et al., *The Birds of British Columbia: Volume I. Non-passerines. Introduction and Loons through Waterfowl*, vol. I (Victoria, B.C.: Royal British Columbia Museum, 1990), passim; O. Slaymaker, M. Bovis, M. North, T. R. Oke, and J. Ryder, "The Primordial Environment," in *Vancouver and Its Region*, ed. Graeme Wynn and Timothy Oke (Vancouver: UBC Press, 1992), 36–37.

15   Arthur R. Kruckeberg, *The Natural History of Puget Sound Country* (Seattle: University of Washington Press, 1991), 276–84; Matthew W. Klingle, *Emerald City: An Environmental History of Seattle* (New Haven, Conn.: Yale University Press, 2007), 22–89.

16   John A. Kadlec and Loren M. Smith, "The Great Basin Marshes," in *Habitat Management for Migrating and Wintering Waterfowl in North America*, ed. Loren M. Smith, Roger L. Pederson, and Richard M. Kaminski (Lubbock: Texas Tech University Press, 1989), 451–56. See also Donald K. Grayson, *Desert's Past: A Natural Prehistory of the Great Basin* (Washington, D.C.: Smithsonian Institution Press, 1993); Fred A. Ryser Jr., *Birds of the Great Basin: A Natural History* (Reno: University of Nevada Press, 1985), 1–14; Joseph R. Jehl Jr., "Changes in Saline and Alkaline Lake Avifaunas in Western North America in the Past 150 Years," in *A Century of Avifaunal Change in Western North America*, ed. Joseph R. Jehl Jr. and Ned K. Johnson, Studies in Avian Biology No. 15 (Cooper Ornithological Society, 1994), 258–72.

17   Samuel N. Dicken, "Pluvial Lake Modoc, Klamath County, Oregon, and Modoc and Siskiyou Counties, California," *Oregon Geology* 42, no. 11 (1980): 179–87; Grayson, *Desert's Past*, 97–98, 111; and Stephen Trimble, *The Sagebrush Ocean: A Natural History of the Great Basin* (Reno: University of Nevada Press, 1989), 136–40.

18   Grayson, *Desert's Past*, 194–97, 208–21.

19   Technically, the Klamath Basin is just to the west of the Great Basin boundary. Unlike other valleys in the Great Basin, it is drained by a river (the Klamath River, which empties into the Pacific). But as the rest of the discussion shows, the area has many similarities to Great Basin lakes and marshes.

20   Waterfowl population estimates are for the 1950s. USDI Fish and Wildlife Service, Office of Regional Director, Portland 18, Oregon, "Special Report on Waterfowl Requirements: Tule Lake and Lower Klamath

National Wildlife Refuges, Klamath Basin, California and Oregon," Refuge Files, KBNWR-HQ, 15–17; D. S. Gilmer, J. L. Yee, and D. M. Mauser, "Waterfowl Migration on Klamath Basin National Wildlife Refuges, 1953–2001," U.S. Geological Survey, Biological Resources Discipline Biological Science Report, USGS/BRD/BSR, 2004, 1.

21 Stanton B. Turner, "Reclamation—A New Look for the Tule Lake and Klamath Lake Basins," *Journal of the Shaw Historical Library* 2, no. 2 (1988): 30.

22 Norris Hundley Jr., *The Great Thirst: Californians and Water: A History*, rev. ed. (Berkeley: University of California Press, 2001), 5–9; Allan A. Schoenherr, *A Natural History of California* (Berkeley: University of California Press, 1992), 516–19; Mickey E. Heitmeyer, Daniel P. Connelly, and Roger L. Pederson, "The Central, Imperial, and Cochella Valleys of California," in Smith, Pederson, and Kaminski, *Habitat Management*, 475; Baldassarre and Bolen, *Waterfowl Ecology and Management*, 407–10.

23 Heitmeyer, Connelly, and Pederson, "The Central, Imperial, and Cochella Valleys," 476–80.

24 Ann Vileisis, *Discovering the Unknown Landscape: A History of America's Wetlands* (Washington, D.C.: Island Press, 1997), 26, 355.

25 Baldassarre and Bolen, *Waterfowl Ecology and Management*, 407.

26 David S. Gilmer, Michael R. Miller, Richard D. Bauer, and John R. LeDonne, "California's Central Valley Wintering Waterfowl: Concerns and Challenges," *Transactions of the North American Wildlife and Natural Resources Conference* 47 (1982): 441.

27 However, as I will show in future chapters, some of the natural wetlands were replaced by cultivated wetlands such as rice fields, which waterfowl used. The development of cereal crops in the Central Valley also offset the loss of natural wetland foods, since some species of waterfowl (particularly geese) can consume crops such as wheat and barley.

28 Godfrey Sykes, *The Colorado Delta* (Washington, D.C.: Carnegie Institution of Washington and the American Geographical Society of New York, 1937), 1, 3; Edward P. Glenn, Christopher Lee, and Carlos Valdes-Casillas, "Introduction," *Journal of Arid Environments* 49 (2001): 1–4; and Jennifer Pitt, "Can We Restore the Colorado River Delta?" *Journal of Arid Environments* 49 (2001): 211–13.

29 Aldo Leopold, *A Sand County Almanac, and Sketches Here and There* (New York: Oxford University Press, 1949; repr., New York: Oxford University Press, 1989), 146, 148.

30 On the identification of bison and salmon with their environments, see Andrew C. Isenberg, *The Destruction of the Bison: An Environmen-*

tal History, 1750–1920 (Cambridge: Cambridge University Press, 2000); Taylor, *Making Salmon*; and White, *Organic Machine*, 90–92.

31 Baldassarre and Bolen, *Waterfowl Ecology and Management*, 167, 178–89.

32 Although it seems commonsensical for birds to migrate from north to south and back again, this is not the case with birds flying along major migration routes elsewhere in the world. Many species in Europe and Asia, for instance, migrate along an east-west axis. Scott Weidensaul, *Living on the Wind: Across the Hemisphere with Migratory Birds* (New York: North Point Press, 1999), 21, 33.

33 Some mammals, such as caribou, do make annual migrations of hundreds of miles. Yet compared to the thousands of miles covered by many species of migrating birds, the migrations of caribou and other terrestrial mammals are relatively short.

34 Peter Berthold, *Bird Migration: A General Survey*, 2nd ed. (Oxford: Oxford University Press, 2001), 1–2.

35 Hugh Dingle, *Migration: The Biology of Life on the Move* (New York: Oxford University Press, 1996), 23. Another example familiar to many is the migration of salmon from the ocean up rivers and streams. Salmon will continue on their journey without feeding until they arrive at their spawning grounds or die in the process.

36 Ibid., 322–23, 350.

37 Baldassarre and Bolen, *Waterfowl Management*, 178–81.

38 Weidensaul, *Living on the Wind*, 68.

39 Ibid., 68–74.

40 Bellrose, *Ducks, Geese, and Swans*, 112–23.

41 Ibid., 102–9.

42 Ibid., 262–70.

43 "Migration depends upon links—food, safe havens, quiet roost sites, clean water, and a host of other resources, strung out in due measure and regular occurrence along routes that may cross thousands of miles. But we are breaking those links with abandon." Weidensaul, *Living on the Wind*, 27.

2 · ELUSIVE SANCTUARIES

1 Mitsch and Gosselink, *Wetlands*, 84. These figures represent wetland loss up to 1990. However, as this chapter shows, much of the wetland loss occurred before the 1940s. See also Frayer, Peters, and Pywell, "Wetlands of the Central Valley."

2 The Prairie Pothole region was an exception to this rule. However, as

discussed in the previous chapter, the Prairie Pothole was less important overall for Pacific Flyway waterfowl, especially in comparison to birds that migrated along other flyways.

3   Linda Nash, *Inescapable Ecologies: A History of Environment, Disease, and Knowledge* (Berkeley: University of California Press, 2006), 66. On American views toward wetlands, see Ann Vileisis, *Discovering the Unknown Landscape: A History of America's Wetlands* (Washington, D.C.: Island Press, 1997), 51–69.

4   Peter Steinhart coined the phrase "draining the skies." Blake and Steinhart, *Tracks in the Sky*, 108.

5   T. R. Oke, M. North, O. Slaymaker, and D. G. Steyn, "Primordial to Prim Order: A Century of Environmental Change" in Wynn and Oke, *Vancouver and Its Region*; Cole Harris, "The Lower Mainland, 1820–81," in ibid., 149–70; Alfred H. Siemens, "The Process of Settlement in the Lower Fraser Valley—In Its Provincial Context," in *Lower Fraser Valley: Evolution of a Cultural Landscape*, ed. Alfred H. Siemens (Vancouver: Tantalus Research Limited, 1968), 27–39; George R. Winter, "Agricultural Development in the Lower Fraser Valley," in ibid., 101–16; Barry Leach, "Waterfowl on a Pacific Estuary: A Natural History of Man and Waterfowl on the Lower Fraser River," British Columbia Provincial Museum Special Publication no. 5 (Victoria: British Columbia Provincial Museum, 1982); Laura Cameron, *Openings: A Meditation on History, Method, and Sumas Lake* (Montreal and Kingston: McGill-Queen's University Press, 1997).

6   Cameron, *Openings*, 50–57. Sumas Lake lay within the Railway Belt, an area twenty miles wide on each side of the Canadian Pacific Railway line. British Columbia ceded land within the belt to the dominion in 1883, but in 1896, the dominion returned Sumas Lake to the province.

7   Ibid., 60–74; James Murton, *Creating a Modern Countryside: Liberalism and Land Resettlement in British Columbia* (Vancouver: UBC Press, 2007), 109–35.

8   Historian James Murton discusses the emergence of the new liberal order and its environmental implications in *Creating a Modern Countryside*, 1–17, 109–33.

9   Quotation in W. R. Derrick Sewell, *Water Management and Floods in the Fraser River Basin*, Department of Geography, Research Paper No. 100 (Chicago: The University of Chicago, 1965), 49.

10 Sewell, *Water Management*, 37–59; Ellis Ladner, *Above the Sand Heads: A Vivid Account of Life on the Delta of the Fraser River, 1868–1900* (Cloverdale, B.C.: D. W. Friesen & Sons Ltd., 1979), 37–38; Slaymaker et al.,

"The Primordial Environment," 37–38; Oke et al., "Primordial to Prim Order," 153–54; Wendy J. Hales, "The Impact of Human Activity on Deltaic Sedimentation, Marshes of the Fraser River Delta, British Columbia" (PhD diss., University of British Columbia, 2000), 20–23, 42–46. Salt marshes continue to form on the leading edge of the Fraser River Delta, which compensates somewhat for the marshes lost to diking and drainage. Information about the effect of riprap on wetland formation obtained from Wendy Hales, personal communication, 18 February 2003, and Darren Ham, personal communication, 19 February 2003. The original dikes did not have riprap to protect them. It was installed later, though the exact timing is unclear.

11 Vileisis, *Discovering the Unknown Landscape*, 72–73, 76–78; Benjamin Horace Hibbard, *A History of the Public Land Policies* (New York: The Macmillan Company, 1924; repr., Madison: University of Wisconsin Press, 1965), 269–88.

12 Major floods affected the Sacramento repeatedly from the 1850s to the 1880s (1853, 1867–68, 1871–72, 1873, 1875, and 1881). Robert Kelley, *Battling the Inland Sea: American Political Culture, Public Policy, and the Sacramento Valley, 1850–1986* (Berkeley: University of California Press, 1989), 16, 83, 118–19, 160–61, 168–70, 217.

13 Kelley, *Battling the Inland Sea*, 45–154; Vileisis, *Discovering the Unknown Landscape*, 128–31; Hundley, *Great Thirst*, 79–84. Philip Garone provides a thorough analysis of the destruction of wetlands in the Sacramento Valley and the development of the flood control project. See "The Fall and Rise of the Wetlands of California's Great Central Valley: A Historical and Ecological Study of an Endangered Resource of the Pacific Flyway," (PhD diss., University of California–Davis, 2006), 179–210.

14 Kelley, *Battling the Inland Sea*, 249–302; Hundley, *Great Thirst*, 237–40.

15 Karen M. O'Neill, *Rivers by Design: State Power and the Origins of U.S. Flood Control* (Durham, N.C.: Duke University Press, 2006), 3–12.

16 Since natural resources are a provincial responsibility in Canada, the Canadian federal government had less jurisdiction over flood control than the U.S. federal government did over such matters in the United States.

17 The San Joaquin is the southern portion of the Central Valley. Although the Central Valley is the collective name for the Sacramento and San Joaquin valleys, the two sub-valleys have important climatological and hydrological differences. The San Joaquin Valley is drier than the Sacramento Valley (the former receiving less than ten inches precipitation

annually, the latter between ten and twenty inches), and the San Joaquin River is much smaller in terms of discharge than the Sacramento River.

18 The Miller & Lux properties in the San Joaquin Valley were extensive but not contiguous. The company also owned land in Nevada and Oregon (which is included in the acreage total cited), but most of its holdings were in California. See David Igler, *Industrial Cowboys: Miller & Lux and the Transformation of the Far West, 1850–1920* (Berkeley: University of California Press, 2001), 6.

19 Cited in William L. Preston, *Vanishing Landscape: Land and Life in the Tulare Lake Basin* (Berkeley: University of California Press, 1981), 158.

20 Ibid., 136–44, 158–61; Igler, *Industrial Cowboys*, 112–13, 115, 117.

21 Robert A. Sauder, *The Lost Frontier: Water Diversions in the Growth and Destruction of Owens Valley Agriculture* (Tucson: University of Arizona Press, 1994), 96–97, 164; Richard White, *"It's Your Misfortune and None of My Own": A New History of the American West* (Norman: University of Oklahoma Press, 1991), 423–25; Hundley, *Great Thirst*, 141–67, 353–59; David E. Babb, "History of Early Water Diversions and Their Impact of Owens Lake," in *The History of Water: Eastern Sierra Nevada, Owens Valley, White-Inyo Mountains*, ed. C. A. Hall, Jr., V. Doyle-Jones, and B. Widawski, White Mountain Research Station Symposium, vol. 4, 263–67 (Los Angeles: White Mountain Research Station, 1992); Peter Vorster, "The Development and Decline of Agriculture in the Owens Valley," in ibid., 269–84. Dust storms became more severe decades later when the Los Angeles Department of Water and Power began pumping groundwater out of Owens Valley, leading to the destruction of riparian areas along the lower reaches of the Owens River.

22 San Francisco Bay Area Wetlands Ecosystem Goals Project, "Baylands Ecosystem Habitat Goals: A Report of Habitat Recommendations Prepared by the San Francisco Bay Area Wetlands Ecosystem Goals Project," U.S. Environmental Protection Agency, San Francisco, California/San Francisco Bay Regional Water Quality Control Board, Oakland, California (San Francisco: 1999), 21–27; California Department of Water Resources, "Suisin Marsh Facts," Suisin Marsh Program, http://www.iep.water.ca.gov/suisun/facts/history.html (accessed June 2009).

23 William deBuys provides the best account of the creation of the Salton Sea. See William deBuys and Joan Meyers, *Salt Dreams: Land and Water in Low-Down California* (Albuquerque: University of New Mexico Press, 1999), 77–82, 90–95, 98–121. See also Worster, *Rivers of Empire*, 194–97, and Hundley, *Great Thirst*, 207–8.

24 On Lux v. Haggin, see Igler, *Industrial Cowboys*, 92–121. On the controversies surrounding the diversion of water to Los Angeles and the damming of Hetch Hetchy, see White, *"It's Your Misfortune and None of My Own,"* 412–13, 423–24; Runte, *National Parks*, 78–81, 89–99; and Robert W. Righter, *The Battle over Hetch Hetchy: America's Most Controversial Dam and the Birth of Modern Environmentalism* (New York: Oxford University Press, 2005).

25 On the "double agenda," see Vileisis, *Discovering the Unknown Landscape*, 167–94.

26 The phrase "irrigated Eden" comes from Mark Fiege's book of the same name about reclamation and water development in Idaho.

27 Turner, "Reclamation," 25–26; Robbins, *Landscapes of Promise*, 250–51.

28 "Dewater" is awkward, but there is no good substitute for the word. Irrigators and the Reclamation Service rarely drained western marshes. Rather, they dammed or diverted water that fed shallow lakes, such as Lower Klamath or Tule. In the hot dry climate, the water evaporated—as was the case for Tulare and Owens lakes in southern California. Melting snow pack from the Cascade Mountains was the source of water for most of the lakes in the Klamath Basin. The exception to this was Tule Lake, which received water from Clear Lake via the Lost River.

29 Worster, *Rivers of Empire*, 130–31, 160–70; Marc Reisner, *Cadillac Desert: The American West and Its Disappearing Water* (New York: Penguin Books, 1986), 115–20; Carl Abbott, "The Federal Presence," in *The Oxford History of the American West*, ed. Clyde A. Milner II, Carol A. O'Connor, and Martha A. Sandweiss (New York: Oxford University Press, 1994), 471; Pisani, *Water and American Government*, 1.

30 Even though Tule Lake had no surface outlet, some engineers and hydrologists suspected that water drained through permeable vesicular basalt at the southern end of the lake in what is now Lava Beds National Monument. See Turner, "Reclamation," 30.

31 Turner, "Reclamation," 30, 32; U.S. Reclamation Service, "History of the Klamath Project, Oregon-California (from May 1, 1903 to December 31, 1912)," report on file in the Bureau of Reclamation, Klamath Irrigation Project Headquarters, Klamath Falls, Oregon (1912).

32 Donald J. Pisani, *From Family Farm to Agribusiness: The Irrigation Crusade in California and the West, 1850–1931* (Berkeley: University of California Press, 1984), 320–24; Turner, "Reclamation," 28–29. The Reclamation Service also considered constructing an irrigation project in the Malheur Basin, which contained Malheur Lake, another important wetland area

for migratory birds. It abandoned the plan due to contested water rights on the rivers that fed the lake and due to soil surveys that suggested the lake would be unfit for agriculture. See Langston, *Where Land and Water Meet*, 58–60, 71–72.

33 Barrow, *A Passion for Birds*, 133–34; Frank Graham Jr., *The Audubon Ark: A History of the National Audubon Society* (New York: Alfred A. Knopf, 1990), 19–22.

34 Barrow, *A Passion for Birds*, 117–20, 126–34; Graham, *Audubon Ark*, 28–33.

35 Robin W. Doughty, *Feather Fashions and Bird Preservation: A Study in Nature Protection* (Berkeley: University of California Press, 1975), 109–10.

36 William L. Finley, "Hunting Birds with a Camera: A Record of Twenty Years of Adventure in Obtaining Photographs of Feathered Wild Life in America," *National Geographic* 1923, 188. Quotation in Betty Lou Byrne-Shirley, "The Refuges," *The Journal of the Modoc County Historical Society*, no. 18 (1996): 31–32.

37 For a discussion of Finley and Bohlman's trip to Malheur Lake, see Langston, *Where Land and Water Meet*, 63–64.

38 On Finley's approach to filming nature and his contributions to wildlife filmmaking, see Gregg Mitman, *Reel Nature: America's Romance with Wildlife on Film* (Cambridge, Mass.: Harvard University Press, 1999), 96–99. Ansel Adams is undoubtedly the most famous American photographer of nature in the twentieth century. Jonathan Spaulding examines Adams's immense influence on nature photography and his role in modern environmentalism in *Ansel Adams and the American Landscape: A Biography* (Berkeley: University of California Press, 1995).

39 Photographs from Finley and Bohlman's trips are located in the William L. Finley Collection, Oregon Historical Society archives, Portland, Oregon. See also Worth Mathewson, *William L. Finley: Pioneer Wildlife Photographer* (Corvallis: Oregon State University Press, 1986). For accounts of this journey and others to the Oregon lakes, see William L. Finley, "In Search of the Plume Hunters," *Atlantic Monthly*, September 1905, 374–75; ibid., "Cruising the Klamath," *Bird Lore*, Nov.–Dec. 1915, 485–91; ibid., "Hunting Birds with a Camera," 160–201. Richard White discusses the connection between work and play in nature in "'Are You an Environmentalist or Do You Work for a Living?': Work and Nature," in *Uncommon Ground: Toward Reinventing Nature*, ed. William Cronon (New York: W. W. Norton & Company, 1995), 171–85.

40 Finley met Roosevelt during the president's visit to Portland, Oregon, in 1903. Over the years they became friends, and the president encouraged

Finley's work. In 1906, Finley went to Washington, D.C., to meet with Roosevelt in the White House and to show him photographs from his visit with Bohlman to the Klamath Basin. See Douglas Brinkley, *The Wilderness Warrior: Theodore Roosevelt and the Crusade for America*, (New York: HarperCollins, 2009), 715–18, 743–49.

41 Graham, *Audubon Ark*; Ira N. Gabrielson, *Wildlife Refuges* (New York: The Macmillan Company, 1943), 8–13; Albert M. Day, *North American Waterfowl* (New York: Stackpole and Heck, Inc., 1949), 148–49.

42 Reports from Finley were published annually in the November–December issue of *Bird Lore*. For Finley's views and his summaries of the bird protection efforts in the region, see his reports in volumes 13–18 (1911–1916).

43 Theodore Roosevelt, Executive Order, No. 924 (8 August 1908), Refuge Files, KBNWR-HQ.

44 The Bureau of Biological Survey (or the Fish and Wildlife Service) has received little attention from scholars. Information about the agency can be found in Jenks Cameron, *The Bureau of Biological Survey: Its History, Activities and Organization* (Baltimore: Johns Hopkins University Press, 1929); Donald Worster, *Nature's Economy: A History of Ecological Ideas*, 2nd ed. (Cambridge: Cambridge University Press, 1994), 262–65; Matthew D. Evenden, "The Laborers of Nature: Economic Ornithology and the Role of Birds as Agents of Biological Pest Control in North American Agriculture, ca. 1880–1930," *Forest & Conservation History* 39 (October 1995): 172–83; and Barrow, *A Passion for Birds*, 59–61, 171–72. Like many federal conservation agencies, this agency changed its name many times. The agency became a bureau in 1905 and continued to be called the Bureau of Biological Survey until merging with the Bureau of Fisheries to become the Fish and Wildlife Service in 1940. The full administrative history of the agency can be found on the National Archives and Records Administration, Records of the U.S. Fish and Wildlife Service web site, http://www.archives.gov/research_room/federal_records_guide/fish_and_wildlife_service_rg022.html#, 22.1. (accessed 20 August 2009).

45 William L. Finley to William Dutcher, 18 September 1908, Wildlife Refuge Reference List, Division of Wildlife Refuges, Bureau of Biological Survey Records, RG 22, NA-CP. Lewis chose this line of work due to an illness, although he never specified what kind. See L. Alva Lewis to Wm. L. Finley, 5 May 1909, and L. Alva Lewis to T. S. Palmer, 3 April 1910, ibid.

46   L. Alva Lewis, "Month Ending August 31, 1909," ibid.

47   L. Alva Lewis, "Month Ending October 31, 1909," ibid.

48   L. Alva Lewis, "Month Ending August 31, 1909," ibid.

49   L. Alva Lewis to Mr. Finley, 15 May 1909, ibid. The Indians Lewis encoun-
       tered were most likely Klamath or Modoc from the Klamath Reserva-
       tion north of Klamath Falls.

50   Price, *Flight Maps*, 57–109; Doughty, *Feather Fashions and Bird
       Preservation*.

51   On the work and death of Guy Bradley, see Graham, *Audubon Ark*, 28–43.
       Louis Warren examines the often violent resistance to the enforcement
       of game laws in *Hunter's Game*, 21–47.

52   L. Alva Lewis, "Report of the Warden of the Klamath Lake Reservation
       for the Month Ending May 31, 1910," *Reports of the Wardens, 1910*, A-173,
       National Audubon Society Records, New York Public Library, New York,
       189.

53   L. Alva Lewis, "Report of the Warden of the Klamath Lake Reservation
       for the Month Ending April 30, 1910," and "Report of the Warden of the
       Klamath Lake Reservation for the Month Ending November 30, 1910,"
       Wildlife Refuge Reference List, Division of Wildlife Refuges, Bureau of
       Biological Survey Records, RG 22, NA-CP.

54   L. Alva Lewis to William L. Finley, 5 May 1909, ibid.

55   Ann E. Huston, "A History of the Lower Klamath National Wildlife Ref-
       uge," in *A River Never the Same: A History of Water in the Klamath Basin*,
       ed. Shaw Historical Library (Klamath Falls: Oregon Institute of Tech-
       nology, 1999), 61, and Robbins, *Landscapes of Promise*, 252–53.

56   It is unclear whether these fires were purposely set or if they were acci-
       dental. Homesteaders or the Reclamation Service may have set the fires
       to clear the dead vegetation in order to prepare the land for settlement.

57   Frederick C. Lincoln, "Western Field Trip, 9/7–10/20/35," Records of
       the Bureau of Sport Fisheries and Wildlife, Records of the Division of
       Wildlife Research, Office Files of Frederick C. Lincoln, 1917–60, RG 22,
       NA-CP.

58   By 1922, Lower Klamath Lake covered only 365 acres. Prior to drain-
       age, the lake was approximately 54,000 acres, though the precise extent
       of the lake varied somewhat from year to year. "Memorandum: Lower
       Klamath Lake, Klamath Irrigation Project, Oregon-California," 3 March
       1932, File 301.2, Klamath Project Marsh Lands, Lower Klamath Lake,
       1930–1932, Bureau of Reclamation Correspondence File, 1930–1945, RG
       115, National Archives and Records Administration, Rocky Mountain

Region, Denver, Colo., 1, 21. For bird deaths, see ibid., 32. According to the Biological Survey, the birds died from alkali poisoning, a common malady affecting migratory waterfowl in the western United States. Later research confirmed that botulism, not alkali salts, was the real cause of the disease. I discuss botulism and other avian diseases more fully in the next chapter.

59   "Agreement Between Reclamation Service and Klamath Drainage District," William L. Finley, "Report of William L. Finley, Field Agent for the Pacific Coast States," *Bird-Lore*, Nov.-Dec. 1919, 412–14; ibid., "Passing of the Marshlands," *Nature Magazine*, March 1926, 173. The Bureau of Reclamation noted the poor soil conditions repeatedly in its own documents between 1909 and 1925. For a summary, see "Memorandum: Lower Klamath Lake, Klamath Irrigation Project, Oregon-California," 9, 18, 23–25.

60   Executive Orders No. 2200 (14 May 1915), No. 3187 (2 Dec. 1919), No. 3422 (28 March 1921), KBNWR-HQ.

61   Ira N. Gabrielson to E. W. Nelson, Chief Bureau of Biological Survey, November 1922, and Smith Riley to E. W. Nelson, (no date) 1922, Clear Lake, 1922–24, Wildlife Refuges Reference File, Division of Wildlife Refuges, RG 22, NA-CP.

62   Langston, *Where Land and Water Meet*, 66–83.

63   William L. Finley, "Report of William L. Finley, Field Agent for the Pacific Coast States," *Bird-Lore*, Nov.-Dec. 1918, 407–8; ibid., Nov.-Dec. 1919, 412–14; ibid., Nov.-Dec. 1920, 393; Finley, "Passing of the Marshlands," 173.

64   Quotation from Langston, *Where Land and Water Meet*, 77.

65   William L. Finley, "Report of William L. Finley, Field Agent for the Pacific Coast States," *Bird-Lore*, Nov.-Dec. 1923, 452.

66   H. F. Stone, "Report of Inspection Trip, 1920," General Reservations, 1920–1935, Wildlife Refuges Reference File, Division of Wildlife Refuges, Fish and Wildlife Service, RG 22, NA-CP.

67   The Reclamation Service changed its name to the Bureau of Reclamation in 1923.

68   Bureau of Reclamation, "Lower Klamath Lake, Klamath Project, Oregon." *New Reclamation Era*, November 1925, 172, and Elwood Mead, "Memorandum for the Secretary of the Interior," 30 January 1926, Box 7, WFP.

69   "Memorandum: Lower Klamath Lake, Klamath Irrigation Project, Oregon-California," 29–30, 35.

70 L. T. Jessup, "Report on the Proposed Reflooding of a Portion of Lower Klamath Lake California," Bureau of Biological Survey, October 1927, Box 7, WFP.

71 Ibid., 12–15; "Reflooding of Lower Klamath Lake Held Impracticable," Press Release, U.S. Department of Agriculture, Office of Information and Press Service, 5 November 1927, Box 7, WFP.

72 Copley Amory, "Agriculture and Wild Fowl Conservation at Lower Klamath Lake," *New Reclamation Era*, May 1926, 80–82.

73 Gabrielson, *Wildlife Refuges*, 184–85.

74 Quotation from E. W. Nelson, "Unwise Drainage," *Bulletin of the American Game Protective Association* 13, no.1 (1924): 8–9, 11. See also William L. Finley, "Game Refuges," *Nature Magazine*, May 1926, 305.

75 H. M. Worcester to Chief, Bureau of Biological Survey, 4 August 1934, Box 7, WFP; B. E. Hayden to Commissioner, 9 October 1934, Box 8, WFP; Elwood Mead to William Finley, 22 October 1934, ibid.; William Finley to Elwood Mead, 27 December 1934, ibid..

76 H. M. Worcester to Chief, Bureau of Biological Survey, 13 Sept. 1933 and 19 Sept. 1933; W. E. Crouch to J. N. Darling, 12 Oct. 1934, Box 152, "Tule Lake, 1934–1944" file, Reservations, Bureau of Biological Survey General Correspondence, 1890–1956, RG 22, NA-CP.

77 Quote from William Finley to J. N. Darling, 27 September 1934, ibid. See also William Finley to Harold Ickes, 30 June 1934, and U.S. Game Conservation Officer to Paul Redington, 14 December 1933, ibid.

78 William Finley to Elwood Mead, 5 September 1934, Box 7, WFP.

79 William Finley to H. M. Worcester, 27 September 1934 and 25 August 1934, Box 7, WFP; H. M. Worcester to Mr. A. Fungate, 21 August 1934, ibid.

80 Elwood Mead to William Finley, 13 April 1934, ibid.; Finley to Mead, 24 April 1934, 2 July 1934, 30 July 1934, 20 August 1934, ibid. The Bureau of Reclamation explains why reflooding Lower Klamath Lake is impossible in M. A. Schnurr to Finley, 9 July 1934, ibid.

3 · PLACES IN THE GRID

1 Langston, *Where Land and Water Meet*, 116.

2 Ibid., 91. Historian Jared Orsi questions whether bird populations were falling as much as conservationists thought they were in the 1930s. See Jared Orsi, "From Horicon to Hamburgers and Back Again: Ecology,

Ideology, and Wildfowl Management, 1917–1935," *Environmental History Review,* Winter (1994): 27–28.

3   Vileisis, *Discovering the Unknown Landscape,* 167–75; James B. Trefethen, *An American Crusade for Wildlife: Highlights in Conservation Progress* (Harrisburg, Pa.: The Stackpole Company, 1961), 251–64.

4   On the social and economic effects of the Great Depression, see David M. Kennedy, *Freedom from Fear: The American People in Depression and War, 1929–1945* (New York: Oxford Univ. Press, 1999), 160–217, and Donald Worster, *Dust Bowl: The Southern Plains in the 1930s* (New York: Oxford University Press, 1979), 99–164

5   Theodore Saloutos, *The American Farmer and the New Deal* (Ames: Iowa State University Press, 1982), 194–98, 259; Minutes of a Meeting with the Senate Wild Life Committee at the Capitol, Washington, D.C., 9 January 1934, Bureau of Biological Survey Records, Office Files of J. N. "Ding" Darling, 1930–35, RG 22, NA-CP. See also Orsi, "From Horicon to Hamburgers and Back Again," 30–33.

6   Trefethen, *An American Crusade for Wildlife,* 264–67.

7   W. G. Leitch, *Ducks and Men: Forty Years of Co-Operation in Conservation* (Winnipeg, Manitoba: Ducks Unlimited, 1978), 13–15; Curt Meine, *Aldo Leopold: His Life and Work* (Madison: University of Wisconsin Press, 1988), 314–15, 318–19; David E. Lendt, *Ding: The Life of Jay Norwood Darling* (Ames: Iowa State University Press, 1989), 36–37.

8   Aldo Leopold, *Game Management* (New York: Charles Scribner's Sons, 1933), and Meine, Aldo Leopold, 316–17. For a detailed study of Leopold's views on keeping wildlife public, see Warren, *Hunter's Game,* 71–73, 80–81.

9   On Darling's life and work, see Lendt, *Ding;* Philip A. DuMont and Henry M. Reeves, "The Darling-Salyer Team," in *Flyways: Pioneering Waterfowl Management in North America,* ed. A. C. Hawkins, R. C. Hanson, H. K. Nelson, and H. M. Reeves (Washington, D.C.: United States Department of the Interior, Fish and Wildlife Service, 1984), 107–12; Peter Matthiessen, *Wildlife in America* (New York: Viking Press, 1959), 220; and Meine, *Aldo Leopold,* 318–19.

10   U.S. Department of Agriculture, "Report of the President's Committee on Wild-Life Restoration," Original Copy of President's Committee on Wildlife Restoration, Bureau of Biological Survey Records, Office Files of J. N. "Ding" Darling, 1930–1935, RG 22, NA-CP, 1–6, 22–23. The committee singled out the draining of Lower Klamath Lake as a glaring example of an ill-planned draining scheme.

11   It is not clear whether Wallace asked Redington to step down. No doubt he recognized that the report showed the Biological Survey's inability to halt the decline in waterfowl populations and that it called Redington's leadership into question. See Lendt, *Ding*, 67.

12   Lendt, *Ding*, 69-70, 75-77; U.S. Department of Agriculture, Bureau of Biological Survey, Report of the Chief of the Bureau of Biological Survey, 1934 (Washington, D.C.: Government Printing Office, 1934), 2; Trefethen, *An American Crusade for Wildlife*, 263-64.

13   U.S. Department of Agriculture, *Report of the Chief of the Bureau of Biological Survey, 1935*, 5.

14   Richard Lowitt, *The New Deal and the West* (Bloomington: Indiana University Press, 1984), 75-80; Neil M. Maher, "A New Deal Body Politic: Landscape, Labor, and the Civilian Conservation Corps," *Environmental History* 7, no. 3 (2002): 435-61.

15   Surveys of the Bureau of Reclamation and water development projects during the New Deal include Lowitt, *The New Deal and the West*, 81-99; Worster, *Rivers of Empire*, 209-11, 237-45; White, *"It's Your Misfortune and None of My Own,"* 483-87; Hundley, *Great Thirst*, 201-72; Gerald D. Nash, *The Federal Landscape: An Economic History of the Twentieth-Century West* (Tucson: University of Arizona Press, 1999), 24-27.

16   Steve Chase and Mark Madison, "The Expanding Ark: 100 Years of Wildlife Refuges," *Wild Earth*, Winter (2003-2004): 20-24.

17   Frederick C. Lincoln, "Bird Banding," in *Fifty Years' Progress in American Ornithology, 1883–1933*, ed. Frank M. Chapman and T. S. Palmer (Lancaster, Pa.: American Ornithologists' Union, 1933), 65-87; Keir B. Sterling, "Builders of the U.S. Biological Survey, 1885-1930," *Journal of Forest History* 33, no. 4 (1989): 180-87; Barrow, *Passion for Birds*, 184-90; Evenden, "Laborers of Nature," 172-83.

18   Frederick C. Lincoln, *Bird-Banding: Its First Decade Under the Biological Survey*, U.S. Bureau of Biological Survey (Washington, D.C.: Government Printing Office, 1931), 29; Barrow, *Passion for Birds*, 165-72.

19   Bruno Latour, *Science in Action* (Cambridge, Mass.: Harvard University Press, 1987), 219-37.

20   Day, *North American Waterfowl*, 71-88.

21   Henry M. Reeves, "Alexander Wetmore," in Hawkins, Hanson, Nelson, and Reeves, *Flyways*, 75.

22   Ibid., 76.

23   Ibid., 77; Baldassarre and Bolen, *Waterfowl Ecology and Management*, 308.

24 Baldassarre and Bolen, *Waterfowl Ecology and Management*, 301–4.

25 U.S. Department of the Interior, Bureau of Sport Fisheries and Wild-life, "Report on Effects of 1959 Water Levels on Wildlife Values and Public and Economic Uses of Tule Lake," 2 December 1959, *Tule Lake National Wildlife Refuge, 1959*, NR-KBNWR, 33–34; *Lower Klamath Lake National Wildlife Refuge, Jan.–April, 1961*, KBNWR-HQ, 2.

26 U.S. Department of Agriculture, Office of Information, Press Service, "Bear River Marshes, Utah, Saved for Migratory Birds: President Approves Measure to Establish Refuge for Wild Fowl," 3 May 1928. For a brief summary of the refuge's history, see Vanez T. Wilson and Rachel L. Carson, *Bear River: A National Wildlife Refuge*, Conservation in Action Series, No. 8 (Washington, D.C.: Department of the Interior, Fish and Wildlife Service, 1950).

27 "Vanishing Migratory Birds," *Saturday Evening Post*, 19 February 1927.

28 Fitzhugh L. Minnigerode, "Vanishing Water Fowl Have a New Sanctuary," *New York Times*, 8 January 1933.

29 Wayne I. Jensen and Cecil S. Williams, "Botulism and Fowl Cholera," in Linduska, *Waterfowl Tomorrow*, 333–41; E. R. Quorturup and R. L. Sudheimer, "Field Notes on Botulism, Bear River Refuge, Utah, Season 1942," 12 December 1942, Research Reports, 1912–1951, Records of the Branch of Wildlife Research, RG 22, NA-CP; E. R. Quortrup, "The Value of Antitoxin in the Treatment of Ducks Afflicted with Botulism," 11 December 1943, and "Memorandum for Regional Directors and Project Leaders Concerned with Botulism, Use of Antitoxin for Birds Afflicted with Botulism," 20 May 1944, ibid.; Bill Jenkins, "Tulelake Duck Hospital Saves Botulism Victims," *Klamath Falls (Ore.) Herald and News*, 31 August 1949.

30 Frayer, Peters, and Pywell, *Wetlands of the California Central Valley*, 6.

31 Walter W. Bennett to J. C. Salyer, 29 April 1935, FF 17 Los Banos Refuge, 1925–1937, Box 2, Salyer Papers; Vice-President, Miller & Lux to Walter W. Bennett, 8 May 1935, ibid.; A. V. Beronio to J. N. Darling, 31 July 1935, ibid.; J. Clark Salyer II to A. V. Beronio, 5 August 1935, ibid; A. V. Beronio to J. Clark Salyer, 6 December 1935, ibid. For more on Miller & Lux, see Igler, *Industrial Cowboys*.

32 L. M. Winsor to Chief, Biological Survey, 24 August 1939, Box 6, FF 20, Ruby Lake Material, J. Clark Salyer Papers.

33 "Excerpt from a letter to Mr. Salyer from Mr. Walter W. Bennett, dated May 27, 1935, in regard to Franklin and Ruby Lakes in Nevada," Box 6, Ruby Lake Material, FF 32, J. Clark Salyer Papers; L. M. Winsor, "Sup-

plemental Report, Ruby Lakes Project, Nevada," 15 July 1936, ibid.; J. C. Salyer to Chief, Bureau of Biological Survey, 30 November 1936, ibid.; L. M. Winsor to S. H. McCrory, Chief, Bureau of Agricultural Engineering, 31 January 1938, ibid.

34 Cynthia F. Davis, *Where Water Is King: The Story of the Glenn-Colusa Irrigation District* (Willows, Calif.: Glenn-Colusa Irrigation District, 1984), 89–96.

35 S. A. Young, "Spalding Ranch," Records of the Pacific Northwest Regional Office, Portland, Oregon, 1937–67, RG 22, NA-S, 2–3.

36 Ibid., 3–10.

37 L. M. Winsor to Chief of U.S. Dept. of Agriculture Bureau of Engineering S. H. McCrory, 1 July 1936 and 6 July 1936, Historical Files, NR-SNWR-HQ; L. M. Winsor, "Report: Construction Program for Spalding Ranch (Sacramento Migratory Waterfowl Refuge)," 11 May 1937, ibid.

38 Young, "Spalding Ranch," RG 22, NA-S, 15.

39 L. M. Winsor, "Report on Investigations, Surveys and Development Plans for the Sacramento Migratory Waterfowl Refuge (Spalding Ranch) California," U.S. Department of Agriculture, Bureau of Agricultural Engineering, 1936, Historical Files, NR-SNWR-HQ, 4–8.

40 S. J. Hankins to Brice McBride, 15 February 1938, Historical Files, NR-SNWR-HQ; L. M. Winsor to Brice McBride, Memorandum, 19 August 1938, ibid.

41 The Bureau of Biological Survey was transferred from the Department of Agriculture to the Department of the Interior in 1939 and renamed the U.S. Fish and Wildlife Service in 1940.

42 J. Clark Salyer II to Leo Laythe, 7 June 1943, Historical Files, NR-SNWR-HQ. On FWS public relations in the Sacramento Valley, see J. Clark Salyer II to Leo Laythe, 28 April 1943, ibid. For water conflicts between the Biological Survey/FWS and the Glenn-Colusa Irrigation District, see A. C. Elmer to Albert Day, 14 April 1943, ibid.; Peter J. Van Huizen to Leo Laythe, 31 May 1943, ibid.; Leo Laythe to FWS Director, 3 June 1943, ibid.; J. Clark Salyer to Harry M. Creech, 7 June 1943, ibid.; J. Clark Salyer to Leo Laythe, 7 June 1943, ibid.; Memorandum of Agreement Between Glenn-Colusa Irrigation District and the Fish and Wildlife Service, May 1943, ibid.

43 Frank Arthur Hall Jr., "An Environmental History of the Sacramento National Wildlife Refuge" (M.A. thesis, California State University-Chico, 1975), 7–10, 112–14.

44 U.S. Department of Commerce, Bureau of the Census, *United States*

Census of Agriculture: 1935 (Washington, D.C.: Government Printing Office, 1936), vol. 1, pt. 3, and *United States Census of Agriculture: 1950* (Washington, D.C.: Government Printing Office, 1952), vol. 1, part 33.

45   Albert Day to Leo Laythe and E. E. Horn, 11 March 1944, Historical Files, NR-SNWR-HQ.

46   George L. Otterson to Senator Hiram Johnson, 30 March 1944, ibid.

47   Minutes of Meeting of Joint Wildlife Management Committee of California, 3 March 1944, ibid.; Arthur T. Evans, Associated Sportsmen of California, to Harold Ickes, 22 March 1944, ibid.; H. L. Betten, "Rod and Gun," *San Francisco Examiner*, 12 March 1944.

48   During the early 1940s, the FWS was forced to move its headquarters from Washington, D.C., to a warehouse in Chicago to make room for the growth in federal bureaucracy during the Second World War. Ira Gabrielson, chief of the FWS, argued strenuously against the move, saying that it would hamper wildlife conservation and make management of the agency even more difficult. See Ira Gabrielson, "Memoirs of Ira M. Gabrielson (and What Others Have Said About Him), 1889–1977," unpublished manuscript, National Conservation Training Center, Shepherdstown, West Virginia. On the reduction of staff and funds during the war, see United States Department of the Interior, Fish and Wildlife Service, *Annual Report of the Fish and Wildlife Service to the Secretary of the Interior, 1943* (Washington, D.C.: Government Printing Office, 1943), 225–26, 254.

49   E. E. Horn to Director, FWS, 15 March 1944, Historical Files, NR-SNWR-HQ; ibid., 20 March 1944; ibid., 23 March 1944.

50   On the 1932 flood, see "Farmers Meet, Flood Problem Grows Serious," *Klamath Falls (Ore.) Evening Herald*, 18 June 1932; B. E. Hayden to Commissioner, "Break in Cox Bros.' Dike," 21 June 1932, Entry 7, General Correspondence and Project Correspondence, 1930–1945, National Archives and Records Administration, Denver, Colorado, Record Group 115, United States Bureau of Reclamation; Elwood Mead to B. E. Hayden, 25 June 1932, ibid. For the 1937 flood, see L. M. Winsor to W. M. Rush, 11 April 1938, NR-KBNWR-HQ; L. M. Winsor, *Narrative Report: Clear Lake Camp, Tule Lake Camp*, January–April 1938, Tualatin National Wildlife Refuge, Tualatin, Oregon.

51   USDI, Bureau of Reclamation, "Report on Tule Lake Reclamation, Klamath Project, Oregon, Report #5" (April 1938), NR-KBNWR-HQ; USDI, Bureau of Reclamation, "Klamath Project, Modoc Unit, California, Report #5A" (September 1944), ibid., 1–5; W. M. Rush, C. G. Fairchild, and L. M. Windsor, "Memo for Dr. Ira N. Gabrielson," 4 February 1938, ibid., 1–6.

52 Mark Fiege discusses hybrid irrigated landscapes in *Irrigated Eden*, 205–7, 208–9.

53 For an account of FWS work on other refuges during this era, see Gabrielson, *Wildlife Refuges*, 133–81. The FWS also undertook major restoration work at Malheur National Wildlife Refuge, the other large migratory waterfowl refuge in Oregon. See Langston, *Where Land and Water Meet*, 91–113.

54 Gabrielson, "Memoirs," 298–300.

55 J. Clark Salyer II to Regional Director Leo L. Laythe, 3 June 1942, "Tule Lake, 1934–1944," Bureau of Biological Survey General Correspondence, 1890–1956, RG 22, NA-CP.

56 Chas. E. Jackson, Acting Director, to William Finley, 24 June 1942, "Tule Lake, 1934–1944," ibid.

57 See "Memorandum of Understanding Between the Director of the War Relocation Authority and the Secretary of the Interior," undated (internal evidence suggests April 1942), "Tule Lake, 1934–1944," ibid.

58 Memorandum, J. Clark Salyer II to Mr. Day, Mr. Chaney, and Mr. Gardner, October 23, 1942, Box 152, "Tule Lake, 1934–1944," ibid.; Dillon to Leo Laythe, Telegram, November 13, 1942, ibid.; Memorandum, J. Clark Salyer II to Dr. Gabrielson, January 26, 1943, "Tule Lake, 1934–1944," ibid.

59 J. Clark Salyer, Chief, Division of Wildlife Refuges, to Leo Laythe, Regional Director, FWS, Portland, June 12, 1942, FF20, Box 2, J. Clark Salyer Papers; Paul T. Kreager, Regional Refuge Supervisor to Director, Fish and Wildlife Service, FF13, Box 11, 27 May 1942, 29 May 1942, 5 June 1942; C. G. Fairchild, Refuge Manager, to Leo L. Laythe, Regional Director, 23 June 1942, FWS; A. C. Elmer, Assistant Chief, Division of Wildlife Refuges, to Leo L. Laythe, Regional Director, 13 July 1942, ibid.

60 Scott, *Seeing Like a State*.

4 · DUCK FARMS

1 Day, *North American Waterfowl*, 169.

2 "Sale of Federal Duck Stamps in California, 1934–2003," U.S. Fish and Wildlife Service, Federal Duck Stamp Program, http://www.fws.gov/duckstamps/federal/sales/images/California34-03.gif (accessed October 27, 2008).

3 Johnson A. Neff, Peter J. Van Huizen, and James C. Savage, "Rice and Ducks in the Sacramento Valley of California, Season of 1942," 28 Janu-

ary 1943, Research Reports, 1912–1951, Records of the Branch of Wildlife Research, RG 22, NA-CP; California Farm Bureau Federation, "Statement of Position of California Farm Bureau Federation on Crop Damage Caused by Migratory Wild Fowl," 27 May 1943, ibid., 3.

4   Clinton H. Lostetter, "They've Got to Eat Someplace," in Hawkins, Hanson, Nelson, and Reeves, *Flyways,* 461–62; Neff, Van Huizen, and Savage, "Rice and Ducks in the Sacramento Valley"; California Farm Bureau Federation, "Statement of Position of California Farm Bureau Federation on Crop Damage Caused by Migratory Wild Fowl."

5   E. E. Horn, "The Duck Problem," 6 January 1944, Office Files of Frederick C. Lincoln, 1917–60, Records of the Bureau of Sport Fisheries and Wildlife, Records of the Branch of Wildlife Research, RG 22, NA-CP.

6   Neff, Van Huizen, and Savage, "Rice and Ducks in the Sacramento Valley," 8–11.

7   Ibid., 13–14.

8   Ibid.

9   Ibid., 16. Some advocated for the abolishment of the refuges. See NR-SNWR, September–December 1947, SNWR-HQ, 22–23.

10 Neff, Van Huizen, and Savage, "Rice and Ducks in the Sacramento Valley," 17. The reference to market hunters is unusual, since there is no mention of them in other parts of this report or in the annual reports of the Sacramento Refuge from this period.

11 Horn, "Duck Problem," and Johnson A. Neff, "Sacramento Valley Rice—Duck Studies," 7 December 1943, Research Reports, 1912–1951, Records of the Branch of Wildlife Research, RG 22, NA-CP.

12 Sharecropping was very common on private rice farms throughout the Sacramento Valley. See Mary Beth Pudup and Michael J. Watts, "Growing Against the Grain: Mechanized Rice Farming in the Sacramento Valley, California," in *Comparative Farming Systems,* ed. B. L. Turner II and Stephen B. Brush (New York: The Guilford Press, 1987), 368–77.

13 Horn, "Duck Problem."

14 The Sutter By-Pass was one the main canals of the Sacramento Flood Control Project. Except in times of flood, this canal was mostly dry.

15 "Waterfowl Pose California Problem," *Outdoor California,* September 1935, 1, 3; J. Clark Salyer II and Francis G. Gillet, "Federal Refuges," in Linduska, *Waterfowl Tomorrow,* 504; Day, *North American Waterfowl,* 168, 173.

16 "Summary of Year's Activities," NR-KBNWR, 1944, KBNWR-HQ, 3; "Summary of Year's Activities," ibid., 1945; "Annual Summary," ibid., 1947; "Annual Summary," ibid., 1948.

17 The FWS sent six box carloads by rail to these California refuges in 1948. NR-KBNWR, January–March, 1947, KBNWR-HQ, 2; and Paul T. Kreager to Regional Director Laythe, 25 July 1945, Tule Lake National Wildlife Refuge, F.Y. 1946–49, Wildlife Refuges, 1946–1955, RG 22, NA-S.

18 Day, *North American Waterfowl*, 170–71.

19 "Summary of Year's Activities," 1944; "Annual Summary," 1947, 4.

20 Tule Lake National Wildlife Refuge, NR-KBNWR, September–December, 1955, KBNWR-HQ, 24.

21 E. E. Horn, "Suggested Program—Bird Depredations," Memo to Regional Director, Portland, Oregon, 3 June 1948, California, USFWS—Pacific Region, Wildlife Refuges, 1946–1955, RG 22, NA-S.

22 Ibid.

23 Norris A. Bleyhl, "A History of the Production and Marketing of Rice in California," (Ph.D. diss., University of Minnesota, 1955), 151–53, 175–77, 269–70; Ann Foley Scheuring, *A Guidebook to California Agriculture* (Berkeley: University of California Press, 1983), 116–17. On mechanization in California agriculture, see Walker, *Conquest of Bread*, 164–71.

24 Sacramento National Wildlife Refuge Complex, NR-SNWR, 1964, SNWR-HQ, 3–4.

25 On the ecological commons, see Fiege, *Irrigated Eden*, 60–61, 69–73; Fiege, "Private Property and Ecological Commons in the American West," in Wilson and Groth, *Everyday America*.

26 NR-SNWR, 1939, SNWR-HQ.

27 This was likely part of the Chemical Warfare Service's attempts to find peaceful uses for gases employed after World War I. See Edmund P. Russell III, "'Speaking of Annihilation': Mobilizing for War against Human and Insect Enemies," *Journal of American History* 82, no. 4 (1996): 1510–18.

28 Evenden, "Laborers of Nature," 172–83; Thomas R. Dunlap, *Saving America's Wildlife* (Princeton, N.J.: Princeton University Press, 1988), 38, 76, 112–14; Worster, *Nature's Economy*, 263–64.

29 E. R. Kalmbach, "Report on Experiments in the Use of War Gases as Bird Control Agencies, Conducted at the Edgewood, Md. Arsenal of the Chemical Warfare Service," War Gases as Bird Control Agencies [sic], Research Reports, 1912–1951, Records of the Fish and Wildlife Service, 1922–1961, Records of the Branch of Wildlife Research, RG 22, NA-CP.

30 Sacramento National Wildlife Refuge, 1947, 13.

31 Ibid., 1951, 10; 1953, 29.

32 Rossalius C. Hanson, Pilot-Biologist, to Regional Director, Portland, Ore., "Report on Use of Herbicides on Sacramento Refuge," 28 Decem-

ber 1950, Habitat Improvement, Division of Wildlife Refuges, RG 22, NA-CP; Warren S. Bourn to Regional Director, Portland, Ore., "Procurement and Use of Herbicides," 31 March 1953, Sacramento, 1945–55, ibid.; Sacramento National Wildlife Refuge, May–August, 1953, 9. For herbicide use on the Malheur National Wildlife Refuge, see Langston, *Where Land and Water Meet*, 106–8 and fig. 7. FWS weed control efforts were similar to those undertaken by farmers and irrigators. See Fiege, *Irrigated Eden*, 66–69.

33 Warren S. Bourn, "2,4-D and Its Uses, Memorandum from Dr. Warren S. Bourn," 25 January 1949, Control-General, Wildlife Refuges, 1946–1955, RG 22, NA-S.

34 "Highlights of the Year's Activities," Sacramento National Wildlife Refuge, 1951, 1.

35 Sacramento National Wildlife Refuge, January–April, 1949, 12; ibid., May–August, 1949, 4. See Baldassarre and Bolen, *Waterfowl Ecology and Management*, 202–3, 226, 459–60, and Fiege, *Irrigated Eden*, 49.

36 On the Tule Lake Refuge during World War II, the FWS allowed trappers to use buildings at the former CCC camp nearby to skin the animals and prepare the fur for shipment. This stopped after the federal government turned the facilities into a German prisoner-of-war camp and, later, into a jail for disruptive Japanese internees from the Tule Lake War Relocation Center. Clinton S. Fairchild, Refuge Manager, "Five Year Development Program for the Clear Lake Migratory Bird Refuge, Upper Klamath Wildlife Refuge, Lower Klamath Refuge and the Tule Lake Refuge," 1938, Wildlife Refuge Management Plans, 1938–1945, RG 22, NA-S, 67–68, 111–13; ibid., "Five-Year Plan: Tule Lake National Wildlife Refuge"; ibid., "Summary of Year's Activities," NR-KBNWR, 1944, KBNWR-HQ.

37 Edmund Russell III, *War and Nature: Fighting Humans and Insects with Chemicals from World War I to Silent Spring* (New York: Cambridge University Press, 2001), 86. On the development of insecticides during this period, see John H. Perkins, *Insects, Experts, and the Insecticide Crisis: The Quest for New Pest Management Strategies* (New York: Plenum Press, 1982), 3–22.

38 Russell, *War and Nature*, 95–118, 165–75.

39 The federal government supported research into DDT during the 1950s under the direction of the FWS. Thomas R. Dunlap, *DDT: Scientists, Citizens, and Public Policy* (Princeton, N.J.: Princeton University Press, 1981), 76–97.

40 Bleyhl, "History of the Production and Marketing of Rice in California," 182–83; Sacramento National Wildlife Refuge, May–August, 1953, 5, 9. On the characteristics of the pesticide dieldrin, see Shirley A. Briggs and the staff of Rachel Carson Council, *Basic Guide to Pesticides: Their Characteristics and Hazards* (Washington, D.C.: Hemisphere Publishing Corporation, 1992), 134, 212–13.

41 "Memorandum of Understanding Between the U.S. Department of Interior, Fish and Wildlife Service and the U.S. Department of Agriculture, Plant Pest Control Branch," 16 July 1956, Tule Lake National Wildlife Refuge, NR-KBNWR, September–December, 1956, KBNWR-HQ, 13–14.

42 The FWS also characterized the loss of fish as "severe." However, refuge officials were unconcerned by this since "the kill was predominantly rough fish and the resultant loss to fishermen was considered not too important." The FWS did not participate in this spraying. Sacramento National Wildlife Refuge, May–August, 1953, 2, 5, 9.

43 Richard E. Griffith to Regional Director, Portland, Ore., 3 July 1953, Sacramento, 1945–55, Habitat Improvement, Division of Wildlife Refuges, RG 22, NA-CP.

44 The results of the laboratory analyses can be found in the Klamath Basin refuges report from the following year. See Tule Lake National Wildlife Refuge, May–August, 1961, 7–8, 16.

45 Rachel Carson, *Silent Spring* (Boston: Houghton Mifflin Company, 1962), 49–50.

46 Linda Lear discusses Carson's duties and experience working for the Fish and Wildlife Service in *Rachel Carson: Witness for Nature* (New York: Henry Holt and Company, 1997), 95–96, 102, 106–11, 132–33, 138–46.

47 Tule Lake National Wildlife Refuge, May–August, 1963, 9–10; ibid., September–December, 1963, 11. The FWS also considered testing the insecticides Dibram, Diazinon, Dipterex, and Methoxychlor, though there is no indication in agency records whether refuge managers actually did so. See ibid., January–April, 1961, 16.

48 Baldassarre and Bolen, *Waterfowl Ecology and Management*, 291–93.

49 Jensen and Williams, "Botulism and Fowl Cholera," in Linduska, *Waterfowl Tomorrow*, 333–41; E. R. Quorturup and R. L. Sudheimer, "Field Notes on Botulism, Bear River Refuge, Utah, Season 1942," 12 December 1942, Research Reports, 1912–1951, Records of the Branch of Wildlife Research, RG 22, NA-CP; E. R. Quortrup, "The Value of Antitoxin in the Treatment of Ducks Afflicted with Botulism," 11 December 1943, ibid.; "Memoran-

dum for Regional Directors and Project Leaders Concerned with Botulism, Use of Antitoxin for Birds Afflicted with Botulism," 20 May 1944, ibid.; Bill Jenkins, "Tulelake Duck Hospital Saves Botulism Victims," *Herald and News (Klamath Falls, Ore.)*, 31 August 1949, 15.

50   On hunting enclosures, see Paul Robbins and April Luginbuhl, "The Last Enclosure: Resisting Privatization of Wildlife in the Western United States," *Capitalism, Nature, Socialism* 16, no. 1 (2005): 45–61.

51   "Annual Summary," NR-KBNWR, 1947, 4, KBNWR-HQ. National parks experienced a similar surge in use immediately following the war. See Sellars, *Preserving Nature in the National Parks: A History* (New Haven, Conn.: Yale University Press, 1997), 173.

52   Tule Lake National Wildlife Refuge, September–December,1949, 12–14; Lower Klamath National Wildlife Refuge, NR-KBNWR, September–December, 1949, KBNWR-HQ, 9–11. Records from this era show that very few women hunted on the Klamath Basin refuges. Only 8 to 12 percent of hunters were women. Tule Lake National Wildlife Refuge, September–December, 1953, 40.

53   Tule Lake National Wildlife Refuge, September–December, 1955.

54   The FWS calculated these totals through hunter surveys. The actual number killed or crippled by hunters was likely far greater; see ibid., 25.

55   Walter T. Shannon, Director—California Department of Fish and Game to Daniel H. Janzen, Director—Bureau of Sport Fisheries and Wildlife, 13 August 1963, Historical Files, SNWR-HQ.

56   Lansing A. Parker to Walter T. Shannon, 9 September 1963, ibid.

57   Paul T. Quick to The Director, Washington, D.C., 11 April 1963, ibid.

58   "Reasons for and Against Keeping the Sacramento National Wildlife Refuge Closed to Hunting," ibid.

59   Everett D. Ivey to J. Clark Salyer II, 5 May 1962, ibid. See also J. Clark Salyer II to Dr. Everett D. Ivey, 1 June 1962, ibid.

60   Emmet Main, President, Willow Creek Mutual Water Company to Director Daniel H. Janzen, Director, Bureau of Sport Fisheries and Wildlife, 3 August 1964, ibid. The FWS comments on opposition by private hunting clubs in Richard E. Griffith to Director, Bureau of Sport Fisheries and Wildlife, 27 March 1964, ibid., 2.

61   Ira N. Gabrielson to Daniel H. Janzen, 26 August 1964, ibid.; Janzen to Gabrielson, 21 September 1964, ibid.; Carl W. Buchheister to Janzen, 10 July 1964, ibid.; Janzen to Buchheister, 21 August 1964, ibid. Devereux Butcher, author of a popular book about the national wildlife refuges, also opposed allowing hunting on the refuge. Devereux Butcher to Stewart

Udall, Secretary of the Interior, 21 July 1964, ibid.; and Udall to Butcher, 21 August 1964, ibid.

62 Since the passage of the Migratory Bird Hunting Stamp Act (commonly known as the Duck Stamp Act) in 1934, Congress had amended the act two times, in 1949 and 1958. The first amendment allowed the Secretary of the Interior to open up to 20 percent of refuges to hunting; the second amendment allowed up to 40 percent. Critics of these amendments noted that many parts of refuges were unfit for waterfowl. Allowing hunting on two-fifths of a refuge might encompass most or all of the duck and goose habitat. This did not happen on the Sacramento Refuge. While much of the refuge was uplands and of little use to waterfowl, the FWS did not just open the best areas to hunters. The northern part of the refuges, which had marshes, ponds, and rice fields, was still closed to hunters. See Daniel H. Janzen, Director, Bureau of Sport Fisheries and Wildlife to Assistant Secretary for Fish and Wildlife, 20 July 1964, Historical Files, SNWR-HQ.

63 Sacramento National Wildlife Refuge, 1964, 26.

64 Robbins and Luginbuhl, "Last Enclosure," 45–61.

65 U.S. Department of the Interior, Bureau of Sport Fisheries and Wildlife, "Report on Effects of 1959 Water Levels on Wildlife Values and Public and Economic Uses of Tule Lake," 2 December 1959, Tule Lake National Wildlife Refuge, September–December, 1959, 24.

66 Ibid., 27–32. See also Jack Curnow, "Someone Must Know Answers," *Los Angeles Times*, 30 October 1959; John D. Chambliss to Asst. Executive Director, Ducks Unlimited, 1 November 1959, Tule Lake, 1945–1960, Reservations, Bureau of Biological Survey General Correspondence, RG-22, NA-CP; Lawrence J. Durkin, Executive Secretary, Ducks Unlimited to Daniel H. Janzen, Director, Bureau of Sport Fisheries and Wildlife, 17 November 1959, ibid.; Crawford F. Carter to Sen. Thomas H. Kuchel, 17 December 1959, ibid.; J. Allen Bray to Fred A. Seaton, 21 December 1959, ibid.; Ross Leffler, Asst. Secretary of the Interior to J. Allen Bray, 13 January 1960, ibid.

67 U.S. Congress, Senate, Hearing Before the Subcommittee on Irrigation and Reclamation of the Committee on Interior and Insular Affairs, 5. *784 and S. 793 Bills to Promote the Conservation of Migratory Waterfowl and Wildlife Resources in the Tule Lake, Klamath, and Clear Lake National Wildlife Refuges in Oregon and California*, 88th Cong., 1st Sess., 24 April 1963.

68 Ibid., 89.

69   Ibid., 89–93.

70   See the testimony of Tule Lake Irrigation District lawyer Alvin Landis, ibid., 83–86, 95–96.

71   It is unclear whether farmers in the Sacramento and Imperial valleys saw this as a major problem. No farming organization from these areas spoke during the hearing for the bill or submitted letters to the subcommittee considering it. See ibid., contents, 101–2; Daniel A Poole, "Crossroads for Western Waterfowl," *National Parks Magazine*, March 1961, 4–7; "Statement of Stewart L. Udall, Secretary of the Interior, on S. 1988 (Kuchel Act) to the Subcommittee on Irrigation and Reclamation, Interior and Insular Affairs, U.S. Senate, February 23, 1962," Historical Files, KBNWR-HQ.

72   Kuchel Act, Public Law 88–567, 88th Cong., 2 September 1964.

73   Charles Wilkinson, *Blood Struggle: The Rise of Modern Indian Nations* (New York: W. W. Norton & Company, 2005), 75–77.

74   White, *"It's Your Misfortune and None of My Own,"* 579–80; Wilkinson, *Blood Struggle*, 57–71.

75   J. Clark Salyer II, Chief, Branch of Wildlife Refuges to Mr. Keith R. McCarthy, Staff Assistant, Office of Assistant Secretary—Fish and Wildlife, "Position of Klamath Marsh (Oregon) in Maintaining the Pacific Flyway," 25 January 1957, FF29, 1955–57, Box 10, J. Clark Salyer Papers.

76   T. B. Watters, Chairman, Management Specialists, Klamath Indian Tribes to Fred A. Seaton, Secretary of the Interior, 19 May 1958, FF 30, Klamath Marsh, 1959–62, Box 10, J. Clark Salyer Papers.

77   Ibid.

78   J. Clark Salyer II, Chief, Branch of Wildlife Refuges to Chief, Division of Wildlife, "Wocus Bay Indian Problem—Klamath Marsh," 22 May 1958, ibid.

79   Patrick Haynal, "Termination and Tribal Survival: The Klamath Tribes of Oregon," *Oregon Historical Quarterly* 101, no. 3 (2000): 296–98.

5 · REFUGES IN CONFLICT

1   Langston, *Where Land and Water Meet*, 91.

2   Integrated Land Management Working Group, "Integrated Land Management on Tule Lake National Wildlife Refuge," 30 October 2000, KBNWR-HQ, 5, 8.

3   Richard White analyzes the breakdown of consensus over public

lands management in "Contested Terrain: The Business of Land in the American West," in *Land in the American West: Private Claims and the Common Good*, ed. William G. Robbins and James C. Foster, (Seattle: University of Washington Press, 2000), 190–206.

4   "State Sales of Federal Duck Stamps 1934–2003," U.S. Fish and Wildlife Service, Federal Duck Stamp Program, http://www.fws.gov/duck-stamps/federal/sales/sales.htm (accessed October 26, 2008).

5   See Mark v. Barrow Jr., "Science, Sentiment, and the Specter of Extinction: Reconsidering Birds of Prey during America's Interwar Years," *Environmental History* 7, no. 1 (2002): 69–98; Isenberg, *Destruction of the Bison*, 164–92.

6   Shannon Peterson, *Acting for Endangered Species: The Statutory Ark* (Lawrence: University Press of Kansas, 2002), 39–118.

7   Congress passed earlier versions of the ESA in 1966 and 1969, but these precursors to the 1973 act were not as stringent. See Michael J. Bean and Melanie J. Rowland, *The Evolution of National Wildlife Law*, 3rd ed. (Westport, Conn.: Praeger Publishers, 1997), 193–99.

8   Peterson, *Acting for Endangered Species*, 21–35; Bonnie B. Burgess, *Fate of the Wild: The Endangered Species Act and the Future of Biodiversity* (Athens: University of Georgia Press, 2001), 3–28.

9   The National Marine Fisheries Service had jurisdiction over marine animals and anadromous fish such as salmon.

10   Norris Hundley Jr. discusses these changes in *Great Thirst*, 303–62. See also Worster, *Rivers of Empire*, 308–26; Marc Reisner, *Cadillac Desert: The American West and Its Disappearing Water* (New York: Penguin Books, 1986), 393–451. Worster's and Reisner's scathing critiques of water development in the West influenced the debate over water policy in the region. For a critical analysis of the arguments and rhetorical strategies used by these two authors, see Donald J. Pisani, "The Irrigation District and the Federal Relationship: Neglected Aspects of Water History in the Twentieth Century," in *The Twentieth-Century West: Historical Interpretations*, ed. Gerald D. Nash and Richard W. Etulain (Albuquerque: University of New Mexico Press, 1989), 261–66. On Americans' changing views toward dams, see Mark W. T. Harvey, *A Symbol of Wilderness: Echo Park and the American Conservation Movement* (Albuquerque: University of New Mexico Press, 1994; repr., Seattle: University of Washington Press, 2000); John McPhee, *Encounters with the Archdruid* (New York: Farrar, Straus and Giroux, 1971), 153–245.

11   Critics also said that servicing the district with water from the Central

Valley Project was a blatant violation of acreage limitation in the Reclamation Act of 1902. See Worster, *Rivers of Empire*, 292–95.

12   Hundley, *Great Thirst*, 429. Salinity, of course, is a problem in all arid regions with irrigated agriculture. However, the shallow clay layers made the salinity problem even worse in the Westlands Irrigation District. The large amounts of irrigation water used on the crops led to an accumulation of sub-surface water. As excess water evaporated from the surface, salts were left behind. See A. Dennis Lemly, "Agriculture and Wildlife: Ecological Implications of Subsurface Irrigation Drainage," *Journal of Arid Environments* 28 (1994): 88 and "Irrigation Drainage," in *Encyclopedia of Deserts*, ed. Michael A. Mares (Norman: University of Oklahoma Press, 1999), 304.

13   Gary R. Zahm, "Kesterson Reservoir and Kesterson Wildlife Refuge: History, Current Problems, and Management Alternatives," *Transactions of the Fifty-First North American Wildlife and Natural Resources Conference* (1986): 325.

14   Hundley, *Great Thirst*, 429; Tom Harris, *Death in the Marsh* (Washington, D.C.: Island Press, 1991), 7.

15   Harris, *Death in the Marsh*, 12–13; National Research Council (U.S.) Committee on Irrigation-Induced Water Quality Problems, *Irrigation-Induced Water Quality Problems: What Can Be Learned from the San Joaquin Valley Experience* (Washington, D.C.: National Academy Press, 1989), 20–21; Lemly, "Irrigation Drainage," 304–7.

16   Robert Lindsey, "Water That Enriched Valley Becomes a Peril in California," *New York Times*, 7 January 1985; Cass Peterson, "Farm Water Poisons Wildlife; California Refuge Contaminated," *Washington Post*, 10 March 1985; National Research Council, *Irrigation-Induced Water Quality Problems*, 22–25; Hundley, *Great Thirst*, 429–31.

17   In the 1990s, the FWS developed new wetlands near the old refuge in an area called the San Luis National Wildlife Refuge, Kesterson Unit. Despite the similarity in name to the original Kesterson Refuge, this new unit was not on the same land, which is still under control of the Bureau of Reclamation. See Phil Garone, "The Tragedy at Kesterson Reservoir: A Case Study in Environmental History and a Lesson in Ecological Complexity," *Environs: Environmental Law and Policy Journal* 22, no. 2 (1999): 107–44.

18   Philip Shabecoff, "Toxic Water Threatens Many Wildlife Refuges," *New York Times*, 30 April 1985; Cass Peterson, "The Interior Department; Various Pollution Problems Troubling Refuges," *Washington Post*, 1 May

1985; National Research Council, *Irrigation-Induced Water Quality Problems*, 2–3, 47–48.

19   Integrated Land Management Working Group, "Integrated Land Management on Tule Lake," KBNWR-HQ, 8–9.

20   R. M. Abney, "A Comparative Study of the Past and Present Conditions of Tule Lake," USFWS, 1964, cited in USFWS, "Briefing Statement: Wetland/Farm Rotational Management, Tule Lake National Wildlife Refuge," undated (presumably late 1990s), no page numbers, KBNWR-HQ.

21   Ibid.

22   USFWS, "Sump Rotation: A Conceptual Plan, Tule Lake National Wildlife Refuge," 22 November 1993, KBNWR-HQ, 7–9; Integrated Land Management Working Group, "Integrated Land Management," ibid., 8–9; USFWS, "Briefing Statement," ibid.

23   Integrated Land Management Working Group, "Integrated Land Management on Tule Lake," KBNWR-HQ, 10–11, 13–14; USFWS, "Sump Rotation: A Conceptual Plan," ibid., 14–16.

24   Lance Robertson and Dustin Solberg, "Reviving a Refuge," *High Country News*, 16 August 1999, 3.

25   The plaintiffs included national organizations such as the Wilderness Society, Audubon Society, and Sierra Club, as well as the Klamath Forest Alliance, a local environmental group based in the southern Oregon town of Ashland.

26   *Klamath Forest Alliance v. Babbit*, 1–4 (United States District Court for Eastern District of California, 1998); Les Line, "Foul Play in the Klamath Basin," *Audubon Magazine*, May–June 1997, 119–20.

27   The FWS discusses its IPM program on Klamath Basin refuge lands in U.S. Fish and Wildlife Service, "Integrated Pest Management Plan and Environmental Assessment for the Leased Lands at Lower Klamath and Tule Lake National Wildlife Refuges Oregon/California" (workbook; 1998), 3–4. http://www.klamathnwr.org/IpmPLan.htm. For an examination of the aims of IPM, see Joel Bourne, "Bugging Out," *Audubon Magazine*, March–April 1999, 71–73. Some have claimed that IPM is a vacuous term and that IPM programs in the United States have done little to reduce pesticide use or to change conventional farming practices. See Lester E. Ehler and Dale G. Bottrell, "The Illusion of Integrated Pest Management," *Issues in Science and Technology* (Spring 2000): 61–64.

28   Tupper Ansel Blake, Madeleine Graham Blake, and William Kittredge, *Balancing Water: Restoring the Klamath Basin* (Berkeley: University of

California Press, 2000), 129. Kittredge has written many other books about his years in the region and the environmental consequences of irrigated agriculture. See William Kittredge, *Owning It All* (St. Paul, Minn.: Graywolf Press, 1987), 55–71; and *Hole in the Sky: A Memoir* (New York: Vintage Books, 1992).

29 Quoted in Blake, Blake, and Kittredge, *Balancing Water*, 128. The ONRC changed its name to Oregon Wild in 2006.

30 Lawrence W. Powers and Karen Adams, "Contemporary Use of Water Resources in the Klamath Basin," in *A River Never the Same: A History of Water in the Klamath Basin*, ed. Shaw Historical Library (Klamath Falls, Ore.: Shaw Historical Library, Oregon Institute of Technology, 1999), 96–102.

31 Oregon Water Resources Department, "Resolving the Klamath," http://www.wrd.state.or.us/programs/klamath/summary.shtml.

32 On occasion, the Tulelake Irrigation District diverted water to the Tule Lake Refuge when the FWS requested it and if the district could spare it.

33 Water supplies for the Tule Lake and Lower Klamath Lake Refuges are discussed in U.S. Fish and Wildlife Service, "Draft Environmental Assessment: Implementation of the Agricultural Program on Tule Lake National Wildlife Refuge," 19 January 2001, 1.1–1.2, 1.8–1.14, http://www.klamathnwr.org/AgProgramEa.pdf. I discuss the different ways the Bureau of Reclamation and the FWS see the basin's waterscape in Robert Wilson, "Klamath's Federal Agencies Map Different Realities," *High Country News*, 13 August 2001.

34 The ONRC changed its name to Oregon Wild in 2005.

35 Both the ONRC and the Wilderness Society have been closely involved with environmental issues in the Klamath Basin. Their web sites detail the positions of each organization on water use and wildlife management in the Klamath Basin. Oregon Natural Resources Council, "Klamath Basin," http://www.onrc.org/programs/klamath.html#KBCbackground; The Wilderness Society, "The Klamath Basin: A Western Everglades," http://www.wilderness.org/WhereWeWork/Oregon/klamath.cfm.

36 Michael Milstein, "Fish Center of Swirling Storm," *Oregonian*, 8 May 2001.

37 The Klamath Tribes' claim to water was based on the Winters Doctrine, which states that Indian tribes have reserved rights to water that flow through their reservations. This doctrine applies even when the federal government has terminated the reservation, as was the case with the

Klamath Reservation in 1954. See David H. Getches, *Water Law in a Nut-shell*, 3rd ed. (St. Paul, Minn.: West Publishing Co., 1997), 310–11, 316–17; Charles F. Wilkinson, *American Indians, Time, and the Law: Native Societies in a Modern Constitutional Democracy* (New Haven, Conn.: Yale University Press, 1987), 70–71.

38 Fish and Wildlife Service Regional Director, Region 1, Portland, Oregon, "Formal Consultation on the Effects of the Long-Term Operation of the Klamath Project on the Lost River Sucker, Shortnose Sucker, Bald Eagle and American Peregrine Falcon," 1992, KBNWR-HQ.

39 This listing applied only to coho in northern California and southern Oregon. National Research Council, "Interim Report from the Committee on Endangered and Threatened Fishes in the Klamath River Basin, Scientific Evaluation of Biological Opinions on Endangered and Threatened Fishes in the Klamath River Basin" (Washington, D.C.: National Academy Press, 2002), 5. Joseph Taylor III discusses the effects of landscape changes on Oregon salmon in "Burning the Candle at Both Ends: Historicizing Overfishing in Oregon's Nineteenth-Century Salmon Fisheries," *Environmental History* 4 (January 1999): 54–79; and *Making Salmon*, 39–67.

40 Although the legal rulings affirmed the rights of the Klamath Tribes to some of the basin's water, the amount of their entitlement had to be determined by the State of Oregon. Since 1975, the state has been in the process of adjudicating the water rights of Indian tribes and federal agencies who claim the basin's water. Oregon Water Resources Department, "Resolving the Klamath."

41 Ron Hathaway and Teresa Welch, "Background," in *Water Allocation in the Klamath Reclamation Project, 2001: An Assessment of Natural Resource, Economic, Social, and Institutional Issues with a Focus on the Upper Klamath Basin*, ed. William S. Braunworth Jr., Teresa Welch, and Ron Hathaway (Corvallis: Oregon State University Extension Service, 2002), 31–43, 48; Michael Milstein, "Tensions Flare over Water Rights," *Oregonian*, 5 May 2001, and "Fish Center of Swirling Storm."

42 Michael Milstein, "Klamath Refuges Go Thirsty," *Oregonian*, 13 July 2001; Dave Mauser (refuge biologist), "Severe Water Shortages Expected for Lower Klamath National Wildlife Refuge," *Words from the Wetlands*, Spring 2001, KBNWR-HQ, 1–4.

43 Wilson, "Klamath's Federal Agencies."

44 Douglas Jehl, "Cries of 'Save the Suckerfish' Rile Farmers' Allies," *New York Times*, 20 June 2001; Dan Hansen, "Phrase Takes Root in For-

est Struggle," *Spokesman-Review (Spokane, Wash.)*, 23 February 2003. Hansen credits the origin of the phrase to Ron Arnold, executive vice-president of the Center for Free Enterprise, a Wise Use group based in Bellevue, Washington.

45 See Brad Knickerbocker, "Fish vs. Farmers Presents Test Case for Bush," *Christian Science Monitor*, 11 July 2001 and "West's Long, Hot Summer Flares up over Land Use," *Christian Science Monitor*, 9 August 2001; Seth Zuckerman, "Klamath Water Wars: Systems Out of Sync," *Christian Science Monitor*, 27 July 2001; "Oregon's Water War," *New York Times*, 15 July 2001; Eric Brazil, "Klamath Livelihoods Wither: Water Shut-Off Along Oregon Border Takes Toll on Farmers," *San Francisco Chronicle*,   16 July 2001; Nancy Solomon, "Klamath River," *Weekend Edition*, NPR, 16 June 2001, http://discovernpr.org/features/feature.jhtml?wfId=1124508; Elizabeth Arnold, "Klamath Basin, Oregon," *All Things Considered*, NPR, 16 July 2001, http://discover.npr.org/features/feature.jhtml?wfId=1125959; Andy Bowers, "Klamath Basin Protest," *All Things Considered*, NPR, 21 August 2001, http://discover.npr.org/features/feature.jhtml?wfId=1127763; Lee Hochberg, "Fish Vs. Farmers," *The Newshour with Jim Lehrer*, PBS, 20 August 2001.

46 "Klamath Basin Bucket Brigade: 50 Buckets of Defiance," *Klamath Falls Herald and News*, May 2001, 4.

47 Eric Brazil, "Farmers Protest Loss of Water," *San Francisco Chronicle*, 8 May 2001.

48 Protesters opened the head gates on two occasions before July 4th, 2001, but the Independence Day opening attracted the largest number of protesters and the greatest media attention. Associated Press, "Farmer's Reopen Canal Gates in Face of Federal Ban," *New York Times*, 4 July 2001; "Farmers Force Open Canal in Fight with U.S. Over Water," *New York Times*, 6 July 2001; Douglas Jehl, "Officials Loath to Act as Farmers Divert Water Meant for Endangered Fish," *New York Times*, 9 July 2001; Craig Welch, "Both Sides Harden in Oregon Water Dispute," *Seattle Times*, 9 July 2001.

49 See Milstein, "Klamath Refuges Go Thirsty."

50 Jehl, "Officials Loath to Act as Farmers Divert Water Meant for Endangered Fish." See also Brazil, "Klamath Livelihoods Wither."

51 On the connection between work and nature, see Richard White, "'Are You An Environmentalist or Do You Work for a Living?'" 171–85. White also discusses anti-federal government sentiment in the contemporary rural West in "The Current Weirdness in the West," *Western Historical Quarterly* 28 (Spring 1997): 5–16.

52   Bald eagles wintering in the basin feed on the carcasses of dead or dying waterfowl on the Lower Klamath Refuge. Environmentalists and the FWS feared that without adequate water, waterfowl would not use the refuge and, as a consequence, bald eagles would either starve or be forced to search for food elsewhere.

53   Michael Milstein, "Drought Has Little Effect on Birds," *Oregonian*, 5 December 2001.

54   The National Academy of Sciences (NAS) was created by presidential order in the nineteenth century to investigate matters of scientific importance and to offer opinions on scientific controversies when requested to by government agencies. In the case of the Klamath dispute, the National Research Council, an organization affiliated with the NAS, coordinated the investigation.

55   Eric Bailey, "Outside Group to Review Status of 3 Klamath Fish Species," *Los Angeles Times*, 3 October 2001.

56   Nancy Langston, "The Suckers, the Salmon, and the Historian," conference presentation, American Society for Environmental History Annual Meeting, 27 March 2003. Langston was a member of the National Resource Council committee.

57   National Research Council, "Interim Report," 11–25. See also its executive summary of the final report, Committee on Endangered and Threatened Fishes in the Klamath River Basin, "Endangered and Threatened Fishes in the Klamath River Basin, 1–16.

58   Associated Press, "Report Will Affect Klamath Water Allocations, Norton Says," *Seattle Post-Intelligencer*, 5 February 2002; Andrew C. Revkin, "Study Discounts Halting Irrigation to Protect Fish," *New York Times*, 5 February 2002. The fact that the committee's mandate for the interim report was narrow and that the committee would provide a broader set of recommendations in the final report was lost to most commentators. However, see "Fish Wars," *New York Times*, 14 February 2002; and "Move Slowly on Klamath: Report Proves Need for Better Science," *Register-Guard (Eugene, Ore.)*, 11 February 2002.

59   Timothy Egan, "As Thousands of Salmon Die, Fight for River Erupts Again," *New York Times*, 28 September 2002; John Driscoll, "Fish Kill Has Throttled the Klamath People," *Eureka (Calif.) Times-Standard*, 2 October 2002; Andy Dworkin and Michelle Cole, "Scene: Die-Off Could Affect Klamath River for Years," *Oregonian*, 27 September 2002.

60   Douglas Jehl, "Wetland Protection Fades," *New York Times*, 11 February 2003 and "On Environmental Rules, Bush Sees a Balance, Critics a Threat," *New York Times*, 23 February 2003.

61 A senior National Marine Fisheries Service (NFS) scientist also accused the agency and the Bureau of Reclamation of suppressing information that countered the bureau's goal of releasing more water to irrigators. See Laura Paskus, "'Sound Science' Goes Sour," *High Country News*, 23 June 2003.

62 Quote from Ted Kerasote, "Running on Empty," *Audubon Magazine*, October 2001, 23. See also Jeff Barnard, "Wildlife Refuge Asks Farmers for Water for Ducks," *San Francisco Chronicle*, 27 August 2002; Michael Milstein, "Suit: Klamath Refuge Water Belongs to Wildlife," *Oregonian*, 30 October 2002; Jeff Barnard, "Lawsuit Seeks to Force Farms Off Klamath Refuges," *Statesman Journal (Salem, Ore.)*, 30 October 2002. Refuge manager Phil Norton is no relation to Secretary of the Interior Gale Norton.

63 U.S. Fish and Wildlife Service, "Draft Environmental Assessment: Implementation of the Agricultural Program on Tule Lake," 1–2; Oregon Water Resources Department, "Resolving the Klamath."

64 Eric Bailey, "Bill Tackles Klamath River Woes," *Los Angeles Times*, 25 October 2002.

65 DeBuys and Meyers, *Salt Dreams*, 244; U.S. Fish and Wildlife Service, Department of the Interior, "Saving the Salton Sea: A Research Needs Assessment," 1997, 1–2. The phrase "the sump at the end of the West" is from Debuys and Meyers, *Salt Dreams*, 9.

66 DeBuys and Meyers, *Salt Dreams*, 224–32; U.S. Department of the Interior, Bureau of Reclamation, Lower Colorado Region, "Salton Sea Study: Status Report," Boulder City, Nevada, (January 2003), 9–26.

67 Quote from DeBuys and Meyers, *Salt Dreams*, 224. The Salton Sea National Wildlife Refuge is now called the Sonny Bono Salton Sea National Wildlife Refuge. Sonny Bono, best known to most Americans as a pop singer and former husband of Cher, was a U.S. Congressman representing the area in the mid-1990s. While in office, he led efforts to try to restore the sea. He died in a skiing accident in early 1998. In honor of his work on behalf of the sea, the refuge was renamed after him later that year.

68 Ibid., 232–42. Indeed, the Salton Sea seemed to attract writers who saw the area as a particularly vivid example of America's environmental and social problems of the late twentieth and early twenty-first centuries. For instance, see Robert H. Boyle, "Life—or Death—for the Salton Sea?" *Smithsonian*, June 1996, 86–94; and Clara Jeffery, "Go West, Old Man," *Harper's Magazine*, November 2002, 52–60.

69 Weidensaul, *Living on the Wind*, 239–46.

70 The compact was signed in 1922, but unratified by most of the states until 1928 (Arizona did not sign until 1944). Hundley, *Great Thirst*, 214–15; Reisner, *Cadillac Desert*, 129–31.

71 The city already draws some of its water from the Colorado River via an aqueduct, so the transfer would not entail constructing new infrastructure to convey the water to the coast.

72 Matt Jenkins, "The Royal Squeeze," *High Country News*, 16 September 2002, and "The Efficiency Paradox," ibid., 5 February 2007.

73 Jenkins, "Royal Squeeze," 14; Daniel B. Wood, "In Water Transfer, Farmers vs. Sprawl," *Christian Science Monitor*, 11 December 2002; Dean E. Murphy, "In a First, U.S. Puts Limits on California's Thirst," *New York Times*, 5 January 2003.

74 Edward P. Glenn, Christopher Lee, Richard Felger, and Scott Zengel, "Effects of Water Management of the Wetlands of the Colorado River Delta, Mexico," *Conservation Biology* 10, no. 4 (1996): 1175–86; Edward P. Glenn, Francisco Zamora-Arroyo, Pamela L. Nagler, Mark Biggs, William Shaw, and Karl Flessa, "Ecology and Conservation Biology of the Colorado River Delta, Mexico," *Journal of Arid Environments* 49 (2001): 5–15; Jennifer Pitt, "Can We Restore the Colorado River Delta?" *Journal of Arid Environments* 49 (2001): 211–20.

75 "Unflooded," but not dry. Winter is the rainy season in the Central Valley, so rice fields accumulate some water during this time.

76 Advisory Committee on Alternatives to Rice Straw Burning, "Report of the Advisory Committee on Alternatives to Rice Straw Burning," (October 1997), California Air Resources Board, http://www.arb.ca.gov/smp/rice/phsdown/altfin2.pdf, 59–75; Marc Reisner, "Deconstructing the Age of Dams," *High Country News*, 27 October 1997; Glen Martin, "Waterfowl Device Helps Ducks, Rice Farmers," *San Francisco Chronicle*, 29 March 1993.

EPILOGUE

1 Eryn Gable, "At Century Celebration, Refuge System in Disrepair," *Greenwire*, 14 March 2003. U.S. Fish and Wildlife Service, Arctic National Wildlife Refuge, "Wildlife and Wild Landscapes," http://arctic.fws.gov/wildlife_habitat.htm#section1 (accessed 25 August 2008).

2 Scott, *Seeing Like a State*, 11–52.

3 Donald J. Pisani, *Water, Land, and Law in the West* (Lawrence: University Press of Kansas, 1996), 119–23, and *Water and American Government*.

4 Quoted in Pisani, *Water, Land, and Law in the West*, 123.

5 For a cautionary note on using Scott's theories in an American political context, see Morton Keller, "Looking at the State: An American Perspective," *American Historical Review* (February 2001): 114–18. Pisani discusses Scott's work in relation to the Bureau of Reclamation's failed efforts at social planning in *Water and American Government*, 294–95.

6 William C. Ashe, "The Dilemma of the National Wildlife Refuge System: Opening Remarks," *Transactions of the Fifty-Seventh North American Wildlife and Natural Resources Conference* (1992): 541–44; W. Alan Wentz and Frederic A. Reid, "Managing Refuges for Waterfowl Purposes and Biological Diversity: Can Both Be Achieved?" ibid., 581–85; Michael J. Bean, "Biological Diversity and the Refuge System: Beyond the Endangered Species Act in Fish and Wildlife Management," ibid., 577–80; Robert J. Shallenberger, Mary Anne Young, and Nancy J. Roper, "Changing the Way We Look at the Land," *Transactions of the Fifty-Ninth North American Wildlife and Natural Resources Conference* (1994): 532–40.

7 Tim P. Barnett et al. "Human-Induced Changes in the Hydrology of the Western United States," *Science* 319, no. 5866 (2008): 1080–83.

8 For an overview of the effects of climate change on migratory species, see Humphrey Q. P. Quick, "Migratory Wildlife in a Changing Climate," in *Migratory Species and Climate Change: Impacts of a Changing Environment on Wild Animals*, CMS UNEP, DEFRA, (Bonn, Germany: UNEP/CMS, 2006), 40–45.

9 Warren, *Hunter's Game*; Taylor, *Making S)almon*; Jacoby, *Crimes against Nature*; Bruce Braun, *The Intemperate Rainforest: Nature, Culture, and Power on Canada's West Coast* (Minneapolis: University of Minnesota Press, 2002).

10 Wilcove, *No Way Home*, 1–12.

BIBLIOGRAPHY

ARCHIVAL COLLECTIONS AND REFUGE HOLDINGS

California State Archives, Sacramento, California. Division of Fish and Game.

Denver Public Library, Western History and Genealogy Collection, Denver, Colorado. J. Clark Salyer Papers

National Archives and Records Administration, College Park, Maryland. Record Group 22, Bureau of Biological Survey and United States Fish and Wildlife Service.

National Archives and Records Administration, Denver, Colorado. Record Group 115, United States Bureau of Reclamation.

National Archives and Records Administration, Pacific Alaska Region, Seattle, Washington. Record Group 22, Bureau of Biological Survey and United States Fish and Wildlife Service.

New York Public Library, Rare Books and Manuscripts. National Audubon Society Collection.

Oregon State University, Special Collections. William L. Finley Papers.

United States Fish and Wildlife Service National Wildlife Refuges.
Klamath Basin National Wildlife Refuges Complex, Tulelake, California.
Sacramento National Wildlife Refuge Complex, Willows, California.
Tualatin National Wildlife Refuge, Tualatin, Oregon.

BOOKS, ARTICLES, THESES, GOVERNMENT DOCUMENTS

Abbott, Carl. "The Federal Presence." In *The Oxford History of the American West*, ed. Clyde A. Milner II, Carol A. O'Connor and Martha A. Sandweiss, 469–99. New York: Oxford University Press, 1994.

Alerstam, Thomas. *Bird Migration*. Cambridge: Cambridge University Press, 1990.

Amory, Copley. "Agriculture and Wild Fowl Conservation at Lower Klamath Lake." *New Reclamation Era*, May 1926, 80–82.

Ashe, William C. "The Dilemma of the National Wildlife Refuge System: Opening Remarks." *Transactions of the Fifty-Seventh North American Wildlife and Natural Resources Conference* (1992): 541–44.

Associated Press. "Farmer's Reopen Canal Gates in Face of Federal Ban." *New York Times*, 4 July 2001.

———. "Report Will Affect Klamath Water Allocations, Norton Says." *Seattle Post-Intelligencer*, 5 February 2002.

Babb, David E. "History of Early Water Diversions and Their Impact on Owens Lake." In *The History of Water: Eastern Sierra Nevada, Owens Valley, White-Inyo Mountains*, ed. C. A Hall Jr., V. Doyle-Jones, and B. Widawski, 263–67. White Mountain Research Station Symposium, vol. 4. Los Angeles: White Mountain Research Station, 1992.

Bailey, Eric. "Outside Group to Review Status of 3 Klamath Fish Species." *Los Angeles Times*, 3 October 2001.

———. "Bill Tackles Klamath River Woes." *Los Angeles Times*, 25 October 2002.

Baldassarre, Guy A., and Eric G. Bolen. *Waterfowl Ecology and Management*. 2nd ed. Malabar, Fla.: Krieger Publishing Company, 2006.

Banks, Richard C., and Paul F. Springer. "A Century of Population Trends of Waterfowl in Western North America." *Studies in Aviation Biology* 15 (1994): 134–46.

Barcott, Bruce. "What's a River For?" *Mother Jones*, June 2003, 44–51.

Barnard, Jeff. "Wildlife Refuge Asks Farmers for Water for Ducks." *San Francisco Chronicle*, 27 August 2002.

———. "Lawsuit Seeks to Force Farms Off Klamath Refuges." *Statesman Journal (Salem, Ore.)*, 30 October 2002.

Barnett, Tim P., David W. Pierce, Hugo G. Hidalgo, Celine Bonfils, Benjamin D. Santer, Tapash Das, Govindasamy Bala, Andrew W. Wood, Toru Nozawa, Arthur A. Mirin, Daniel R. Cayan, and Michael D. Dettinger.

"Human-Induced Changes in the Hydrology of the Western United States." *Science* 319, no. 5866 (2008): 1080–83.

Barrow, Mark V. Jr. *A Passion for Birds: American Ornithology after Audubon.* Princeton, N.J.: Princeton University Press, 1998.

———. "Science, Sentiment, and the Specter of Extinction: Reconsidering Birds of Prey during America's Interwar Years." *Environmental History* 7, no. 1 (2002): 69–98.

Batt, Bruce D. J., Michael G. Anderson, C. Diane Anderson, and F. Dale Caswell. "The Use of Prairie Potholes by North American Ducks." In *Northern Prairie Wetlands*, ed. Arnold van der Valk, 204–27 (Ames: Iowa State University Press, 1989).

Bean, Michael J. "Biological Diversity and the Refuge System: Beyond the Endangered Species Act in Fish and Wildlife Management." *Transactions of the Fifty-Seventh North American Wildlife and Natural Resources Conference* (1992): 577–80.

Bean, Michael J., and Melanie J. Rowland. *The Evolution of National Wildlife Law.* 3rd ed. Westport, Conn.: Praeger Publishers, 1997.

Bellrose, Frank C. *Ducks, Geese, and Swans of North America.* Harrisburg, Pa: Stackpole Books, 1980.

Benson, Reed D. "Giving Suckers (and Salmon) an Even Break: Klamath Basin Water and the Endangered Species Act." *Tulane Environmental Law Journal* 15, no. 2 (2002): 197–238.

Berthold, Peter. *Bird Migration: A General Survey.* 2nd ed. Oxford: Oxford University Press, 2001.

Blake, Tupper Ansel, Madeleine Graham Blake, and William Kittredge. *Balancing Water: Restoring the Klamath Basin.* Berkeley: University of California Press, 2000.

Blake, Tupper Ansel, and Peter Steinhart. *Tracks in the Sky: Wildlife and Wetlands of the Pacific Flyway.* San Francisco: Chronicle Books, 1987.

Bleyhl, Norris A. "A History of the Production and Marketing of Rice in California." PhD diss., University of Minnesota, 1955.

Blomley, Nick. "Property Rights." In *The Dictionary of Human Geography*, ed. R. J. Johnston, Derek Gregory, Geraldine Pratt, and Michael Watts, 651. 4th ed. Oxford: Blackwell Publishers, 2000.

Bourne, Joel. "Bugging Out." *Audubon Magazine*, March/April 1999, 71–73.

Boyle, Robert H. "Life—or Death—for the Salton Sea?" *Smithsonian*, June 1996, 86–94.

Braun, Bruce. *The Intemperate Rainforest: Nature, Culture, and Power on Canada's West Coast.* Minneapolis: University of Minnesota Press, 2002.

Brazil, Eric. "Klamath Livelihoods Wither: Water Shut-Off Along Oregon Border Takes Toll on Farmers." *San Francisco Chronicle*, 16 July 2001.

Briggs, Shirley A., and the staff of Rachel Carson Council. *Basic Guide to Pesticides: Their Characteristics and Hazards*. Washington, D.C.: Hemisphere Publishing Corporation, 1992.

Brinkley, Douglas. *The Wilderness Warrior: Theodore Roosevelt and the Crusade for America*. New York: HarperCollins, 2009.

Bureau of Reclamation. "Lower Klamath Lake, Klamath Project, Oregon." *New Reclamation Era*, November 1925.

Burgess, Bonnie B. *Fate of the Wild: The Endangered Species Act and the Future of Biodiversity*. Athens: University of Georgia Press, 2001.

Burnett, J. Alexander. *A Passion for Wildlife: The History of the Canadian Wildlife Service*. Vancouver: UBC Press, 2003.

Byrne-Shirley, Betty Lou. "The Refuges." *Journal of the Modoc County Historical Society*, no. 18 (1996): 31–48.

Cameron, Jenks. *The Bureau of the Biological Survey: Its History, Activities and Organization*. Baltimore: Johns Hopkins University Press, 1929.

Cameron, Laura. *Openings: A Meditation on History, Method, and Sumas Lake*. Montreal and Kingston: McGill-Queen's University Press, 1997.

Carson, Rachel. *Silent Spring*. New York: Houghton Mifflin Company, 1962.

Cart, Theodore W. "The Lacey Act: America's First Nationwide Wildlife Statute." *Forest History* (October 1973): 4–13.

———. "'New Deal' for Wildlife: A Perspective on Federal Conservation Policy, 1933–1940." *Pacific Northwest Quarterly* 63, no. 3 (1972): 113–20.

Cartmill, Matt. *A View to a Death in the Morning: Hunting and Nature through History*. Cambridge, Mass.: Harvard University Press, 1993.

Castree, Noel. "The Production of Nature." In *A Companion to Economic Geography*, ed. Eric Sheppard and Trevor J. Barnes. Oxford: Blackwell Publishers Ltd., 2000.

Cawley, R. McGreggor. *Federal Land, Western Anger: The Sagebrush Rebellion and Environmental Politics*. Lawrence: University Press of Kansas, 1993.

Chandler, William J. "Migratory Bird Protection and Management." In *Audubon Wildlife Report, 1985*, ed. Roger L. Di Silvestro, 26–71. New York: The National Audubon Society, 1985.

Chang, Gordon H., ed. *Morning Glory, Evening Shadow: Yamato Ichihashi and His Internment Writings, 1942–1945*. Stanford, Calif.: Stanford University Press, 1997.

Chase, Steve, and Mark Madison. "The Expanding Ark: 100 Years of Wildlife Refuges." *Wild Earth*, Winter 2003–2004, 18–27.

Cosgrove, Denis E. *Social Formation and Symbolic Landscape.* Madison: University of Wisconsin Press, 1984. Reprint, Madison: University of Wisconsin Press, 1998.

Cox, George W. "The Evolution of Avian Migration Systems between the Temperate and Tropical Regions of the New World." *The American Naturalist* 126, no. 4 (1985): 451–74.

Davis, Charles, ed. *Western Public Lands and Environmental Politics.* Boulder: Westview Press, 1997.

Davis, Cynthia F. *Where Water Is King: The Story of the Glenn-Colusa Irrigation District.* Willows, Calif.: Glenn-Colusa Irrigation District, 1984.

Day, Albert M. *North American Waterfowl.* New York: Stackpole and Heck, Inc., 1949.

DeBuys, William, and Joan Meyers. *Salt Dreams: Land and Water in Low-Down California.* Albuquerque: University of New Mexico Press, 1999.

Dicken, Samuel N. "Pluvial Lake Modoc, Klamath County, Oregon, and Modoc and Siskiyou Counties, California." *Oregon Geology* 42, no. 11 (1980): 179–87.

Dicken, Samuel N., and Emily Dicken. *The Legacy of Ancient Lake Modoc: A Historical Geography of the Klamath Lakes Basin.* Eugene: University of Oregon Bookstore, 1985.

———. *The Making of Oregon: A Study in Historical Geography.* Portland: Oregon Historical Society, 1979.

Dingle, Hugh. *Migration: The Biology of Life on the Move.* New York: Oxford University Press, 1996.

Doherty, Jim. "Refuges on the Rocks." *Audubon*, July 1983, 74–117.

Dorsey, Kurkpatrick. *The Dawn of Conservation Diplomacy: U.S.-Canadian Wildlife Protection Treaties in the Progressive Era.* Seattle: University of Washington Press, 1998.

———. "Scientists, Citizens, and Statesmen: U.S.-Canadian Wildlife Protection Treaties in the Progressive Era." *Diplomatic History* 19, no. 3 (1995): 407–29.

Doughty, Robin W. *Feather Fashions and Bird Preservation: A Study in Nature Protection.* Berkeley: University of California Press, 1975.

Driscoll, John. "Fish Kill Has Throttled the Klamath People." *Eureka (Calif.) Times-Standard*, 2 October 2002.

DuMont, Philip A., and Henry M. Reeves. "The Darling-Salyer Team." In *Flyways: Pioneering Waterfowl Management in North America*, ed. A. S. Hawkins, R. C. Hanson, H. K. Nelson, and H. M. Reeves, 107–12. Washington, D.C.: United States Department of the Interior, Fish and Wildlife Service, 1984.

Dunlap, Thomas R. *DDT: Scientists, Citizens, and Public Policy.* Princeton: Princeton University Press, 1981.

———. *Saving America's Wildlife: Ecology and the American Mind, 1850–1990.* Princeton, N.J.: Princeton Univ. Press, 1988.

Dworkin, Andy, and Michelle Cole. "Scene: Die-Off Could Affect Klamath River for Years." *(Portland) Oregonian,* 27 September 2002.

Egan, Timothy. "As Thousands of Salmon Die, Fight for River Erupts Again." *New York Times,* 27 September 2002.

Ehler, Lester E., and Dale G. Bottrell. "The Illusion of Integrated Pest Management." *Issues in Science and Technology* (Spring 2000): 61–64.

Evenden, Matthew D. "The Laborers of Nature: Economic Ornithology and the Role of Birds as Agents of Biological Pest Control in North American Agriculture, ca. 1880–1930." *Forest & Conservation History* 39 (October 1995): 172–83.

Ewan, Rebecca Fish. *A Land Between: Owens Valley, California.* Baltimore: Johns Hopkins University Press, 2000.

"Farmers Force Open Canal in Fight with U.S. Over Water." *New York Times,* 6 July 2001.

Fiege, Mark. *Irrigated Eden: The Making of an Agricultural Landscape in the American West.* Seattle: University of Washington Press, 1999.

———. "Private Property and Ecological Commons in the American West." In *Everyday America: Cultural Landscape Studies after J. B. Jackson,* ed. Chris Wilson and Paul Groth, 219–31. Berkeley: University of California Press, 2003.

———. "The Weedy West: Mobile Nature, Boundaries, and Common Space in the Montana Landscape." *Western Historical Quarterly* 36, no. 1 (2005).

Finley, William L. "Cruising the Klamath." *Bird Lore,* Nov.–Dec. 1915, 485–91.

———. "Game Refuges." *Nature Magazine,* May 1926, 305.

———. "Hunting Birds with a Camera: A Record of Twenty Years of Adventure in Obtaining Photographs of Feathered Wild Life in America." *National Geographic,* August 1923, 160–201.

———. "In Search of the Plume Hunters." *Atlantic Monthly,* September 1905, 374–75.

———. "Passing of the Marshlands." *Nature Magazine,* March 1926, 173.

———. "Report of William L. Finley, Field Agent for the Pacific Coast States," *Bird-Lore,* Nov.–Dec., 1918–1923.

———. "The Trail of the Plume Hunter." *Atlantic Magazine,* September 1910, 374–75.

"Fish Wars." *New York Times,* 14 February 2002.

Foster, Doug. "Refuges and Reclamation: Conflicts in the Klamath Basin, 1904–1964." *Oregon Historical Quarterly* 103, no. 2 (2002): 150–87.

Foster, Janet. *Working for Wildlife: The Beginnings of Preservation in Canada.* 2nd ed. Toronto: University of Toronto Press, 1998.

Frayer, W. E., Dennis D. Peters, and H. Ross Pywell. "Wetlands of the Central Valley: Status and Trends, 1939 to Mid-1980s." Portland, Ore.: United States Fish and Wildlife Service, 1989.

Gabrielson, Ira N. *Wildlife Refuges.* New York: The Macmillan Company, 1943.

Garone, Philip. "The Fall and Rise of the Wetlands of California's Great Central Valley: A Historical and Ecological Study of an Endangered Resource of the Pacific Flyway." PhD diss., University of California–Davis, 2006.

———. "The Tragedy at Kesterson Reservoir: A Case Study in Environmental History and a Lesson in Ecological Complexity." *Environs: Environmental Law and Policy Journal* 22, no. 2 (1999): 107–44.

Getches, David H. *Water Law in a Nutshell.* 3rd ed. St. Paul, Minn.: West Publishing Co., 1997.

Gill, Frank B. *Ornithology.* 2nd ed. New York: W. H. Freeman and Company, 1995.

Gilmer, D. S., J. L. Yee, D. M. Mauser, and J. M. Hainline. "Waterfowl Migration on Klamath Basin National Wildlife Refuges 1953–2000." U.S. Geological Survey, Biological Resources Discipline Biological Science Report, USGS/BRD/BSR, 2004.

Gilmer, David S., Michael R. Miller, Richard D. Bauer, and John R. LeDonne. "California's Central Valley Wintering Waterfowl: Concerns and Challenges." *Transactions of the North American Wildlife and Natural Resources Conference* 47 (1982): 441–52.

Glenn, Edward P., Christopher Lee, Richard Felger, and Scott Zengel. "Effects of Water Management of the Wetlands of the Colorado River Delta, Mexico." *Conservation Biology* 10, no. 4 (1996): 1175–86.

Glenn, Edward P., Christopher Lee, and Carlos Valdes-Casillas. "Introduction." *Journal of Arid Environments* 49 (2001): 1–4.

Glenn, Edward P., Francisco Zamora-Arroyo, Pamela L. Nagler, Mark Biggs, William Shaw, and Karl Flessa. "Ecology and Conservation Biology of the Colorado River Delta, Mexico." *Journal of Arid Environments* 49 (2001): 5–15.

Graham, Frank Jr. *The Audubon Ark: A History of the National Audubon Society.* New York: Alfred A. Knopf, 1990.

Grayson, Donald K. *Desert's Past: A Natural Prehistory of the Great Basin.* Washington, D.C.: Smithsonian Institution Press, 1993.

Haggerty, Julia, and William Travis. "Out of Administrative Control: Absentee Owners, Resident Elk and the Shifting Nature of Wildlife Management in Southwestern Montana." *Geoforum* 37, no. 5 (2006): 816–30.

Hales, Wendy J. "The Impact of Human Activity on Deltaic Sedimentation, Marshes of the Fraser River Delta, British Columbia." PhD diss., University of British Columbia, 2000.

Hall, C. A. Jr., V. Doyle-Jones, and B. Widawski, eds. *The History of Water: Eastern Sierra Nevada, Owens Valley, White-Inyo Mountains*. White Mountain Research Station Symposium, vol. 4. Los Angeles: White Mountain Research Station, 1992.

Hall, Frank Arthur Jr. "An Environmental History of the Sacramento National Wildlife Refuge." M.A. Thesis, California State University, Chico, 1975.

Hansen, Dan. "Phrase Takes Root in Forest Struggle." *Spokesman-Review (Spokane, Wash.)*, 23 February 2003.

Hardwick, Susan W., and Donald G. Holtgrieve. *Valley for Dreams: Life and Landscape in the Sacramento Valley*. Lanham, Md.: Rowman & Littlefield, 1996.

Harris, Cole. "The Lower Mainland, 1820–81." In *Vancouver and Its Region*, ed. Graeme Wynn and Tim Oke, 149–70. Vancouver: UBC Press, 1992.

Harris, Tom. *Death in the Marsh*. Washington, D.C.: Island Press, 1991.

Harvey, Mark W. T. *A Symbol of Wilderness: Echo Park and the American Conservation Movement*. Albuquerque: University of New Mexico Press, 1994. Reprint, Seattle: University of Washington Press, 2000.

Hathaway, Ron, and Teresa Welch. "Background." In *Water Allocation in the Klamath Reclamation Project, 2001: An Assessment of Natural Resource, Economic, Social, and Institutional Issues with a Focus on the Upper Klamath Basin*, ed. William S. Braunworth Jr., Teresa Welch, and Ron Hathaway, 31–43. Corvallis, Ore.: Oregon State University Extension Service, 2002.

Hawkins, A. S., R. C. Hanson, H. K. Nelson, and H. M. Reeves, eds. *Flyways: Pioneering Waterfowl Management in North America*. Washington, D.C.: United States Department of the Interior, Fish and Wildlife Service, 1984.

Haynal, Patrick. "Termination and Tribal Survival: The Klamath Tribes of Oregon." *Oregon Historical Quarterly* 101, no. 3 (2000): 270–301.

Hays, Samuel P. *Beauty, Health, and Permanence: Environmental Politics in the United States, 1955–1985*. New York: Cambridge University Press, 1987.

———. *Conservation and the Gospel of Efficiency: The Progressive Conservation Movement, 1890–1920*. Cambridge, Mass.: Harvard University Press, 1959.

———. *A History of Environmental Politics since 1945*. Pittsburgh: University of Pittsburgh Press, 2000.

Heitmeyer, Mickey E., Daniel P. Connelly, and Roger L. Pederson. "The Central, Imperial, and Cochella Valleys of California." In *Habitat Management for Migrating and Wintering Waterfowl in North America*, ed. Loren M. Smith, Roger L. Pederson, and Richard M. Kaminski, 475–505. Lubbock: Texas Tech University Press, 1989.

Henderson, George L. *California and the Fictions of Capital*. New York: Oxford University Press, 2000.

Hibbard, Benjamin Horace. *A History of the Public Land Policies*. New York: The Macmillan Company, 1924. Reprint, Madison: University of Wisconsin Press, 1965.

Hirt, Paul W. *A Conspiracy of Optimism: Management of the National Forests since World War II*. Lincoln: University of Nebraska Press, 1994.

Hundley, Norris Jr. *The Great Thirst: Californians and Water: A History*. Rev. ed. Berkeley: University of California Press, 2001.

Huston, Ann E. "A History of the Lower Klamath National Wildlife Refuge." In *A River Never the Same: A History of Water in the Klamath Basin*, ed. Shaw Historical Library, 59–68. Klamath Falls, Ore.: Oregon Institute of Technology, 1999.

Igler, David. *Industrial Cowboys: Miller & Lux and the Transformation of the Far West, 1850–1920*. Berkeley: University of California Press, 2001.

Isenberg, Andrew C. *The Destruction of the Bison: An Environmental History, 1750–1920*. Cambridge: Cambridge University Press, 2000.

Jacoby, Karl. *Crimes against Nature: Squatters, Poachers, Thieves, and the Hidden History of American Conservation*. Berkeley: University of California Press, 2001.

Jeffery, Clara. "Go West, Old Man." *Harper's Magazine*, November 2002, 52–60.

Jehl, Douglas. "Cries of 'Save the Suckerfish' Rile Farmers' Political Allies." *New York Times*, 20 June 2001.

———."Officials Loath to Act as Farmers Divert Water Meant for Endangered Fish." *New York Times*, 9 July 2001.

———. "On Environmental Rules, Bush Sees a Balance, Critics a Threat." *New York Times*, 23 February 2003.

———. "Wetland Protection Fades." *New York Times*, 11 February 2003.

Jehl, Joseph R. Jr. "Changes in Saline and Alkaline Lake Avifaunas in Western North America in the Past 150 Years." In *A Century of Avifaunal Change in Western North America*, ed. Joseph R. Jehl Jr. and Ned K. Johnson, 258–72. *Studies in Avian Biology*, no. 15. Cooper Ornithological Society, 1994.

Jelinek, Lawrence J. *Harvest Empire: A History of California Agriculture*. San Francisco: Boyd & Fraser Publishing Company, 1979.

Jenkins, Bill. "Tulelake Duck Hospital Saves Botulism Victims." *Klamath Falls (Ore.) Herald and News*, 31 August 1949.

Jenkins, Matt. "The Efficiency Paradox." *High Country News*, 5 February 2007.

"The Royal Squeeze." *High Country News*, 16 September 2002.

Jensen, Wayne I., and Cecil S. Williams. "Botulism and Fowl Cholera." In *Waterfowl Tomorrow*, ed. Joseph P. Linduska, 333–41. Washington, D.C.: United States Department of the Interior, Bureau of Sport Fisheries and Wildlife, Fish and Wildlife Service, 1964.

Johnson, Stephen, Gerald Haslam, and Robert Dawson. *The Great Central Valley: California's Heartland*. Berkeley: University of California Press, 1993.

Kadlec, John A., and Loren M. Smith. "The Great Basin Marshes." In *Habitat Management for Migrating and Wintering Waterfowl in North America*, ed. Loren M. Smith, Roger L. Pederson, and Richard M. Kaminski, 451–74. Lubbock: Texas Tech University Press, 1989.

Keller, Morton "Looking at the State: An American Perspective." *American Historical Review* (February 2001): 114–18.

Kelley, Robert. *Battling the Inland Sea: American Political Culture, Public Policy, and the Sacramento Valley, 1850–1986*. Berkeley: University of California Press, 1989.

Kennedy, David M. *Freedom from Fear: The American People in Depression and War, 1929–1945*. New York: Oxford University Press, 1999.

Kerasote, Ted. "Running on Empty." *Audubon Magazine*, October 2001, 22–23.

Kittredge, William. *Owning It All*. Saint Paul, Minn.: Graywolf Press, 1987.

———. *Who Owns the West?* San Francisco: Mercury Press, 1996.

Klingle, Matthew. *Emerald City: An Environmental History of Seattle*. New Haven, Conn.: Yale University Press, 2007.

Knickerbocker, Brad. "Fish vs. Farmers Presents Test Case for Bush." *Christian Science Monitor*, 11 July 2001.

———. "West Makes a Battle Cry of Klamath Basin." *Christian Science Monitor*, 27 August 2001.

———. "West's Long, Hot Summer Flares up over Land Use." *Christian Science Monitor*, 9 August 2001.

Krech, Shepard III, John R. McNeill, and Carolyn Merchant, eds. *Encyclopedia of World Environmental History*. New York: Routledge, 2004.

Ladner, T. Ellis. *Above the Sand Heads: A Vivid Account of Life on the Delta of the Fraser River, 1868–1900*. Cloverdale, B.C.: D. W. Friesen & Sons Ltd., 1979.

Langston, Nancy. *Forest Dreams, Forest Nightmares: The Paradox of Old Growth in the Inland West.* Seattle: University of Washington Press, 1995.

———. *Where Land and Water Meet: A Western Landscape Transformed.* Seattle: University of Washington Press, 2003.

Latour, Bruno. *Science in Action.* Cambridge, Mass.: Harvard University Press, 1987.

———. *We Have Never Been Modern.* Cambridge, Mass.: Harvard University Press, 1993.

Leach, Barry A. "Waterfowl on a Pacific Estuary: A Natural History of Man and Waterfowl on the Lower Fraser River." British Columbia Provincial Museum Special Publication, no. 5. Victoria: British Columbia Provincial Museum, 1982.

Lear, Linda. *Rachel Carson: Witness for Nature.* New York: Henry Holt and Company, 1997.

Leitch, W. G. *Ducks and Men: Forty Years of Co-Operation in Conservation.* Winnipeg, Manitoba: Ducks Unlimited, 1978.

Lemly, A. Dennis. "Agriculture and Wildlife: Ecological Implications of Subsurface Irrigation Drainage." *Journal of Arid Environments* 28 (1994): 85–94.

———. "Irrigation Drainage." In *Encyclopedia of Deserts*, ed. Michael A. Mares, 304–7. Norman: University of Oklahoma Press, 1999.

Lendt, David E. *Ding: The Life of Jay Norwood Darling.* Ames: Iowa State University Press, 1989.

Leopold, Aldo. *Game Management.* New York: Charles Scribner's Sons, 1933.

———. *A Sand County Almanac, and Sketches Here and There.* New York: Oxford University Press, 1949. Reprint, New York: Oxford University Press, 1989.

Lincoln, Frederick C. "Bird Banding." In *Fifty Years' Progress in American Ornithology, 1883–1933*, ed. Frank M. Chapman and T. S. Palmer. Lancaster, Pa.: American Ornithologists' Union, 1933.

———. *Bird-Banding: Its First Decade Under the Biological Survey.* U.S. Bureau of Biological Survey. Washington, D.C.: Government Printing Office, 1931.

———. *The Migration of American Birds.* New York: Doubleday, Doran, & Company, Inc., 1939.

Lindsey, Robert. "Water That Enriched Valley Becomes a Peril in California." *New York Times*, 7 January 1985.

Linduska, Joseph P., ed. *Waterfowl Tomorrow.* Washington, D.C.: United States Department of the Interior, Bureau of Sport Fisheries and Wildlife, Fish and Wildlife Service, 1964.

Line, Les. "Foul Play in the Klamath Basin." *Audubon Magazine*, May–June 1997, 119–20.

Loo, Tina. *States of Nature: Conserving Canada's Wildlife in the Twentieth Century.* Vancouver: UBC Press, 2006.

Lostetter, Clinton H. "They've Got to Eat Someplace." In *Flyways: Pioneering Waterfowl Management in North America*, ed. A. S. Hawkins, R. C. Hanson, H. K. Nelson and H. M. Reeves, 461–71. Washington, D.C.: United States Department of the Interior, Fish and Wildlife Service, 1984.

Lowitt, Richard. *The New Deal and the West.* Bloomington: Indiana University Press, 1984.

Madison, Mark. "Conserving Conservation: Field Notes from an Animal Archive." *Public Historian* (2004): 145–56.

Maher, Neil M. "A New Deal Body Politic: Landscape, Labor, and the Civilian Conservation Corps." *Environmental History* 7, no. 3 (2002): 435–61.

Martin, Glen. "Waterfowl Device Helps Ducks, Rice Famers." *San Francisco Chronicle*, 29 March 1993.

Mathewson, Worth. *William L. Finley: Pioneer Wildlife Photographer.* Corvallis: Oregon State University Press, 1986.

Matthiessen, Peter. *Wildlife in America.* New York: The Viking Press, 1959.

Mauser, Dave. "Severe Water Shortages Expected for Lower Klamath National Wildlife Refuge." *Words from the Wetlands*, Spring 2001.

McPhee, John. *Encounters with the Archdruid.* New York: Farrar, Straus and Giroux, 1971.

Meine, Curt. *Aldo Leopold: His Life and Work.* Madison: University of Wisconsin Press, 1988.

Meinig, Donald W. *The Interpretation of Ordinary Landscapes.* Oxford: Oxford University Press, 1979.

———. *The Shaping of America: A Geographical Perspective on 500 Years of History.* Volume 3: Transcontinental America, 1850–1915. New Haven, Conn.: Yale University Press, 1998.

Merrill, Karen R. "In Search of the 'Federal Presence' in the American West." *Western Historical Quarterly* 30 (Winter 1999): 449–73.

Milner, Clyde A. II, Carol A. O'Connor, and Martha A. Sandweiss, eds. *The Oxford History of the American West.* New York: Oxford University Press, 1994.

Milstein, Michael. "Competing Water Demands Threaten River." *(Portland) Oregonian*, 11 April 2003.

———. "Crisis Smothers Economy." *(Portland) Oregonian*, 7 May 2001.

———. "Drought Has Little Effect on Birds." *(Portland) Oregonian*, 5 December 2001.

———. "Feds Seek Water for Klamath Salmon." *(Portland) Oregonian*, 2 April 2003.

———. "Fish Center of Swirling Storm." *(Portland) Oregonian*, 8 May 2001.

———. "Klamath Refuges Go Thirsty." *(Portland) Oregonian*, 13 July 2001.

———. "Suit: Klamath Refuge Water Belongs to Wildlife." *(Portland) Oregonian*, 30 October 2002.

———. "Tensions Flare over Water Rights." *(Portland) Oregonian*, 5 May 2001.

———. "Water Quality, Future Murky." *(Portland) Oregonian*, 9 May 2001.

Minnigerode, Fitzhugh L. "Vanishing Water Fowl Have a New Sanctuary." *New York Times*, 8 January 1933.

Mitchell, Don. *Cultural Geography: A Critical Introduction*. Malden, Mass.: Blackwell Publishing, 2000.

———. *The Lie of the Land: Migrant Workers and the California Landscape*. Minneapolis: University of Minnesota Press, 1996.

Mitman, Gregg. *Reel Nature: America's Romance with Wildlife on Film*. Cambridge, Mass.: Harvard University Press, 1999. 2nd ed., Seattle: University of Washington Press, 2009.

Mitsch, William J., and James G. Gosselink. *Wetlands*. 3rd ed. New York: John Wiley & Sons, Inc., 2000.

"Move Slowly on Klamath: Report Proves Need for Better Science." *Register-Guard (Eugene, Ore.)*, 11 February 2002.

Murton, James. *Creating a Modern Countryside: Liberalism and Land Resettlement in British Columbia*. Vancouver: UBC Press, 2007.

Murphy, Dean E. "In a First, U.S. Puts Limits on California's Thirst." *New York Times*, 5 January 2003.

Nash, Gerald D. *The Federal Landscape: An Economic History of the Twentieth-Century West*. Tucson: University of Arizona Press, 1999.

Nash, Linda. *Inescapable Ecologies: A History of Environment, Disease, and Knowledge*. Berkeley: University of California Press, 2006.

National Research Council (U.S.) Committee on Irrigation-Induced Water Quality Problems. "Interim Report from the Committee on Endangered and Threatened Fishes in the Klamath River Basin, Scientific Evaluation of Biological Opinions on Endangered and Threatened Fishes in the Klamath River Basin." Washington, D.C.: National Academy Press, 2002.

———. *Irrigation-Induced Water Quality Problems: What Can Be Learned from the San Joaquin Valley Experience*. Washington, D.C.: National Academy Press, 1989.

Nelson, E. W. "Unwise Drainage." *Bulletin of the American Game Protective Association* 13, no. 1 (1924): 8–9, 11.

Oke, T. R., M. North, O. Slaymaker, and D. G. Steyn. "Primordial to Prim Order: A Century of Environmental Change." In *Vancouver and Its Region*, ed. Graeme Wynn and Tim Oke, 147-70. Vancouver: UBC Press, 1992.

O'Neill, Karen M. *Rivers by Design: State Power and the Origins of U.S. Flood Control*. Durham: Duke University Press, 2006.

"Organize Against Huge Refuge." *Evening Herald (Klamath Falls, Ore.)*, 12 October 1928.

Orsi, Jared. "From Horicon to Hamburgers and Back Again: Ecology, Ideology, and Wildfowl Management, 1917-1935." *Environmental History Review* (Winter 1994): 19-40.

Paskus, Laura. "'Sound Science' Goes Sour." *High Country News*, 23 June 2003.

Perkins, John H. *Insects, Experts, and the Insecticide Crisis: The Quest for New Pest Management Strategies*. New York: Plenum Press, 1982.

Peterson, Cass. "Farm Water Poisons Wildlife; California Refuge Contaminated." *Washington Post*, 10 March 1985.

———. "The Interior Department; Various Pollution Problems Troubling Refuges." *Washington Post*, 1 May 1985.

Peterson, Shannon. *Acting for Endangered Species: The Statutory Ark*. Lawrence: University Press of Kansas, 2002.

Philo, Chris, and Chris Wilbert, eds. *Animal Spaces, Beastly Places: New Geographies of Human-Animal Relations*. London: Routledge, 2000.

Pincetl, Stephanie S. *Transforming California: A Political History of Land Use and Development*. Baltimore: Johns Hopkins University Press, 1999.

Pisani, Donald J. "Federal Water Policy and the Rural West." In *The Rural West Since World War II*, ed. R. Douglas Hurt. Lawrence: University Press of Kansas, 1998.

———. *From Family Farm to Agribusiness: The Irrigation Crusade in California and the West, 1850–1931*. Berkeley: University of California Press, 1984.

———. "The Irrigation District and the Federal Relationship: Neglected Aspects of Water History in the Twentieth Century." In *The Twentieth-Century West: Historical Interpretations*, ed. Gerald D. Nash and Richard Etulain, 257-92. Albuquerque: University of New Mexico Press, 1989.

———. *To Reclaim a Divided West: Water, Law, and Public Policy, 1848–1902*. Albuquerque, NM: University of New Mexico Press, 1992.

———. *Water and American Government: The Reclamation Bureau, National Water Policy, and the West, 1902–1935*. Berkeley: University of California Press, 2002.

———. *Water, Land, and Law in the West*. Lawrence: University Press of Kansas, 1996.

Pitt, Jennifer. "Can We Restore the Colorado River Delta?" *Journal of Arid Environments* 49 (2001): 211–20.

Powers, Lawrence W., and Karen Adams. "Contemporary Use of Water Resources in the Klamath Basin." In *A River Never the Same: A History of Water in the Klamath Basin*, ed. Shaw Historical Library, 91–103. Klamath Falls, Ore.: Shaw Historical Library, Oregon Institute of Technology, 1999.

Preston, William L. "Serpent in the Garden: Environmental Change in Colonial California." In *Contested Eden: California before the Gold Rush*, ed. Ramón Gutiérrez and Richard J. Orsi. Berkeley: University of California Press, 1998.

———. *Vanishing Landscape: Land and Life in the Tulare Lake Basin*. Berkeley: University of California Press, 1981.

Price, Jennifer. *Flight Maps: Adventures with Nature in Modern America*. New York: Basic Books, 1999.

Proctor, Noble S., and Patrick J. Lynch. *Manual of Ornithology: Avian Structure and Function*. New Haven, Conn.: Yale University Press, 1993.

Pudup, Mary Beth, and Michael Watts. "Growing against the Grain: Mechanized Rice Farming in the Sacramento Valley, California." In *Comparative Farming Systems*, ed. B. L. Turner II and S. Brush, 345–84. New York: The Guilford Press, 1987.

Pyne, Stephen J. *Fire in America: A Cultural History of Wildland and Rural Fire*. Princeton, N.J.: Princeton University Press, 1982.

Quick, Humphrey Q. P. "Migratory Wildlife in a Changing Environment." In *Migratory Species and Climate Change: Impacts of a Changing Environment on Wild Animals*, ed. CMS, UNEP, DEFRA, 40–45. Bonn, Germany: UNEP/CMS, 2006.

Reeves, Henry M. "Alexander Wetmore." In *Flyways: Pioneering Waterfowl Management in North America*, ed. A. S. Hawkins, R. C. Hanson, H. K. Nelson, and H. M. Reeves, 75–81. Washington, D.C.: United States Department of the Interior, Fish and Wildlife Service, 1984.

Reiger, John F. *American Sportsmen and the Origins of Conservation*. 3rd ed. Corvallis: Oregon State University Press, 2001.

Reisner, Marc. *Cadillac Desert: The American West and Its Disappearing Water*. New York: Penguin Books, 1986.

———. "Deconstructing the Age of Dams." *High Country News*, 27 October 1997.

Revkin, Andrew C. "Study Discounts Halting Irrigation to Protect Fish." *New York Times*, 5 February 2002.

Riebsame, William, James J. Robb, and University of Colorado at Boulder

Center of the American West, eds. *Atlas of the New West: Portrait of a Changing Region.* New York: W. W. Norton & Company, 1997.

Righter, Robert W. *The Battle over Hetch Hetchy: America's Most Controversial Dam and the Birth of Modern Environmentalism.* New York: Oxford University Press, 2005.

Robbins, Paul, and April Luginbuhl. "The Last Enclosure: Resisting Privatization of Wildlife in the Western United States." *Capitalism, Nature, Socialism* 16, no. 1 (2005): 45–61.

Robbins, William. *Landscapes of Promise: The Oregon Story, 1800–1940.* Seattle: University of Washington Press, 1997.

Robertson, Lance, and Dustin Solberg. "Reviving a Refuge." *High Country News,* 16 August 1999.

Rose, Gene. *San Joaquin: A River Betrayed.* Fresno, Calif.: Linrose Publishing Co., 1992.

Rothman, Hal. *America's National Monuments: The Politics of Preservation.* Lawrence: University Press of Kansas, 1989.

Runte, Alfred. *National Parks: The American Experience.* 3rd ed. Lincoln: University of Nebraska Press, 1997.

Russell, Edmund P. III. "'Speaking of Annihilation': Mobilizing for War against Human and Insect Enemies." *Journal of American History* 82, no. 4 (1996): 1505–29.

———. *War and Nature: Fighting Humans and Insects with Chemicals from World War I to Silent Spring.* New York: Cambridge University Press, 2001.

Ryser, Fred A. Jr. *Birds of the Great Basin: A Natural History.* Reno: University of Nevada Press, 1985.

Saloutos, Theodore. *The American Farmer and the New Deal.* Ames: Iowa State University Press, 1982.

Salyer, J. Clark II, and Francis G. Gillet. "Federal Refuges." In *Waterfowl Tomorrow,* ed. Joseph P. Linduska, 497–508. Washington, D.C.: United States Department of the Interior, Bureau of Sport Fisheries and Wildlife, Fish and Wildlife Service, 1964.

Sauder, Robert A. *The Lost Frontier: Water Diversions in the Growth and Destruction of Owens Valley Agriculture.* Tucson: University of Arizona Press, 1994.

Sauer, Carl. "The Morphology of Landscape." In *Land and Life: A Selection from the Writings of Carl Ortwin Sauer,* ed. John Leighly. Berkeley: University of California Press, 1965.

Sayre, Nathan F. *Ranching, Endangered Species, and Urbanization in the Southwest: Species of Capital.* Tucson: University of Arizona Press, 2002.

Scheuring, Ann Foley. *A Guidebook to California Agriculture*. Berkeley: University of California Press, 1983.

Schoenherr, Allan A. *A Natural History of California*. Berkeley: University of California Press, 1992.

Scott, James C. *Seeing Like a State: How Certain Schemes to Improve the Human Condition Have Failed*. New Haven, Conn.: Yale University Press, 1998.

Sellars, Richard West. *Preserving Nature in the National Parks: A History*. New Haven, Conn.: Yale University Press, 1997.

Sewell, W. R. Derrick. *Water Management and Floods in the Fraser River Basin*. Department of Geography, Research Paper No. 100. Chicago: University of Chicago, 1965.

Shabecoff, Philip. "Toxic Water Threatens Many Wildlife Refuges." *New York Times*, 30 April 1985.

Shallenberger, Robert J., Mary Anne Young, and Nancy J. Roper. "Changing the Way We Look at the Land." *Transactions of the Fifty-Ninth North American Wildlife and Natural Resources Conference* (1994): 532–40.

Siemens, Alfred H. "The Process of Settlement in the Lower Fraser Valley— In Its Provincial Context." In *Lower Fraser Valley: Evolution of a Cultural Landscape*, ed. Alfred H. Siemens, 27–39. Vancouver: Tantalus Research Limited, 1968.

Slaymaker, O., M. Bovis, M. North, T. R. Oke, and J. Ryder. "The Primordial Environment." In *Vancouver and Its Region*, ed. Graeme Wynn and Timothy Oke, 17–37. Vancouver: UBC Press, 1992.

Smith, Allen G., Jerome H. Stoudt, and J. Bernard Gollop. "Prairie Potholes and Marshes." In *Waterfowl Tomorrow*, ed. Joseph P. Linduska, 39–50. Washington, D.C.: United States Department of the Interior, Bureau of Sport Fisheries and Wildlife, Fish and Wildlife Service, 1964.

Smith, Loren M., Roger L. Pederson, and Richard M. Kaminski, eds. *Habitat Management for Migrating and Wintering Waterfowl in North America*. Lubbock: Texas Tech University Press, 1989.

Smith, Robert H., Frank Dufresne, and Henry A. Hansen. "Northern Watersheds and Deltas." In *Waterfowl Tomorrow*, ed. Joseph P. Linduska, 51–66. Washington, D.C.: United States Department of the Interior, Bureau of Sport Fisheries and Wildlife, Fish and Wildlife Service, 1964.

Spaulding, Jonathan. *Ansel Adams and the American Landscape: A Biography*. Berkeley: University of California Press, 1995.

Spence, Mark David. *Dispossessing the Wilderness: Indian Removal and the Making of the National Parks*. New York: Oxford University Press, 1999.

Steinberg, Ted. *Down to Earth: Nature's Role in American History*. New York: Oxford University Press, 2002.

Sterling, Keir B. "Builders of the U.S. Biological Survey, 1885–1930." *Journal of Forest History* 33, no. 4 (1989): 180–87.

Stoll, Steven. *The Fruits of Natural Advantage: Making the Industrial Country-side in California*. Berkeley: University of California Press, 1998.

Swanson, George A., and Harold F. Duebbert. "Wetland Habitats of Water-fowl in the Prairie Pothole Region." In *Northern Prairie Wetlands*, ed. Arnold van der Valk, 228–67 (Ames: Iowa State University Press, 1989).

Sykes, Godfrey. *The Colorado Delta*. Washington, D.C.: Carnegie Institution of Washington and the American Geographical Society of New York, 1937.

Taylor, Joseph E. III. "Burning the Candle at Both Ends: Historicizing Over-fishing in Oregon's Nineteenth-Century Salmon Fisheries." *Environmental History* 4 (1999): 54–79.

———. *Making Salmon: An Environmental History of the Northwest Fisheries Crisis*. Seattle: University of Washington Press, 1999.

Tober, James. *Who Owns the Wildlife? The Political Economy of Conservation in Nineteenth-Century America*. Westport, Conn.: Greenwood Press, 1981.

Trefethen, James B. *An American Crusade for Wildlife: Highlights in Conservation Progress*. Harrisburg, Pa.: The Stackpole Company, 1961.

Trimble, Stephen. *The Sagebrush Ocean: A Natural History of the Great Basin*. Reno: University of Nevada Press, 1989.

Turner, Stanton B. "Reclamation—A New Look for the Tule Lake and Klamath Lake Basins." *Journal of the Shaw Historical Library* 2, no. 2 (1988): 25–70.

———. *The Years of Harvest: A History of the Tule Lake Basin*. Eugene, Ore.: 49th Avenue Press, 1987.

Tyrrell, Ian R. *True Gardens of the Gods: Californian-Australian Environmental Reform, 1860–1930*. Berkeley: University of California Press, 1999.

U.S. Congress. Senate. Subcommittee on Irrigation and Reclamation of the Committee on Interior and Insular Affairs. *S. 784 and S. 793, Bills to Promote the Conservation of Migratory Waterfowl and Wildlife Resources in the Tule Lake, Klamath, and Clear Lake National Wildlife Refuges in Oregon and California*. 88th Cong., 1st Sess., 24 April 1963.

U.S. Department of Agriculture. Bureau of Biological Survey. *Report of Chief of Biological Survey*. Washington, D.C.: Government Printing Office, 1927; 1932; 1934; 1935.

U.S. Department of Commerce. Bureau of the Census. *United States Census of Agriculture: 1935*. Washington, D.C.: Government Printing Office, 1936.

———. *United States Census of Agriculture: 1950*. Washington, D.C.: Government Printing Office, 1952.

U.S. Department of the Interior. Bureau of Reclamation, Lower Colorado Region. "Salton Sea Study: Status Report." Boulder City, Nev., 2003.

U.S. Department of the Interior. Fish and Wildlife Service. *Annual Report of the Fish and Wildlife Service to the Secretary of the Interior, 1943*. Washington, D.C.: Government Printing Office, 1943.

———. "Briefing Statement: Wetland/Farm Rotational Management," [1999].

———. Klamath Basin National Wildlife Refuges. "Draft Environmental Assessment: Implementation of the Agricultural Program on Tule Lake National Wildlife Refuge."19 January 2001.

———. Regional Director. Region 1. "Formal Consultation on the Effects of the Long-Term Operation of the Klamath Project on the Lost River Sucker, Shortnose Sucker, Bald Eagle and American Peregrine Falcon," 22 July 1992.

———. "Saving the Salton Sea: A Research Needs Assessment." 1997.

Vale, Thomas R. *The American Wilderness: Reflections on Nature Protection in the United States*. Charlottesville: University of Virginia Press, 2005.

van der Valk, Arnold, ed. *Northern Prairie Wetlands*. Ames: Iowa State University Press, 1989.

"Vanishing Migratory Birds." *Saturday Evening Post*, 19 February 1927.

Vileisis, Ann. *Discovering the Unknown Landscape: A History of America's Wetlands*. Washington, D.C.: Island Press, 1997.

Vorster, Peter. "The Development and Decline of Agriculture in the Owens Valley." In *The History of Water: Eastern Sierra Nevada, Owens Valley, White-Inyo Mountains*, ed. C. A. Hall Jr., V. Doyle-Jones, and B. Widawski, 269–84. White Mountain Research Station Symposium, vol. 4. Los Angeles: White Mountain Research Station, 1992.

Walker, Richard A. *The Conquest of Bread: 150 Years of Agribusiness in California*. New York: The New Press, 2004.

Warren, Louis S. *The Hunter's Game: Poachers and Conservationists in Twentieth-Century America*. New Haven, Conn.: Yale University Press, 1997.

"Waterfowl Pose California Problem." *Outdoor California* (September 1935): 1, 3–11.

Watkins, T. H. *Righteous Pilgrim: The Life and Times of Harold L. Ickes, 1874–1952*. New York: Henry Holt and Company, 1990.

Weidensaul, Scott. *Living on the Wind: Across the Hemisphere with Migratory Birds*. New York: North Point Press, 1999.

Welch, Craig. "Both Sides Harden in Oregon Water Dispute." *Seattle Times*, 9 July 2001.

Weller, Milton W. *Freshwater Marshes: Ecology and Wildlife Management.* 3rd ed. Minneapolis: University of Minnesota Press, 1994.

———. *Wetland Birds: Habitat Resources and Conservation Implications.* Cambridge: Cambridge University Press, 1999.

Wentz, W. Alan, and Frederic A. Reid. "Managing Refuges for Waterfowl Purposes and Biological Diversity: Can Both Be Achieved?" *Transactions of the Fifty-Seventh North American Wildlife and Natural Resources Conference* (1992): 581–85.

White, Richard. "Animals and Enterprise." In *The Oxford History of the American West*, ed. Clyde A. Milner II, Carol A. O'Connor, and Martha A. Sandweiss, 236–73. New York: Oxford University Press, 1994.

———. "'Are You an Environmentalist or Do You Work for a Living?': Work and Nature." In *Uncommon Ground: Toward Reinventing Nature*, ed. William Cronon, 171–85. New York: W. W. Norton & Company, 1995.

———. "Contested Terrain: The Business of Land in the American West." In *Land in the American West: Private Claims and the Common Good*, ed. William G. Robbins and James C. Foster, 190–206. Seattle: University of Washington Press, 2000.

———. "The Current Weirdness in the West." *Western Historical Quarterly* 28 (Spring 1997): 5–16.

———. *"It's Your Misfortune and None of My Own": A New History of the American West.* Norman: University of Oklahoma Press, 1991.

———. *The Organic Machine: The Remaking of the Columbia River.* New York: Hill and Wang, 1995.

Wilcove, David S. *No Way Home: The Decline of the World's Great Animal Migrations.* Washington, D.C.: Island Press, 2007.

Wilkinson, Charles. *American Indians, Time, and the Law: Native Societies in a Modern Constitutional Democracy.* New Haven, Conn.: Yale University Press, 1987.

———. *Blood Struggle: The Rise of Modern Indian Nations.* New York: W. W. Norton & Company, 2005.

Wilson, Robert. "Klamath's Federal Agencies Map Different Realities." *High Country News*, 13 August 2001.

Winter, George R. "Agricultural Development in the Lower Fraser Valley." In *Lower Fraser Valley: Evolution of a Cultural Landscape*, ed. Alfred H. Siemens. Vancouver: Tantalus Research Limited, 1968.

Wolch, Jennifer. "Anima urbis." *Progress in Human Geography* 26, no. 6 (2002): 721–42.

Wolch, Jennifer, and Jody Emel, eds. *Animal Geographies: Place, Politics, and Identity in the Nature-Culture Borderlands.* London: Verso, 1998.

Wolch, Jennifer R., Kathleen West, and Thomas E. Gaines. "Transpecies Urban Theory." *Environment and Planning D: Society and Space* 13 (1995): 735–60.

Wood, Daniel B. "In Water Transfer, Farmers vs. Sprawl." *Christian Science Monitor*, 11 December 2002.

Worster, Donald. *Dust Bowl: The Southern Plains in the 1930s.* New York: Oxford University Press, 1979.

———. *Nature's Economy: A History of Ecological Ideas.* 2nd ed. Cambridge: Cambridge University Press, 1994.

———. *Rivers of Empire: Water, Aridity, and the Growth of the American West.* New York: Pantheon Books, 1985.

Wylie, John. *Landscape.* New York: Routledge, 2007.

Wynn, Graeme, and Timothy Oke, eds. *Vancouver and Its Region.* Vancouver: UBC Press, 1992.

Zahm, Gary R. "Kesterson Reservoir and Kesterson Wildlife Refuge: History, Current Problems, and Management Alternatives." *Transactions of the Fifty-First North American Wildlife and Natural Resources Conference* (1986): 324–29.

Zuckerman, Seth. "Klamath Water Wars: Systems Out of Sync." *Christian Science Monitor*, 27 July 2001.

INDEX

Quick, Paul T., 120–21

Reclamation Act of 1902, 46,
  205–6n11
reclamation board, State of California, 40
Reclamation Service, U.S., 35–36, 45,
  46–48, 52, 56. *See also* Reclamation, U.S. Bureau of
Reclamation, U.S. Bureau of:
  engineering solutions, 92–93, 138;
  homesteading on refuges, 123–26;
  Klamath Basin conflict and, 146,
  149–50, 151, 152, 154; livestock
  grazing and, 61–63; Lower Klamath Lake and, 58–59; during the
  New Deal, 72; opposition from
  environmentalists, 137–38, 166;
  wastewater sump creation, 96–97,
  138; water allocation, 90. *See also*
  Reclamation Service, U.S.
Redington, Paul, 70
refuges. *See* wildlife refuges
rice cultivation. *See* grain
  cultivation
Rice Straw Burning Reduction Act,
  163
Robbins, Paul, 123
Roosevelt, Franklin D., 68, 70, 72
Roosevelt, Theodore, 13, 50, 52
Ruby Lake, 82
Ruby Mountains, 82
ruddy ducks, 160

Sacramento Flood Control Project,
  40
Sacramento National Wildlife Refuge: bird deaths on, 115; establishment of, 83–85; grain production
  on, 87–88, 109; hunting and, 104,

120, 121–22; importance to water-
  fowl, 3, 5–6; management of, 102;
  water management on, 85–87
Sacramento River, 5, 26–27, 39, 40,
  86, 101
Sacramento–San Joaquin River
  Delta, 138
Sacramento Valley: flood control
  in, 39–40; hunting in, 118, 121;
  rice farming in, 44, 87, 101–2, 114,
  126, 163; wetlands, 26–27. *See also*
  Central Valley
salmon, 15, 149–50, 155–56
Salton Sea, 42–43, 80, 158–62, 157*fig*,
  166
Salton Sea Authority, 161
Salton Sink, 42
San Francisco Bay, 41–42
San Joaquin River, 26–27, 64
San Joaquin Valley, 26–27, 40, 81,
  149. *See also* Central Valley
San Luis Drain, 138, 139
Sayler, J. Clark II: aquatic plants on
  refuges and, 90; Japanese-Amer-
  ican internment and, 94, 95, 96;
  Klamath Marsh and, 128, 129–30;
  role in refuge program, 66, 73,
  80–81, 97
Scott, James, 97, 167, 168–69
Seattle Fur Exchange, 113
Seeing Like a State, 167, 168–69
selenium, 139
Shasta Dam, 40
Sheepy Ridge, 92, 93
shortnose suckerfish, 148
Sierra Club, 44
Silent Spring, 115–16
Silvies River, 57
Skagit River, 23
Slave River, 20

Design and composition by Pamela Canell. Typeset in Minion, a font created by Robert Slimbach in 1990, and Gotham, a font created by Jonathan Hoefler and Tobias Frere-Jones in 2000. Printed and bound by Thomson-Shore, Chelsea, Michigan, on 50# Natures Natural.